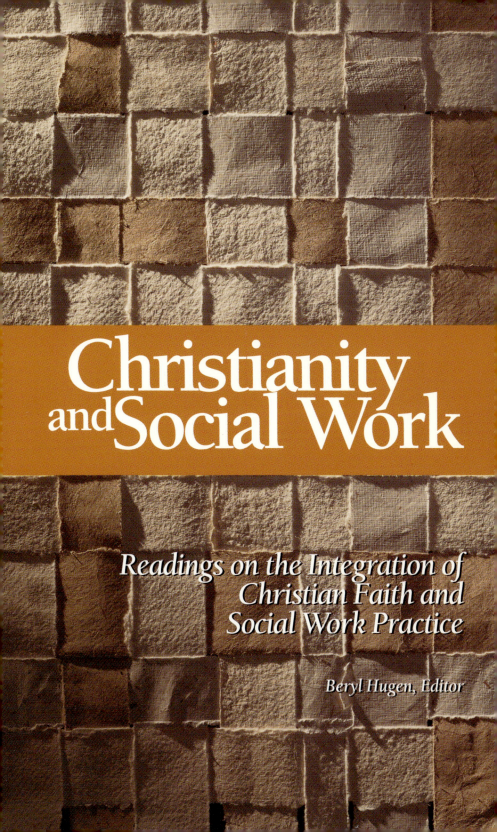

Christianity
and Social Work

*Readings on the Integration of
Christian Faith and
Social Work Practice*

Beryl Hugen, Editor

Christianity and
Social Work

Christianity and Social Work

Readings on the Integration of Christian Faith and Social Work Practice

Editor
Beryl Hugen

Copyright 1998
North American Association of Christians in Social Work
P.O. Box 121
Botsford, CT 06404-0121

ISBN 0-9623634-6-4

CONTENTS

Worldviews and Plumblines

Spiritual Aspects in the Helping Process

Humility and Competence

PREFACE

I have been teaching social work on the undergraduate level at Christian colleges for several years. While teaching social work, I have used what I felt were the best introductory texts on the market. However, these texts were produced for the secular market and have been at best neutral and at times antagonistic to Christian concerns. For the past few years I have felt a need for a text that would not only offer a Christian perspective on the social work profession as a whole, but also on specific topics within the profession. In discussions with some of my colleagues, I sensed that they saw a similar need.

After some research and discussion it seemed that the best approach was to produce a collection of articles dealing with a variety of topics and issues related to the practice of social work. To accomplish this I decided to recruit Christian social workers from a wide variety of colleges and universities who would address topics in which they were most competent.

The contributors, therefore, represent a variety of academic settings, along with a broad range of theological and social work perspectives. The common denominator for all of them is a commitment to social work as a profession and a commitment to integrating social work with their Christian faith. The contributors were not given a strict outline to follow, but rather were supplied with the basic purpose of the book and general stylistic guidelines. As editor, I have attempted to allow the authors' ideas to stand with as few editorial changes as possible.

This collection has been written so that it may either be used by itself in the classroom, supplemented by lecture material, or used as a supplement to standard texts. Perhaps its best usage is as a text where selected articles are addressed in differing courses throughout the curriculum of the social work program.

The reader may agree with some of the contributors and disagree with others. It is my hope that the reader, whether agreeing or disagreeing, will be stimulated to integrate his or her Christian worldview with the professional social work perspective on helping. I know all the contributors sincerely hope that the reader will catch a glimpse of the potential contributions that being a Christian in social work can make to the competent and wholistic practice of professional social work and, not incidentally, to the furtherance of the gospel of Jesus Christ and the growth of His Kingdom.

Acknowledgements

Special thanks are due the contributors. I have had the entirely enjoyable task of working with a group that without exception not only produced substantive manuscripts, but shared a clear commitment to the integration of Christian faith and social work practice.

I thank my colleagues at Calvin College for their editorial help and the support of the Calvin Faculty Research Fellowship Program. Special thanks go to Carla Goslinga at Dordt College and Maxine Comer at Calvin College for their secretarial assistance along with Bob Alderink from Publishing Services (Calvin College) for his work on the layout.

I also wish to acknowledge the influence of Alan Keith-Lucas on the initial thinking and development of this project. Both his life and writings continue to provide encouragement and motivation for many social workers in the continuing effort to integrate their Christian faith and social work practice.

CHAPTER 1

INTRODUCTION

Beryl Hugen

One of the developments in social work in the second half of the 20th century has been a marked decline in the recognition of the Christian religion in the teaching and practice of professional social work. The secularization of the social work profession, the notion of religion in both an ideological and institutional sense having little or no part in forming or informing the world of social work, has been very extensive. In fact, the profession has at times been outright hostile toward persons and institutions that profess a Christian orientation to practice. Even presently, when spirituality is being recognized by the profession as a legitimate area of inquiry, Christianity, as one spiritual voice, is recognized only hesitantly.

This is unfortunate for a number of reasons. First, social work once used the language of Christianity as a basis for its existence. Historically, such language was widely and eloquently used by both social work educators and practitioners. Second, spirituality, and to a large degree Christian spirituality, is very much part of our culture and continues to play a significant role in providing moral rationale and reasoning to our political, social, and charitable institutions. As a result, many individuals who seek to be social workers want to know what role Christian faith plays in a helping profession—specifically, the professional existence and activities of social work. The purpose of this book is to help respond to this question.

For many in the social work profession, this question of the relationship of Christian faith and social work is inconsequential, irrelevant, and for some, even an inappropriate topic for professional investigation. For others, it is simply outrageous. George Marsden recently published a book entitled, *The Outrageous Idea of Christian Scholarship.* Why is Christian scholarship an outrageous idea? Many academics (including social workers) regard Christian belief as an affront to reason. They argue that people may hold religious beliefs in the privacy of their own homes, but to propose that such antiquated notions should inform one's scholarship and practice is truly outrageous.

Ironically, throughout history and particularly in the history of charity, the opposite has been true. It would be hard for anyone to deny that the Christian church is one of the true originators of charity. Out of ancient Israel's concern for justice and mercy toward the sick, the poor, the orphaned, the widowed — from Micah and Hosea, Jeremiah and Isaiah — grew the compassion of Jesus and the devotion of Paul. The justice and love of God set forth and exemplified in the Judeo-Christian tradition has given drive and direction to much of western culture's charities. Historically the whole shape and operation of organized welfare is inexplicable apart from this religious conviction and commitment. Jewish, Catholic, and Protestant thought have all along continuously shaped the ideological basis of social work practice. One writer has suggested that these religious traditions, along with the secular philosophy of humanism, are the four foundational roots out of which has emerged the value base of the profession (Kohs, 1966). So it is today that many social workers find the assumptions, beliefs, and values of the Christian faith helpful in providing a frame of reference for understanding and responding to both individual and societal problems.

There are many social workers who are Christians who do not hold to the idea that there is such a thing as Christian social work—only Christians in social work (I am one of them). They do believe, however, that one's Christian perspective comes into play in social work practice when one is deciding *what* to do, *when* to do it, *how* to do it, and *why* one should do it. They clearly identify with those who seek to follow Christ in a servant role for the alleviation of pain and suffering and the establishment of justice and peace in the world. It is for this significant group of social workers (perhaps you are one of them), whose motivations to enter the profession and whose desire is to develop approaches to helping that reflect and are informed by their Christian faith, that this book is written.

The Changing Context for Practice

Social work as a profession has undergone a variety of changes in the twentieth century. Many of these reflect both significant material and technological changes in our society, along with a shift in our ideas about the relationship between people and their social environment, particularly government. The early twentieth century was fertile ground for the development and expansion of broad governmental responsibility for social welfare. The idea of the welfare state and of the centrality of government and public service seemed both inevitable and probably necessary.

But the latter part of the twentieth century has been much less hospitable to the concept of the welfare state. The country has lost the political enthusiasm and conviction that problems can be fixed through public processes and public action. Ideas of limited government, volunteerism, and privatization are now in vogue, and seem not to be some passing fancy.

Private, sectarian, and faith-based organizations are now being asked and expected to fill in the gaps left by this shrinking public response. Churches, sectarian agencies, and Christian voluntary organizations are being increasing called upon to participate more fully in providing community-based social welfare services. Social workers, therefore, who are able to understand and relate to both the professional(public) and faith-based communities are now in an important and advantageous position to contribute by developing policies and programs, and delivering services to help meet the social welfare needs in their communities. Several chapters of the book are focused on this changing environment of social work practice.

Worldviews and Plumblines

It is increasingly being recognized that social work, while its preoccupation in the last half century has been with "science" and with developing objective and empirically validated practice techniques, is also a normative discipline (Siporin, 1982, 1983). Normative means that social work also is concerned with how persons ought to behave "on principle," and that the goals of the profession are guided by particular values. A normative principle is an objective rule which when properly applied distinquishes between right and wrong. Such rules may be applied to the behavior of individuals, whether client or professional, or to social processes and their associated outcomes. So when the social work profession advocates for a redistribution of resources that are deemed valuable to society, a philosophical basis or normative principle for such a redistribution is needed. For example, to promote a national health plan because it is believed that adequate health care is a right, requires a standard or principle informing others as to what is the basis for such a right. So also human behavior, both individual and collective, is socially defined as good or bad, normal or deviant. Whether one chooses as a social worker to enforce these norms or advocate for their change, the essential "morality" of these norms or standards requires justification. Social work has always been guided by such normative principles, although they have rarely been clearly and completely explicated.

For the Christian, the standard or "plumbline" (Amos 7:8) used to make judgements has always been the principles set forth in the Bible. Hence it is important and necessary for Christian social workers to relate or test the values of the profession with the principles of a Christian worldview. To be explicit about such moral principles provides an opportunity to reconnect with the profession's religious bearings and roots. To do so may also help recover dimensions of social work teaching and practice that have been alienated from their theological roots. Articulating these Christian principles or "plumblines" — helping the reader develop a Christian worldview related to social work — is another one of the focuses of this book.

Spiritual Aspects in the Helping Process

Today there is also a small but growing movement within the social work profession that affirms that spirituality and religious beliefs are integral to the nature of the person and have a vital influence on human behavior. These spiritual and religious dimensions are being increasingly recognized as important features of social work practice, at all phases of the social work helping process and in all areas of practice. This perspective embraces a holistic conception of the person, with this view more recently being elaborated as the bio-psycho-social-spiritual perspective. This perspective reintroduces spiritual issues as a legitimate practice focus and provides for a more complete understanding of client strengths, weaknesses, and problems. As a result, there is now a need for the development of theoretical frameworks, including assessment tools, intervention models, and evaluation methods that flow from this perspective.

Social work research has also shown that although many social workers see religious and spiritual issues as important parameters in practice and important in their own lives as well as in the lives of their clients, many are hesitant to initiate discussion of spiritual issues with clients (Derezotes & Evans, 1995; Joseph, 1988). Much of this hesitation is due to the lack of knowledge and skill in this area. Greater sensitivity to the concerns of the religious client has also been shown to be related to the social worker's own spiritual awareness — the ability to integrate the personal, spiritual and religious self with the professional self. Again, there has been a reluctance to incorporate such knowledge into social work education, considering such discussions as an intrusion into a private sphere.

With this wider movement within the profession to embrace a bio-psycho-social-spiritual focus in practice and the promotion of a professional learning environment that is more supportive of personal religious and spiritual experiences, Christian social workers now have the opportunity to truly minister to the whole person. Several chapters in the book also address these spiritual aspects of the helping process.

Humility and Competence

These tasks — adapting to the changing landscape in social welfare, articulating the principles of a Christian worldview related to social work, and developing spiritual frameworks related to the differing aspects of the helping process and a professional use of self related to spirituality — also provide challenges. One is to apply a Christian message to the realities of the contemporary practice context, and not assume that a Christian understanding and response to social problems from an earlier time period is applicable for today. This also means that Christians in social work do not have all the answers. The Bible may provide principial guidance, but does not always provide clear and specific direction for the sometimes confusing moral and ethical situations social workers encounter in practice. As Christian social workers, we know that we live and practice in a broken world, and that our only real comfort is that we are not our own, but we belong, body and soul, in life and in death, to our faithful Savior Jesus Christ.

It is also easy to assert the evident Christian goodness of helping people. And it can be easier still to assume that a Christian perspective on the profession of social work furthers that good. But goodness of motivation may be and frequently is unrelated to outcome. There is always the possibility that our Christian perspectives are no more than self-serving rationales (promoting judgmentalism, discrimination and selective helping motiffs) rather than the product of a thoughtful analysis. This book, therefore, attempts to offer a Christian perspective for social work that is within the parameters of contemporary models of social work research and scholarship — clearly the social work profession can also inform the Christian community. The book's final chapter, written in a narrative form, illustrates these themes of humility and competence.

References

Derezotes, D.S. & Evans, K.E.(1995). Spirituality and religiousity in practice: In-depth interviews of social work practitioners. *Social Thought, 18*(1), 39-54.

Joseph, M.V.,(1988). Religion and social work practice. *Social Casework, 60*(7), 443-452.

Kohs, S.C. (1966). *The Roots of Social Work.* Association Press.

Siporin, M.(1982). Moral philosophy in social work today. *Social Service Review, 56,* 516-38.

Siporin, M. (1983). Morality and immorality in working with clients. *Social Thought, 15,*(3/4), 42-52.

CHAPTER 2

CHURCH SOCIAL WORK

Diana R. Garland

Early in my professional career, I went from being a clinical social worker in a small community mental health center to being a clinical social worker in a small church-related counseling center. I continued to work with clients seeking help with marital conflict, grief, troubled and troubling children, chemical addictions, depression, and an assortment of other life challenges. I did not see much difference in the clients and their problems which presented themselves to me in my new practice setting, nor, I must admit, even in the cozy, informal atmosphere of the centers.

The only difference I noticed was the source of referrals. In the community mental health center, clients came from inpatient psychiatric referrals and local physicians, or they came on the advice of friends and pastors. In the pastoral counseling center, pastors were far more often the referral sources. The work did not seem to change very much, however. In both settings, clients' problems and strengths were tangled together with the family and community in which they lived, and in the philosophical and spiritual frameworks through which they interpreted their world, themselves, and the meaning of life and suffering. Unfortunately, because I saw no difference in the contexts of my work, I missed opportunities for more effective work with my clients and in the churches and community that supported my work. I simply did in the church-related agency what I had done in the community mental health center.

Over time, however, I began to wonder if anything about my work *should* be different. How should I be defining my responsibilities as a social worker in a church-related setting? In both settings, I dealt with spiritual issues when they came up in relationship to the problems and struggles clients presented. Was it simply that spiritual concerns were more often a part of the focus in the church agency, because clients sought us out as a place where these concerns would be considered appropriate and important? Was it that the staff could initiate discussions of spiritual matters when we felt that spirituality was relevant to the client's presenting problem? Or should there be something different about the very nature and purpose of our work? Should I be defining my work in relationship with the congregations that sent us referrals, or should I let the referrals be the boundaries of my professional responsibility?

Those questions started my search for defining what church social work is and can be, whether it happens in a pastoral counseling agency, a congregation, or denominational headquarters. If I could go back to my practice in that pastoral counseling center now, I would define my role and responsibilities very differently, and I would do that defining in conversation with the churches that related to our agency. As you read this chapter, think about how you would define social work practice in such a setting.

****

More than any other helping profession, social work recognizes that the context for work has a dramatic impact on that work, both in positive and negative ways. The context can be both a barrier and a resource for change. When the context is ignored, barriers remain hidden and resources go unused. Even the value of social work to the host institution itself may be lost in the process.

Congregations can be a tremendous resource in working with social work clients. The congregation can be a community of support that can make all the difference to a family coping with stressful experiences such as chronic illness, for example. The congregation can provide (1) friendship, concern, and the mentoring of others who have been through such experiences, (2) respite care for the ill family member that supports the caregiver and spreads the burden of care to a wider group, (3) hot meals brought to the home and help with household chores, and (4) a framework for interpreting the meaning and significance of the stress the family is experiencing. The church social worker sensitive to these resources can nurture and strengthen them.

Congregations also provide access to social services for persons who would otherwise be difficult for social service agencies to reach. For example, families will involve themselves in educational programs such as parenting classes or marriage seminars offered by their church who might never seek out such a program offered by a community mental health agency.

At the same time, the church context for social work practice can also present significant barriers to practice and complicate a client's difficulties. For example, a family going through a divorce may sense gossip and even rejection instead of compassion and support by a congregation. A single adult may feel odd and out of place in a congregation which emphasizes the nuclear family as the ideal lifestyle ordained by God. A teenager struggling with questions of sexual orientation or a couple in the throes of family violence may consider the church—and a social worker related to the church—the last place where help can be found.

Certainly, the setting of church social work often dictates that the social worker will deal with spiritual and religious issues more often and in more depth than in other practice settings. But there is much more to it than that.

What Is Church Social Work?

Roselee is Director of Christian Social Ministries, a full time staff position at First Baptist Church. Her responsibilities include developing and administering a diversity of programs sponsored by this large congregation, including a counseling center staffed with full-time and part-time mental health professionals, an emergency assistance program, a therapeutic day care program for children who have emotional difficulties as a result of traumatic life experiences, a feeding program for homeless persons, a prison ministry, an after-school recreational program for community teenagers, and a myriad of support groups for persons experiencing a variety of life crises and challenges. Her work includes supervising the professional staff and providing consultation and support for a very large group of volunteers who work in these programs.

David is a social worker in a counseling center supported by the local denominational association of congregations. He provides individual and family counseling for members of the supporting congregations as well as for others in the community. He also leads marriage enrichment, parent education, and other educational programs for congregations too small to have staff able to provide this kind of leadership, and he is organizing a family resource center for the churches to use. It will have videotapes, books, and audiotapes on a variety of topics related to family life.

Martha directs a church-sponsored community center in an inner-city slum. The center offers recreational and after-school tutoring and child-care programs for community children and youths, job placement and training programs for older youths and adults, a resource center and micro-loan program for small business development by residents of the community, crisis counseling and emergency assistance, a variety of support groups, and a food co-op. Martha trains and supervises a whole army of volunteers from suburban churches who provide staff for the various programs.

Often, the Center is involved in organizing the community and its supporting congregations to advocate for the needs of children and their families living in poverty in the community.

Ricardo directs the Christian Social Ministries Department in the national headquarters of the denomination. He supervises the work of staff all over the United States. His board of directors determines which mission sites to found and support, including community centers in inner cities, rural areas, and with various ethnic minority groups. By writing articles in denominational magazines and the curricula of the denomination's educational programs, Ricardo helps churches of his denomination examine the social issues of the day and advocate for justice. He also is a frequent speaker at regional church conferences and meetings.

Church social work is social work which takes place under the auspices of a church organization, whether that organization is a congregation, denominational agency, or ecumenical or parachurch organization. To understand church social work, then, requires understanding the church.

The Church is a Human Organization

Churches are human organizations, sharing many of the characteristics of other human organizations. They have *structures* which divide responsibility and privilege between persons (clergy and lay persons, congregations and denominations, deacons and membership). They have *tasks* to be performed—worship, missions and ministry, care of the membership, outreach/evangelism, and administration of the church's physical and human resources. They have *processes, rules and norms* for performing these tasks; some of these are overt and formal, but many are also informal and unspoken. Finally, churches and church organizations have *bodies of beliefs codified in creeds and doctrines* which define their culture. These characteristics need to be understood in all their particularity in each setting for effective social work practice.

For example, as Martha works with the congregations which partner with her community center, she seeks involvement of the persons who provide leadership to their congregations and can move those congregations toward greater action. That means understanding how roles and power are defined and distributed in each congregation. In some churches, power rests with the pastor, but in others, power may be vested in a women's organization, or the board of deacons. As she works with these various leaders, she describes her work using the language of the church. For example, she describes the community center's work as missions and evangelism, a way that their members can grow and strengthen their faith by serving others.

Depending on the processes of each congregation, Martha may work informally with individual leaders over coffee or provide formal presentations of the work of the center at church committee meetings. She provides ongoing consultation with volunteers, helping them relate their volunteer work to their own faith journeys. As she talks with leaders and members of congregations, she is sensitive to and uses language which is congruent with their doctrine and their use of scripture.

The Church is the Body of Christ

Of course, the church is also something other than a human organization. It is also a creation of God, the Church to which all followers of Jesus Christ in the past, present, and future belong. This Church is the body of Christ, and its parts each have indispensable functions (Romans 12:3-8; 1 Corinthians 12). In another image, Christians together are members of the "household of God" who, with Christ as the cornerstone, serve as a holy temple, a dwelling place for God (Ephesians 2:19-22). The Church is in process of being and becoming this creation, this dwelling place for God. The tension between current reality and theological ideal motivates and guides the continuous modifications and development of church organizations—and thus the context for church social work practice.

Church Social Workers as Leaders of Christian Social Ministries

Church social workers often provide leadership in the social ministries of congregations and denominations. Social ministries are activities carried out by Christians (both professional church leaders and members of congregations) to help persons in need and to work for greater social justice in communities and the larger society. These ministries are considered central responsibilities of the church and of individual Christians, growing out of Jesus' teaching (1) that neighbors are to be loved as we love ourselves and that all persons are our neighbors, (2) that responding to the needs of persons is a way to respond faithfully to God's love, and (3) that God is less concerned with religious ritual than with social justice.

The Settings of Church Social Work

Church social workers practice in various settings. These include congregations and parishes, denominational organizations, ecumenical organizations, and parachurch organizations. Each of these have somewhat different characteristics that give definition to social work practice in that setting. *Congregations* are groups of persons who voluntarily band together for religious purposes, and who share an identity with one another. They often have a central meeting place and may be referred to as the group which meets in that place (First Baptist Church, The Church of the Redeemer) despite the frequent disclaimer that a church is not a building, it is the people. A *parish* is the geographic community served by the congregation. The term parish is often also used to refer to local governmental jurisdictions (like a "county"), reflecting a time when one church body was overwhelmingly the dominant religious institution and when geographic location and congregational membership were synonymous.

A *denomination* is an organization which governs many congregations who share certain beliefs and practices. Denominations vary dramatically in their government structures. In some denominations, congregations are subsystems of the larger denomination and are not seen as independent, autonomous entities apart from the denomination (e.g., Roman Catholic). In other denominations, congregations are independent entities which voluntarily participate in the denomination because the denomination can help them achieve goals which they could not on their own (e.g. Baptist). Because their participation is voluntary, congregations in these denominations can also choose to disaffiliate themselves if they become dissatisfied or alienated by the work or policies of the denomination. Through the denomination, congregations support mission ventures, social service and social action projects, educational institutions (universities and seminaries), publication houses, and financial and other support services for clergy and congregations.

Denominations are often organized into local, state, and national levels of government and service programs. Church social workers are employed by denominational agencies such as residential child care and treatment programs, shelters for homeless persons and families, pregnant teens, and abused family members; community-based family service agencies; housing, nutrition, and socialization programs for aging families; adoption and foster care programs; hospitals; refugee relief programs; and disaster and world hunger relief agencies. Social workers are also commissioned as missionaries with specific cultural groups in this country and in international contexts.

Ecumenical organizations are organizations of denominations, individual congregations, and even individual church members. The organizations attempt to transcend theological, ecclesiological, and historical differences between churches and denominations in order to work toward common purposes. For example, community ministry agencies are local community-based organizations of churches from various denominations who share the same community. The congregations cooperate with one another in the ecumenical community ministry in order to provide social services to their communities which few congregations could provide with only their own resources—child day care, adult day care, emergency assistance, feeding programs for senior adults or homeless persons, counseling services, etc. The National Council of Churches and the World Council of Churches represent the national and global levels of ecumenical organization. These organizations often strive to be inclusive of denominations and religious organizations with a broad spectrum of theological and political viewpoints, sometimes extending to non-Christian faith groups and organizations.

Finally, there are *parachurch organizations*. Parachurch organizations resemble ecumenical organizations in their inclusion of persons and congregations from differing denominations. However, parachurch organizations sometimes are limited to congregations and denominations that consider themselves more conservative theologically and politically than those who are comfortable participating in the diversity present in many ecumenical organizations. Parachurch organizations also are often special interest networks with a specific purpose rather than the comprehensive organizations which ecumenical organizations represent. Examples of parachurch organizations are World Vision, Bread for the World, Youth for Christ, Prison Fellowship, Focus on the Family, and the Christian Coalition.

It should be clear by now that *church social work* and *Christian social work* are not equivalent. The personal faith of the social worker does not define that worker's practice as church social work; church social work is defined by the context in which the social worker practices.

What Makes the Church a Distinctive Context for Social Work Practice?

Churches and their agencies are distinct from other practice settings in that they represent (1) a host, rather than primary, setting for social work; (2) a social community; (3) a source of programs and practices which often become, through a process of secularization, part of the dominant society; and (4) voices of advocacy for social justice. These primary characteristics of the churches and their agencies, taken together, make it a context unlike any other for social work practice.

Churches and their agencies are *host settings* for social services.

Churches are not primarily social service agencies. Instead, they are *host settings*, settings in which social work is a "guest," invited in for a reason. Host settings are those which have purposes other than or beyond the primary purposes of the social work profession, but these purposes which can be enhanced by what social work can offer. For example, hospitals and schools are also "host settings" for social work. They are not primarily social service agencies, but their purposes—treating illness and educating students— are furthered by providing social services to their patients/students. Hospitals use social workers to help plan for care after a patient leaves the hospital, or to help families deal with the crises of difficult diagnoses and with making care plans. Schools use social workers to address family and community factors that keep children from succeeding in school.

If social workers in a host setting forget that they are there to help the organization achieve its goals, and instead try to transform the setting into a *primary* setting, one which is primarily committed to providing social services and advocating for social justice, the welcome of the host setting may be withdrawn. Hospital social workers can address the needs of patients and their families, and may even be able to advocate for their needs with community structures and even the hospital itself. But they probably cannot expect the hospital to support their spending time working with street gangs in order to decrease the violence in the community. Even though such work may be related to the health of patients and their families, the hospital will probably see it as peripheral, not an activity to invest in if it means less energy is directed toward the direct care needs of patients and their families.

Social ministry and social action are central to the mission of the church. Church social workers must keep in mind, however, that social ministry and social action are important for the church because they point to the kingdom of God, because they are the fulfillment of Jesus' teachings, and because engaging in them grows the faith of Christians. Social service and social action are not ends in themselves; they must always be securely anchored in and reflective of the church's mission.

Churches are *social communities*.

A *community* is the set of personal contacts through which persons and families receive and give emotional and interpersonal support and nurture, material aid and services, information, and make new social contacts. The people in a community know us. They are people we can borrow from or who will take care of a child in an emergency. They are the ones from whom we can obtain news and gossip so that we know the significant and not so significant information that gives shape to our lives. Community includes the physical environment that communicates a sense of belonging because it is familiar. The smells of the river or the factory or the pine trees down the street are much like the smell of Grandma's house, part of the canvas of daily experience so familiar that it is hardly noticed until we are in different surroundings and miss them. We sit in the same pew on Sunday and look at the same stained glass windows from the same angle, and can predict who else will sit where. We hardly think about or recognize community until it is changed, or we absent ourselves. Upon return from a long absence, the sights, smells and greetings from familiar people may flood us with emotion. All these point to the familiar niche that community is. It consists of people, organizations, and physical environment that keep us from depending solely on persons within our family to meet all our personal, social, physical, and spiritual needs, and who communicate, "this is your place; you belong here."

The African proverb "It takes a village to raise a child" became a political slogan pointing to the importance of community for children, but it does not quite go far enough. *All* persons, both children and adults, need community. Because children are so dependent on others for their survival, their vulnerability in the absence of community is more apparent. Adults, too, however, need to live in and experience community, although some seem to need community more than others. Even self-sufficient adults living alone seek the company of others, if only for recreation and social support. Even seemingly independent adults need community when they become ill, injured, or feel threatened.

In our world of automobiles and our society of expressways and work and school separated from home and neighborhood, community is frequently no longer defined geographically. In many ways, marking the path of a person's automobile over the course of a week—from work to home to school to recreation to church to extended family and so on—will map that person's community. To the extent that the congregation is a significant emotional and interpersonal node in that tracing, the church is community. It may be the only institution in which all members of a family or friendship group participate together. For many, it is a place where they regularly worship, study, eat, engage in recreation, conduct business, socialize with others, and care and are cared for (Garland, forthcoming).

Both in congregations and in church agencies, church social workers have the task of building and strengthening communities. The most effective outreach ministries of the church (i.e., "evangelism") are those which extend the hospitality and care of the church community to those who do not have such a community. For example, one downtown congregation in a metropolitan area has "adopted" a nearby middle school. They provide tutoring, mentoring, enrichment classes, and stock a reduced-cost store in which students can purchase needed items. In the process, the church members developed relationships with the school's students. A large church-related family service agency trains church volunteers as family mentors and then pairs them with families in crisis. In the Chicago area, church women take gift baskets of baby items and small gifts for new mothers to young single mothers in the hospital whom nurses identify as having few or no visitors. The basket includes coupons for two evenings of free in-home child care by the women of the church and monthly visits to bring toys on loan and to discuss child development. Some of the women have subsequently become friends with these young mothers and "grandmas" to their babies. A program developed by church social workers in Louisville, Kentucky pairs the families of mothers with AIDS with volunteers who will provide support and friendship. They work with the mother to make permanent plans for children in the event of her death. In short, these programs wrap the community around families and individuals both inside and outside the congregation.

The focus of the church social worker is not simply using the community of faith to meet the needs of social work clients, but through service and caregiving, to build and strengthen the community itself. Dieter Hessel concludes that "the primary role of professional church workers is to equip a faithful *community* to intervene compassionately in the social system and to enhance caring interpersonal relations in ways that are consistent with Christian maturity" (Hessel, 1982, p. 125).

Church social workers are often expected to be active members and leaders of the denominations and congregations they serve. In some settings, the social worker may be ordained or in other ways recognized by the church as a leader. Because communities encompass both formal and informal ties between people in a web of relationships, it is difficult to separate formal—professional—relationships from informal relationships. Professional relationships with clients sometimes originate in church activities such as church committees, groups, and church programs led by the social worker. Boundaries of client/professional relationships and between professional and private life therefore are much less well defined then in some other professional contexts. At times, they are virtually absent. Consequently, clients and church members have greater access to the social worker than in other social service settings. The social worker also has greater potential knowledge of clients' and members' social networks and other resources and barriers for intervention. Often, however, the social worker has to cope with personal or organizational confusion of roles and the results of being almost constantly, if informally, "on duty" (Ferguson, 1992; Wikler, 1986; Wikler, 1990; Wigginton, 1997).

Churches *spin off programs and services* to their societal context.

Sometimes churches start ministries which take on a life of their own, outgrowing the congregational setting where they began. For example, All Saints Church in Los Angeles began an AIDS ministry before any programs for AIDS patients and their families existed. Over time, they were able to obtain funding from government and private sources outside the congregation. Volunteers began working with the AIDS ministry from outside the congregation. The program grew and became incorporated separately, and then became independent of the church.

Ed Bacon, Rector of All Saints, has pointed out that when the church gives birth to a ministry, then successfully calls on society to support that ministry, and finally the ministry is secularized and integrated into society, then the church has facilitated social transformation (Bacon, 1996). Many of the child welfare agencies in this nation began through volunteer organizations of church women. Over time they hired professional staff and became increasingly independent of the birthing church (Garland, 1994).

One of the difficult tasks for church social workers is leading the church in deciding when to hold on to ministries and when to let go of them. The church social worker can help this become a decision-making process which is inclusive of both professionals and church members and leaders who have invested themselves in the ministry. The decision needs to be made with clarity about the mission of the church and its purposes in beginning the ministry, and how that mission and sense of purpose have evolved through service.

In many respects, the profession of social work is itself a "spin off" of the church. It was a social transformation begun in the church. Long before the social work profession's birth, the church concerned itself with human needs and served poor, oppressed, and marginalized persons. The direct forerunners of social work were the voluntary societies which church groups and individuals formed in the eighteenth and nineteenth centuries. These societies and agencies addressed the problems of hunger, slum life, unemployment, worker's rights, mental illness, prison reform, and the care of widows and orphans. Many early social workers were ministers and other church leaders. For example, in the early years of the 20th century, Jane Addams rejected a foreign missionary career to become a pioneer social worker in the settlement house movement in Chicago (Garland, 1995; Hinson, 1988). Social work has become increasingly secularized over the past century. The relationship between the church and the social work profession has sometimes been rocky. The church has moved from being the primary host setting for social work practice to being one of many places where social workers practice. Nevertheless, perhaps the church needs to celebrate the social transformation it created by giving birth to and nurturing the social work profession as it became a part of the mainstream of our society.

Churches are (or should be) advocates for the poor and oppressed and committed to social justice.

The church not only serves oppressed persons; it is sometimes their advocate. An advocate is one who pleads the case of another, who speaks out for those who have no voice. Advocates seek to bring about change in unjust social systems in addition to ministering to those who are harmed by the injustice.

For churches, advocacy most often grows out of ministry. For example, the Christian Service Program (CSP) in Canton, Illinois, assists seniors in completing their Medicare and health insurance forms, offers volunteer income tax assistance, and meets similar simple clerical needs. The program is staffed by volunteers. They deny any interest in engaging in "advocacy"; they just want to help senior adults in their community. Social justice is not their chosen priority. But when they learned that the county ambulance service in Canton was being curtailed, they led the charge for a new ambulance service to take its place. When they found some insurance companies were ignoring or hassling their clients, they pressured the companies to improve their care of senior citizens. And when they realized that one of the many forms for the Social Security Administration made no sense, they leaned on the agency until Social Security changed its form (Dudley, 1996).

At other times, churches have been advocates because it was their own people who were victimized by injustice. During the period of slavery and in the time of racist oppression which has followed, the Black Church not only gave birth to new social institutions such as schools, banks, insurance companies, and low income housing, but it also provided the arena for political activity to address the larger society's racism as well as the needs of the community. Black churches had a major role in establishing the black self-help tradition during a time when there were no public social welfare agencies and private philanthropy was reserved for other groups.

One of the most challenging tasks of church social workers is leading congregations and denominations from ministry into advocacy for social justice (Garland, 1994,1996). As Harvie Conn states:

> ...the task of the church, until that glorious day, is to be co-workers with God in the formation of the new creation. This is why the church is not content merely to change individuals: God is not so content. One day soon God will create a wholly new environment in which the righteousness of His people will shine.... We labor in the knowledge that God alone can build it. But, in Pannenberg's words, our "satisfaction is not in the perfection of that with which we begin but in the glory of that toward which we tend...." What will be the instrument of the church in effecting this change? Not simply charity but also justice. Charity is episodic, justice is ongoing. One brings consolation, the other correction. One aims at symptoms, the other at causes. The one changes individuals, the other societies (Conn, 1987, p. 147).

Jesus made the declaration of Jubilee central to his mission and identity. His salvation includes not only deliverance from sin and physical healing; it also involves a gift of economic and social well-being for the poor and downtrodden of the world (Campolo, 1990).

What Else do Church Social Workers Need to Know?

Churches, then, are (1) host settings for social services, (2) social communities, and (3) contributors to the justice and well-being of the world as they spin off services and programs into mainstream society and as they advocate for societal change. To work with congregations and other church practice settings, however, social workers need to know more than how to provide social services in a host setting, how to develop and nurture community, how to help churches determine their ongoing relationship with social services, and how to motivate and lead in advocacy for social justice. Churches are voluntary, mission-driven organizations with a unique culture. Each of these characteristics suggests knowledge and skills needed by the church social worker.

Churches are *voluntary organizations*.

Particularly in American society, church membership and participation is voluntary. If people do not like what is happening in one congregation, they simply move to another, or stop participating altogether. In some denominations, even congregational participation in the denomination is voluntary. If the congregation does not like what the denomination is doing, it may choose to withdraw and to affiliate with another denomination, to remain independent, or simply to withhold its financial support from the denomination. Dealing with conflict and maintaining interpersonal relationships therefore have much greater import in church social work than in other settings.

At the level closest to many church social workers, the work of many church social service and social action programs are carried out by church members—volunteers. Supervising and consulting with volunteers is dramatically different than supervising and consulting with employees. Volunteers have to continue to see the significance of what they do in order to be motivated; there is no paycheck at the end of the week which keeps them coming even when they are tired and discouraged. Just as challenging, volunteers are not hired, so they cannot be fired. Dealing with difficulties in the work of volunteers requires considerable skill and sensitivity.

Nurturing the relationship with congregations and their leaders is an ongoing, significant aspect of church social work. Speaking and writing are arenas of church social work that have much greater import than in other social work specializations. The most effective church social workers often preach or in other ways provide worship leadership to churches and church groups, provide stimulating educational presentations, and write about what they do and about the role of the church in social issues of the day. They write for church newsletters, Christian education curriculum, denominational magazines, and specialized publications.

Churches and their agencies are *mission-driven organizations*.

The church is a mission driven organization. That is, it is not motivated primarily by serving the needs around it but by the mission to which it feels called. The church is not ultimately responsible for effectively meeting all the needs of society. Instead, the church is responsible for being faithful to its mission, a mission of telling the story of its faith and serving as a living witness to the love of God as demonstrated in the life, death, and resurrection of Jesus Christ. Church social workers must first be clear about and then articulate the relationship between their work and this overarching mission of the church.

Too often, social workers approach the church from the perspective of *social work's* mission, which is addressing the needs of persons in their environment and advocating for social justice. When one begins with social work's mission, the church is seen as a resource to be mined in accomplishing the mission of social work. After all, the church has money, and volunteers, and some political clout. The volunteer service of church members is a tremendous resource to social services in our society; it has been estimated that churchgoers donate about 1.8 million hours of services in the United States annually (Filteau, 1993). It is not surprising, then, that social workers try to finesse the church's involvement and support of what they are doing. Sometimes this works, and both the social work professional and the church are enhanced, because their missions are congruent with one another.

On the other hand, sometimes social workers end up strip-mining the church, taking their resources of money for emergency assistance, or volunteers for their social service programs, with little thought for the impact on the church itself. The focus is on getting needed help in the social service program, rather than the reverse—helping the church achieve its mission. The money is spent, but the church may feel little connection with what happened to the money, and they become discouraged that their little bit makes so little difference in a sea of need. Volunteers find the work hard and do not connect that serving the needs of others is a fulfillment of Jesus' teaching, regardless of the response. The harassed social worker may have no time to work with the volunteers, to pray with them, to connect what they are doing with their spiritual lives. As a consequence, the church's resources are diminished rather than nurtured. As for the social worker, there may be a growing resentment over time as the church loses its interest in being involved and the resources dry up.

Church social work, therefore, must begin with the church's mission and how the mission of social work can be used in service of that mission. Working with volunteers must thus be bi-focal—both on the provision of needed services by the volunteer as well as on the nurture of faith and commitment in the volunteer (Garland, 1994).

Churches are *cultural groups*

It should be clear by now that churches are in many respects subcultures. They have their own language, nonverbal symbols, norms, and patterns of relationships. They have historical identities that shape their current understanding of themselves. These identities reflect not only an overarching denominational heritage but also the unique histories of a particular congregation. Like families, churches develop over time, going through organizational stages that partially shape their current life together (Moberg, 1984; Carroll, Dudley, & McKinney, 1986; Garland, 1994).

The church social worker operates within and uses the language
and cultural patterns of the church community. The Bible, theology,
and Christian values are keys to understanding and working effectively
in this context. For example, the concepts of the "family of God" and
Christian hospitality provide the ground for social action in behalf of
homeless and isolated persons and social ministry programs that attempt to include them in the community. Biblical teachings on the value
and role of children provide impetus for child welfare services and child
advocacy. Understanding these distinctive characteristics of the church
context is just as important for effective social work practice as is understanding the culture, history, and current life experiences of an ethnic family requesting family service.

Often, the social worker will find not only commonalities but also
basic conflicts between the values and knowledge of the social work profession and a congregation's or denomination's beliefs and practices. For example, Midgley and Sanzenbach (1989) have spelled out some of the basic
conflicts between social work practice and fundamentalist Christian doctrines. The church social worker must find ways to live with and sometimes to challenge the contradictions inherent in being a social worker and
a church leader. Such conflicts are not unique to the church context for
social work practice but can be found in every host setting.

What are the Qualification for Church Social Work?

Church social work is not for every social worker who is a Christian, just as not every Christian is called to be a church leader. Social
workers are also needed in public and other private, nonsectarian settings where they can live their faith through their work. Church social
work is a highly demanding vocation, and one that requires some specific personal as well as professional qualifications:

1. First and foremost, the church social worker needs to be a Christian who loves the church in all its humanness as well as the ideal
   to which it strives. Churches are like any other human institution;
   there are problems, politics and personal conflicts. Grady Nutt, a
   Christian humorist, once said that the church is like Noah's ark: if
   it weren't for the storm outside, you couldn't stand the stink inside. I would add that church social workers, like other church
   leaders, often work below deck where the bilge can get pretty deep.
   Church leaders, including church social workers, must have a love
   for the church that can transcend the frustrations of fallible organizations and persons.

2. Church social workers often are the only social worker, or one of a very few, in the organization. Their work is often self-defined and requires creativity and the ability to envision what is not and plan and work toward the not-yet. Because so much of the work is often independent practice, a master's degree in social work which develops these abilities is frequently needed.

3. Church social workers are church leaders, relating social service and social action to the culture of the church community, which is rooted in scriptures and the history and doctrine of the church. At least some formal graduate theological education which provides knowledge of the Bible, theology, church history, and spiritual life can be enormously helpful. In addition, understanding the organizational distinctives of a voluntary, mission-driven organization is essential. Some graduate social work programs are now providing courses and concentrations in church social work that include this specialized content.

4. Church social workers do a great deal of public speaking and have opportunity to be influential if they can write for professional and congregational audiences about their work and its relationship to the mission and teachings of the church. They need to be prepared with skills of preaching, teaching, training, and writing.

5. Church social workers need specialized expertise in the arena of ministry in which they are employed, whether that is family therapy in a church child welfare or counseling agency, community organizing in an inner-city community center, administration in a denominational office of Christian social ministries, or any of the other myriad arenas for church social work practice.

6. Church social workers need personal warmth and a love for persons that is felt by others and draws people to them. They often do a lot of informal work with church leaders, members, and volunteers, and they need to be able to inspire, encourage, and motivate others to do the hard work of Christian social ministries.

7. Church social workers need a deep personal faith and a sense of calling to this challenging arena of professional practice. Sometimes church social workers find themselves in the heat of church or denominational conflicts which can be disheartening. Sometimes churches are unconscionably slow in living their mission as a people of faith and service. Sometimes churches are more social communities than they are the body of Christ. Sometimes church social workers see into the

heart of social injustice on the outside and ugly politics on the inside of churches. Church social work is not for the faint of heart, nor is it for those seeking nine- to-five employment.

8. Finally, church social workers need to be able to claim the truth that God does not call Christians, even church social workers, to be all that is required for the work before us; God calls us to be faithful. We are not ultimately judged on how effective our efforts have been to meet the needs of others or to create a just society, but on how faithful we have been to allow God to work through us as we do the best we can with what we have in the place we are.

The biblical stories of God's actions through history are always stories of limited, inadequate persons through whom God worked. These persons courageously lived into God's calling in the place they found themselves—Shiphrah and Puah, a couple of slave midwives who saved the Hebrew baby boys, including Moses; David, a little boy with a sling-shot who felled a giant; Esther, a young Jewish wife of a ruthless king who risked her life to save her people; a nameless boy, a volunteer offering his meager lunch to help feed a hungry crowd of thousands. The great promise for church social workers is that we are not alone in facing the great challenges of social injustice, churches in internal conflict, and our own limitations.

References

Bacon, E. (1996). Presentation : Louisville Institute Conference, Louisville, KY.

Campolo, T. (1990). *The kingdom of God is a party*. Dallas: Word.

Carroll, J. W., Dudley, C. S., & McKinney, W. (Eds.). (1986). *Handbook for congregational studies*. Nashville: Abingdon.

Conn, H. (1987). *A clarified vision for urban mission: Dispelling urban stereotypes*. Grand Rapids: Zondervan.

Dudley, C. S. (1996). *Next steps in community ministry*: Alban.

Ferguson, J. (1992). The congregation as context for social work practice. In D. R. Garland (Ed.), *Church social work* (pp. 36-57). St. Davids: The North American Association of Christians in Social Work.

Filteau, J. (1993). Churches play critical role in national social welfare. *Intercom* (June-July), 5.

Garland, D. R. (1994). *Church agencies: Caring for children and families in crisis*. Washington, D.C.: Child Welfare League of America.

Garland, D. R. (1995). Church social work, *Encyclopedia of Social Work* . Washington, D.C.: National Association of Social Workers.

Garland, D. R. (1996). *Precious in His Sight: A guide to child advocacy for the churches*. (rev. ed.). Birmingham: New Hope.

Garland, D. R. (forthcoming). *Family ministry*. Downers Grove: Intervarsity Press.

Hessel, D. T. (1982). *Social ministry*. Philadelphia: Westminster Press.

Hinson, E. G. (1988). The historical involvement of the church in social ministries and social action. *Review and Expositor, 85*(2), 233-241.

Midgley, J., & Sanzenbach, P. (1989). Social work, religion, and the global challenge of fundamentalism. *International Social Work, 32*, 273-287.

Moberg, D. O. (1984). *The church as a social institution*. Grand Rapids: Baker Book House.

Wigginton, S. (1997). Roping off the pews: Boundary issues in family ministry. *Journal of Family Ministry, 1997*(2).

Wikler, M. (1986). Pathways to treatment: How Orthodox Jews enter therapy. *Social Casework, 67* (2), 113-118.

Wikler, M. (1990). "Fishbowl therapy": Hazards of Orthodox therapists treating orthodox patients. *Journal of Psychology and Judaism, 14* (4), 201-212.

CHAPTER 3

SOCIAL WORK'S LEGACY
THE METHODIST SETTLEMENT MOVEMENT

Sarah S. Kreutziger

Walter Trattner in his social welfare textbook *From Poor Law to Welfare*, critically asserts that religious settlements were little more than "modified missions....bent on religious proselytizing, rigorous Americanization, and the imposition of social conformity on lower class clientele" (1976, p. 17). I believe he vastly underestimates the scope and positive impact of religious settlements on the more highly publicized Social Settlement Movement and on social work itself. Starting in the mid-nineteenth century, in response to the demands of the industrialization of American cities and towns, the religious settlement workers created, financed, and staffed outreach programs to the most marginalized inhabitants of the inner cities. They formed Bible classes, kindergartens, industrial schools, clubs, loan banks, job bureaus, dispensaries, reading rooms, and other programs that laid the groundwork for later social reforms. In the process, they created the foundation for the beginning of modern social work. Religious settlements strengthened the cause of women's rights and paved the way for women to enter careers in social welfare. And, in the South, religious settlers led the campaign for racial and ethnic equality.

Many denominations sponsored these specialized city missions, but perhaps none was as well organized and tenacious as the Methodist Episcopal Church (now the United Methodist Church) in spearheading this form of mission outreach. For that reason, an examination of the Methodist Religious Settlement Movement not only shows the work of religious settlers as part of the religious settlement movement, but highlights as well the tension between the ideologies of Christianity and the emerging tenets of enlightenment liberalism. This tension forms social work values today.

Origins of the Methodist Religious Settlement Movement

City Missions

The religious settlement movement in American Methodism began in New York City "on the 5th of July, 1819, [when] 'a number of females' met at the Wesleyan Seminary...for the purpose of forming an Auxiliary Society to the Missionary Society of the Methodist Episcopal Church, which had been formed the previous April" (Mason, 1870, p. 82). While their original purpose was to support missionaries to the North American Indians, their work gradually focused on problems closer to home. By 1850, "the ladies of the mission," united in evangelistic pragmatism, began their work in the notorious Five Points of New York City surrounded by:

> ...miserable-looking buildings, liquor stores innumerable, neglected children by scores, playing in rags and dirt, squalid-looking women, brutal men with black eyes and disfigured faces, proclaiming drunken brawls and fearful violence. (Mason, 1870, p. 33)

The Five Points Mission was the earliest city mission and the precursor of latter settlement homes and community centers in the United States (Leiby, 1978; Magalis, 1973; Riis, 1962).

Led by evangelist Phoebe Palmer, one of the most famous women of her day, the ladies raised money for a building, appointed a paid missionary, and volunteered to conduct Sunday schools, church services, and a nursery for working women. Later, they opened a reading room as an enticement for men who habitually sought solace in taverns, started a medical dispensary, installed public baths for the tenement dwellers, and provided emergency food and shelter for the poor.

Another project of the Missionary Society was "rescue work." In 1833, the women formed the Moral Reform Society to help women who "were victims of sin and shame" (Ingraham, 1844, p. 39) find ways to support themselves other than prostitution. The Society hired city missionaries who were some of the first female social workers. The first and most famous was Margaret Pryor whose descriptions of her "walks of usefulness" became a best-selling book and did much to publicize their work.

Pryor's and Palmer's pleas to move into social reform were spoken in language of the "woman's sphere of action." This language can be appreciated best when we consider the assigned roles and relationships of that era. As homemakers whose responsibility was to build a "sanctified" (holy) society, women were exhorted by religious leaders to protect theirs' and others' homes by instilling spiritual values and righteous living in their children and other members of the household. Their special providence was to take care of other women and children who did not have similar resources or religious beliefs. It followed then, that other rescue work was directed at children. Charles Loring Brace, founder of a massive foster care system for destitute children, began his career at

Five Points Mission. His work there convinced him that "effective social reform must be done in the source and origin of evil, — in prevention, not cure" (Brace, 1973, p. 78). He founded the Children's Aid Society in 1853; an organization that relocated more than fifty-thousand
children to rural homes to remove them from the real and perceived
dangers of city life.

The Five Points Mission and similar agencies were part of a broader
effort known as the City Mission Movement which had its roots in the
New York Religious Tract Society. The tract societies distributed religious literature to convert the inner-city poor. In the 1830's, members
of the Tract Society began holding prayer meetings and establishing
Sunday schools for the children marked for evangelism (Smith-
Rosenberg, 1971). As the volunteers became familiar with the living
conditions of the residents, they carried food and clothing with them
on their rounds and set up emergency funds. In time, they organized
their welfare work into wards for distribution and created a new organization, the Society for the Relief of the Worthy Poor. This became the
New York Association for Improving the Condition of the Poor. By 1870,
forty full-time salaried missionaries were pioneering model tenements,
summer camps for children, industrial training schools, and systematic
"outdoor" relief. The Association was a forerunner of the New York
Charity Organization Society, a pioneer of early professional social work.

The Institutional Churches

The rapid replication of the programs of the Five Points Mission was
inspired by the challenge of the industrial age and the difficulties experienced by the men and women who immigrated to the United States to
work in its factories. "Between 1860 and 1900, some fourteen million immigrants came to America and about another nine million, mainly from
southern and eastern Europe...arrived between 1900 and 1910" (Trattner,
1979, p.135). The massive crowding, illnesses, and social problems created
by the influx of largely unskilled, illiterate, foreign-speaking individuals
was unparalleled in our history. In New York City, two-thirds of the population lived in tenements in 1890, while Chicago, then the fastest growing
city in the world, packed inner-city residents near the putrid-smelling, un-
sanitary stockyards where slaughtered animal carcasses fouled water and
air. Gangs and petty criminals, fortified by alcohol and other drugs, preyed
on the new arrivals. The "urban frontier, like the rural frontier, was a dangerous place" (Seller, 1981, p. 50).

To the native-born Americans, the newcomers were dangerous in
other ways. Their political attitudes, born out of feudal societies in which

government was an agent of social control provided a challenge to American democracy. In the slums, the immigrants turned to old-world political traditions such as the "padrone," or political boss, who would manipulate the system for personal gain in exchange for votes. American ideals of patriotic civic action on the basis of self-denial and responsibility clashed with these attitudes (Hofstadter, 1955).

Americans were also concerned about the breakdown of traditional Protestant religious customs and beliefs founded on Puritanism which portrayed the United States as a "holy experiment" destined to create a new society as a beacon to the rest of the world (Winthrop, 1960; Woodbridge, Noll, & Hatch, 1979). Living sin-free, disciplined, temperate, hard-working lives was crucial to this cause. The immigrants, mostly Roman Catholic, drank, brought "continental ideas of the Sabbath" with them, displayed nomadic living habits, and wore fancy dress (Strong, 1893, p. 210). These practices severely distressed city evangelists. Even worse for their cause was the reality that many in the mainline denominations were becoming indifferent to the plight of the poor and abandoning the inner city churches.

The solution to these changes was to set up a specialized form of city missions in these abandoned churches to Americanize, and hence Christianize, the new arrivals by offering them resources and support. These citadels against the onslaught of massive social problems were called Institutional Churches. Programs and activities developed in these "open" or "free" churches (because there was no charge for the pews) were adopted by the social settlers and others following in their footsteps (Bremner, 1956). These churches viewed themselves as "institutions" that ministered seven days a week to the physical and spiritual wants of all the people within their reach. [They] sponsored clinics, free Saturday night concerts, self-supporting restaurants and lodging houses, wood yards for the unemployed, "fresh air work" for women and children, and "gold-cure" establishments for drunkards. There was a marked emphasis on practical education. Institutional churches sponsored libraries and literary societies and carried on kindergartens, trade schools, and community colleges (McBride, 1983, p. xi).

Although these churches have been described as similar to the secularized social settlements because they adopted many methods and educational theories of the "new charity" (Abell, 1962, p. 164), there is much evidence that the primary mission of the institutional churches was evangelism. While their programs were similar to non-sectarian charities, their ideology was quite different. The Methodist women who supported institutional work were motivated by Scripture. They were to feed the hungry, care for the sick, and clothe the poor (Tatem, 1960).

Methodist women carried these ideals into their work with the religious settlements and supported all of these missions through the structure and activities of the Home Missionary Societies.

The Home Missionary Societies

Almost without exception, the Home Missionary Societies were made up of white, middle-class women, better educated than most of their female contemporaries and freed from time-consuming house chores by the same industrial revolution that was creating the massive social problems in the cities and towns. While many other denominations were ministering to poor and oppressed individuals, the Methodists were the most zealous and well-organized. By 1844, when the Methodist Episcopal Church separated into the southern and northern branches over slavery, there were already 360 missionaries in the United States and one mission in Liberia supported by these societies (Norwood, 1974).

After the Civil War, the local mission societies joined together to build national organizations within the two divisions. The northern church established its missionary societies first in 1869, followed by the southern church nine years later, to aid foreign missions. The Woman's Home Missionary Society was founded in 1880 in the northern Methodist Episcopal Church to support missions within the United States. Their support of missions in the South, especially for the recently freed slaves, led to the founding of the southern church's Home Mission Society in 1880 (*Home Missions*, 1930).

Much of the philosophy undergirding the mission societies' work came from a societal view of women as the moral guardians of the home. In the North, missionary society members organized under the banner of "evangelical domesticity," the notion that the natural spiritual superiority of women gave them the authority to protect their homes and children from the evil influences of society (Lee, 1981). Countless women echoed the belief that "in every well-regulated family their [sic] mother is the potent influence in molding the little ones committed to her sacred guidance" (*Women's Missionary Society*, 1884, p. 4). Much of the reform activity therefore, was directed toward helping other women and children create barriers against the evils that would destroy the sanctity of the home.

In the South, the drive to purify homes was made more difficult by antebellum ideology. The plantation mentality that enslaved black women kept white women in bondage as well. A rigid, tightly-knit, hierarchical social order demanded obedience and submissiveness. As a result, religious activities for women stressed personal piety rather than the "social holiness" of evangelical service that northern women had channeled into abolition, women's rights, and other reforms (Thompson, 1972; Scott, 1970). The Civil War, despite its devastation, liberated southern women for reform activities previously denied them. Consequently, they poured their energies into "their appointed sphere": the churches. In time, the wives, daughters, and sisters of former slave holders joined with the wives, daughters, and sisters of slaves to establish agencies and organizations that promoted racial harmony and reinforced the cause of women's rights (Hall, 1979; Scott, 1984). A significant product of their work was the Methodist Religious Settlement Movement.

The Religious Settlements

Activities and Staffing

Methodist settlements, like their predecessors, often began as child care facilities for working mothers and expanded into kindergartens, sewing clubs, domestic labor training, homemaker clubs, rescue work for prostitutes, boys' athletic clubs, classes in cooking, play grounds, and religious services. Although they also included reading rooms, public baths, English classes, night school, dispensaries, lectures, concerts, music lessons, bookkeeping and banking classes, military drills, gymnastics, milk stations, saving associations, libraries, and "improvement clubs for men," — they were primarily geared to the needs of mothers and children (Woods & Kennedy, 1911).

The settlement houses were originally sponsored as an expanded mission project of the Women's Home Missionary Society (WHMS), the Chicago Training School for City, Home and Foreign Missions (CTS), and several independent associations. While the goal of the leaders of these organizations was still the sanctification of society through the changed lives of individuals, their work among the poor enlarged their vision of the difficulties that these individuals faced. City missionaries realized that society as a whole must be changed if their goal to evangelize the world was to be reached. Fed by the theology of the social gospel, which saw sin as systemic as well as individual, the city missionaries and their supporters created a broader, more far-reaching attack upon the barriers that kept all people from realizing their God-given potential.

Volunteers from the missionary societies and churches, along with a few paid city missionaries, ran many of the early missions; but the need for better training and education for their expanding work prompted missionary society leaders such as Lucy Rider Meyer, Jane Bancroft Robinson, and Belle Harris Bennett to advocate for biblically-trained women who would live in the neighborhoods among the disadvantaged in the same manner that foreign missionaries lived with citizens in the lands they served. After much planning, hard work, and many setbacks, the efforts of these women and others were realized by the 1880's in a new version of the home missionary: the deaconess.

Deaconesses were distinguished from the city missionaries by the clothing they wore, their communal living arrangements, their formal connection to the church, and their unsalaried service (*Deaconess Advocate*, February 1901). Easily recognized because of their dark dresses, starched bonnets tied with a large white bow, and brisk manner, the deaconesses took their calling seriously. Their task was to "minister to the poor, visit the sick, pray for the dying, care for the orphan, seek the wandering, comfort the sorrowing, [and] save the sinning..." (Thoburn & Leonard in Lee, 1963, p. 37). With the biblical deaconess Phoebe as their model, deaconesses went into the inner cities of the North and the factory towns and rural communities of the South as part of the twentieth century vanguard for the religious settlement movement. In the first thirty years of the Methodist diaconate, the Chicago Training School, founded by Lucy Rider Meyer, sent nearly 4,000 deaconesses and city missionaries to work in hospitals, schools, settlements, rescue homes, and churches. Forty of these institutions were started by CTS graduates (Brown, 1985).

In the South, Methodist settlements constituted from 30% to 100% of all settlements when the first national listing was compiled in 1911 (Woods & Kennedy, 1911). Settlements that served white populations were called Wesley Houses, after Methodism's founder John Wesley, and settlements that served African-Americans were known as Bethlehem Houses (Tatem, 1960). Settlement leaders worked with white American cotton mill employees in Georgia, French-Arcadians families and Italian immigrants in Louisiana, African-American farms workers in Tennessee and Georgia, European seafood workers in Mississippi, and Hispanic migrant workers in Texas and Florida (Nelson, 1909). Many of the settlements were headed by deaconesses who lived in the neighborhoods they served. In 1910, there were six Methodist deaconess training schools and ninety social agencies staffed by 1,069 deaconesses (Glidden, in Dougherty, 1988).

The Deaconess Mother Heart

The religious basis of the beliefs and values of the deaconess sisterhood was the Puritan vision of America's spiritual manifest destiny: America as the beacon to the rest of the world. Deaconess values were also formed from Wesleyan ideals of "perfecting" society through service and mission, cultural definitions of women's position and place, enlightenment views of scientific reasoning, and the emerging social gospel. Their declared goal was the salvation of the "household of faith": American society. The evils of unchurched people, drunkenness, pauperism, and negative influences from foreigners could be wiped out, they believed, with a return to Christian ideals based on the earlier promise of God's covenant with the "New Jerusalem," the United States. This heavenly pattern, imprinted upon America, would ensure the salvation of the world. As deaconess educator Belle Horton declared, "we must 'save America for the world's sake'" (Horton, 1904, p. 41).

Justification for women's entry into this noble endeavor came from church tradition and the Bible as expressed through the metaphor of the Mother Heart. The Mother Heart, as described by Meyer, was the nurturing, caring, feminine side of God understood and possessed by women. Deaconess sisterhood, reinforced by communal living arrangements and church connection, readily integrated the holistic social gospel tenets into their ideological center. Since building the Kingdom of God on earth required the sanctification of each home, it was important for churches to include the work of those whose specific mission was the care of God's "unmothered children": Women. This allowed the deaconesses, and by extension - all females - greater authority to be ministers to the whole of society. This expanded vision of women's role in the church and community helped set the stage for the ordination of women, suffrage, and other forms of women's rights. It also helped pave the way for women to enter paid careers as the profession of social work emerged from its two pioneer branches: the Charity Organization Societies and the Settlement Movements.

Religious Settlements and Social Settlements

The women who staffed the settlement homes and institutions were on the front lines of the home mission field. Because the early city mission and institutional churches had provided the model for service and intervention in the lives of the dispossessed for non-sectarian settlements and associated charities just as they had for the religious settlements, there was a great deal of exchange of information, ideas, education, and services. Meyer was a friend of social settlement leader Jane Addams and each knew and respected the other's work. Addams helped Meyer select the site for the CTS and was involved in the early plans. Meyer had wanted to put Addams on the School's Board of Trustees in 1892, but was voted down because: Hull-House was just then drawing the fire of the churches because it had been thought necessary to eliminate any direct religious teaching from its program and one or two members of the Training School Board protested against the presence of this "unChristian enterprise" (Horton, 1928, p. 182).

Addams discussed this experience in *Twenty Years at Hull-House* (1981) and the embarrassment it caused, in her words, to "the open-minded head of the school" (p. 72). Addams compared the Training School favorably to the activities of the social settlements. Meyer and Addams continued to be friends throughout their careers and Meyer frequently spoke of Addam's work in the *Deaconess Advocate*, the journal of the CTS.

Despite opposition from church members who opposed the non-religious atmosphere of the social settlements, social settlement leaders continued to lecture regularly at the CTS and the students' field work included living as residents at Hull-House and other social settlements (Brown, 1985). By 1913, Meyers had supplemented the biblically-oriented lectures with textbooks by charity organization pioneers Edward J. Devine and Amos Warner (*Bulletin CTS*, January, 1914). By 1918, her students were working in the United Charities and Juvenile Protection Associations as "visitors" (*Bulletin CTS*, December, 1918), and were learning to think in the codified, scientific methods of the "new charity." Although religious motivation and language continued to be part of the curriculum, the new field of sociology and its promise of "perfecting" society through social engineering gradually supplanted the earlier emphasis on evangelism and proselytization in all the training schools. In time, it would become increasingly difficult to distinguish between the ideology and practices of those who graduated from the deaconess training schools and those who graduated from the university-based schools of social work. As deaconess education and values became less and less distinguishable from the values and methods of early professional social work, deaconess organizations began to lose the sponsorship of the church and other financial backers. Consequently, deaconess training schools were merged into schools of theology or schools of social work (Tatem, 1960; Nola Smee, telephone interview, July, 1995; address by Walter Athern, April 26, 1926, Boston University School of Theology Archives).

The Decline of the Methodist Religious Settlement Movement

While the movement toward non-sectarian liberalism characterized by scientifically-trained workers was initially moderated by the religious training of the settlers and other mission workers, the increasing centralization of reform activities and governmental intervention in social reform tipped the balance in favor of secularism. Additionally, "the spontaneous will to serve," so evident in earlier church volunteers, was subverted by the drive for professionalization. Previous values that had stressed compassion, emotional involvement, and vigorous love of humanity, according to social work historian Roy Lubove (1965), were "educated out" in preference for a "scientific trained intelligence and skillful application of technique" (p. 122). This new climate of professionalism at the beginning of the twentieth century changed the relationship between helper and those helped. Agencies became bureaucratic rather than evangelical, more contractual than spontaneous, and more removed from their clients.

One of the defining and continuing differences between the social settlements and the religious settlements was the pressure by churches on sectarian settlements to use their work for proselytizing (Doris Alexander, telephone interview, July, 1995; Davis, 1967). This pressure caused many of the settlements begun under religious auspices to sever their ties with their parent organizations. This was done to solicit community-wide support and to appeal to wealthy industrialists interested in ecumenical charities (Dubroca, 1955; Trolander, 1987). After World War I, with the rise of the Community Chest and other centralized social service funding, social settlement leaders were forced to answer to an organizational hierarchy that could dictate policy and programs. The net result was less emphasis on controversial community action (Trolander, 1987) and religious instruction. Funding from these centralized agencies also reinforced the drive to replace sectarian-trained workers with professional social workers.

Compounding these trends was social work's move into individual treatment and away from community development. Veterans of World War I suffering from battle-fatigue and shell shock required more than friendly neighborly relationships to help them cope with their personal and health-related problems. Red Cross workers treating military families discovered that Freudian psychoanalytic approaches and casework techniques developed by Mary Richmond, pioneer leader of the Charity Organizational Societies, were better suited to their needs. "Friendly visiting" gave way to therapeutic intervention as settlements were changed from community centers into mental health clinics.

This trend continued until by the early 1960's, professional social workers had replaced volunteers and religious settlement workers in many of the centers. The consequences of the move, according to one historian, led to greater emotional detachment between residents and the workers and less mutual concern and care. As she explained:

In place of spontaneity and being available around the clock, [social workers] made appointments and 'treatment plans.' Instead of seeking to do *with* the neighborhood, they sought to do *for* the neighborhood. Their 'professional' detachment from the neighborhood was not only physical, it was psychological. (Trolander, 1987, p. 39)

While Methodists followed similar practices related to staffing, there were some differences. Methodist deaconesses continued to reside in the settlements until the mid 1980's (Nola Smee, telephone interview, July, 1995) which helped to maintain the physical as well as the symbolic presence and sense of involvement in the neighborhoods that is part of the settlement legacy. Even when the settlers moved out, it was not so much because of their lack of dedication as it was from church policy and changing attitudes. The decline of religious settlers paralleled the decline of the deaconess movement as deaconesses began to retire and fewer and fewer women were willing to expend the level of commitment required for the diaconate as other opportunities for ministry and employment opened to women. The success of the deaconess crusade, the right of women to participate fully in the church and community, in other words, contributed to its decline (Betty Purkey, telephone interview, July, 1995).

Implications for the Future

While the history of religious settlements has remained in the shadows of the highly publicized work of social settlements such as Jane Addam's Hull-House (Addams, 1981; Davis, 1967; Leiby, 1979), the fact remains that these sectarian-sponsored organizations contributed much to the origins and success of early social work. Overlooked by most social work chroniclers were the hundreds of religiously-committed women, backed by an army of loyal supporters, who also moved into inner-city and rural neighborhoods to share their talents and service with the less fortunate. Methodist settlement leaders were typical examples of these women and their dreams.

The Methodist religious settlers' vision of society began with evangelical hopes for a holy nation undergirded by mutual concern for each other and love of God. This vision inspired the work that built hundreds of social welfare institutions and provided the support and financial resources to run them. When these front-line city missionaries were forced by the overwhelming task and changing times to create new ways of thinking and practice, they lost part of the religious underpinning that defined their vision. Despite these challenges and the decline of the deaconess movement, many of the original settlement houses survive as community centers and urban outreach stations for the churches. As such, they serve as reminders of what the church is capable of doing when the call for commitment, dedication, and sacrifice is answered. When, in the words of Bellah et al., (1985), we seek "the recovery of our social ecology [that] would allow us to link interests with the common good" (p. 287).

The religious and social settlers faced a society reeling from the effects of "wrecked foundations of domesticity" (Addams, 1972, p. 47) and other problems of societal dislocation and despair. Many contemporary people would agree that this century's end brings similar challenges. Family disorganization, international disruptions, population shifts, some with tragic consequences, and continuing disagreements over race, class, and gender create disunity and loss of purpose. Our country, like religious institutions and other social service professions, seems to be searching for a renewed vision and mission. Social work leaders Harry Specht and Mark Courtney (1994) join others calling for the profession of social work to return to its defining mission in the tradition of the settlement movements and the strong belief in the improvement of society. The history of the Methodist Religious Settlement Movement offers one avenue to reclaim that charge.

Notes

This chapter was rewritten from information from the author's unpublished dissertation research for Tulane University and research from a paper submitted to the School of Divinity at Duke University.

References

Abell, Aaron Ignatius. (1962). *The urban impact on American Protestantism 1861-1900.* Hamden: Archon.

Addams, Jane. (1981). *Twenty years at Hull House.* Phillips Publishing Co., 1910; reprint, New York: Signet Classic.

Addams, Jane. (1972). *The spirit of youth and the city streets.* New York: MacMillan Co., 1909; reprint, Urbana: University of Chicago Press.

Bellah, Robert N., Richard Madsen, William M. Sullivan, Ann Swidler & Steven M. Tipton. (1985). *Habits of the Heart: Individualism and commitment in American life.* Berkeley: University of California Press.

Brace, Charles Loring. (1973). *The dangerous class of New York.* New York: Wynkoop & Hollenbeck, Publisher, 1872; NASW Classic reprint, Washington, DC: NASW.

Bremner, Robert H. (1956). *From the depths: The discovery of poverty in the United States.* New York: New York University Press.

Brown, Irva Calley. (1985). *"In their times": A history of the Chicago Training School on the occasion of its centennial celebration, 1885-1985.* Evanston: Garrett Evangelical Theological Seminary.

Bulletin of the Chicago Training School for City, Home and Foreign Missions. (1914). 15(4).

Bulletin of the Chicago Training School for City, Home and Foreign Missions. (1918). 18(4).

Davis, Allen F. (1967). *Spearheads for reform: The social settlements and the progressive movement 1890-1914.* New York: Oxford University Press.

Deaconess Advocate. Vols. 14-29, 1898-1914.

Dougherty, Mary Agnes. (1979). The Methodist Deaconess, 1885-1918: A study in religious feminism. Ph. D. diss., University of California, Davis.

Dubroca, Isabelle. (1955). *Good neighbor Eleanor McMain of Kingsley House.* New Orleans: Pelican Publishing Co.

Hall, Jacquelyn Dowd. (1979). *Revolt against chivalry: Jessie Daniel Ames and the women's campaign against lynching.* New York: Columbia University Press.

Hofstadter, Richard. (1955). *The age of reform.* New York: Alfred A. Knopf.

Home Missions. (1930). Nashville: Woman's Missionary Council, Methodist Episcopal Church, South.

Horton, Isabelle. (1904). *The burden of the city.* New York: Fleming H. Revell Company.

Horton, Isaabelle. (1928). *High adventure—life of Lucy Rider Meyer.* New York: Methodist Book Concern.

Ingraham, Sarah R. (1844). *Walks of usefulness or reminiscences of Mrs. Margaret Prior.* New York: American Female Moral Reform Society.

Ladies of the Mission. (1854). *The old brewery and the new mission house at the Five Points.* New York: Stringer & Townsend.

Lee, Elizabeth Meredith. (1963). *As among the Methodists: Deaconesses yesterday today and tomorrow.* New York: Woman's Division of Christian Service, Board of Missions, Methodist Church.

Lee, Susan Dye. (1981). Evangelical domesticity: The Woman's Temperance Crusade of 1873-1874. In Hilah Thomas & Rosemary Skinner Keller, (Eds.), *Women in new worlds,* (pp. 293-309). Nashville: Abingdon Press.

Leiby, James. (1978). *A history of social welfare and social work in the United States.* New York: Columbia University Press.

Lubove, Roy. (1965). *The professional altruist: The emergence of social work as a career 1880- 1930.* Cambridge: Harvard University Press.

Magalis, Elaine. (1973). *Conduct becoming to a woman.* New York: Women's Division, Board of Global Ministries, The United Methodist Church.

Mason, Mary. (1870). *Consecrated talents: Or the life of Mrs. Mary W. Mason.* New York: Carlton & Lanahan.

McBride, Esther Barnhart. (1983). *Open church: History of an idea.* U.S.A.: By the author.

Nelson, John. (1909). *Home mission fields of the Methodist Episcopal Church, South.* Home Department, Board of Missions, Methodist Episcopal Church, South.

Norwood, Frederick A. (1974). *The story of American Methodism.* Nashville: Abingdon Press.

Riis, Jacob A. (1962). *How the other half lives: Studies among the tenements of New York.* 1890. Reprint, American Century Series. New York: Hill & Wang.

Scott, Anne Firor. (1970). *The southern lady: From pedestal to politics 1830-1930.* Chicago: University of Chicago Press.

Scott, Anne Firor. (1984). *Making the invisible woman visible.* Urbana: University of Illinois Press.

Seller, Maxine Schwartz. (1981). *Immigrant women.* Philadelphia: Temple University Press.

Smith-Rosenberg, Carroll. (1971). *Religion and the rise of the American city: The New York City Mission Movement, 1812-1870.* Ithaca: Cornell University Press.

Sprecht, Harry & Mark E. Courtney. (1994). *Unfaithful angels: How social work has abandoned its mission.* New York: The Free Press.

Strong, Josiah. (1893). *The new era or the coming kingdom.* New York: Baker & Taylor Co.

Tatum, Noreen Dunn. (1960). *A crown of service: A story of women's work in the Methodist Episcopal Church, South, from 1878-1940.* Nashville: Parthenon Press.

Thompson, Edgar. (1972). God and the southern plantation system. In Samuel Hill, (Ed.), *Religion and the solid South*, (pp. 57-91). Nashville: Abingdon Press.

Trattner, Walter I. (1979). *From poor law to welfare state.* (2nd. ed.), New York: Free Press.

Trolander, Judith Ann. (1987). *Professionalism and social change.* New York: Columbia University Press.

Winthrop, John. (1960). A model of Christian charity. In H. Shelton Smith, Robert T. Handy, & Lefferts A. Loetscher (Eds.), *American Christianity*, (pp. 98-102). New York: Charles Scribner's Sons.

Woman's Missionary Society of the Methodist Episcopal Church, South. (June): 1884.

Woodbridge, John D., Mark A. Noll, & Nathan O. Hatch. (1979). *The gospel in America.* Grand Rapids: Zondervan Publishing House.

Woods, Robert A. & Albert J. Kennedy, (Eds). (1911). *Handbook of settlements.* New York: Charities Publication Committee.

Archives

Boston University School of Theology.
Special Collections, University Libraries,
Boston, Massachusetts

CHAPTER 4

COMMUNITY PRACTICE: LESSONS FOR SOCIAL WORK FROM A RACIALLY-MIXED CENTRAL CITY CHURCH

Janice M. Staral

Social workers in the 21st century face the challenge of creating effective partnerships in order to respond to social problems. Developing these community coalitions requires an understanding of the history of problems and the nature of potential partners. The story of Reformation Lutheran Church, a racially-mixed church located in the central city of Milwaukee, Wisconsin, suggests strategies for developing community. These strategies are rooted in the settlement house tradition and reflect the religious beliefs of the church. This information was gleaned from participant-observer research conducted at the invitation of the church minister from 1991 to the present time.

Reformation Church was chosen as the focus of this study because the leaders of Reformation Church decided to remain at their original church location when faced with the problems of urban change and declining membership. During the past 20 to 30 years, leaders of other similar mainline churches chose to either close or sell their church buildings. Frequently, after the church closings, new churches were built in the outlying Milwaukee suburbs, following the out-migration of many of their church members. An example of this migration is illustrated by another Milwaukee Lutheran Church's decision to leave the central city. A note located in the Memorial Lutheran's 1992 Church Directory explains this movement to the suburbs:

> Rapid changes and population shifts took place in the inner-city during the 1950's and 1960's. In the summer of 1964, an offer to purchase the church by Mt. Moriah Baptist Church was accepted and the property was vacated by June 14, 1964. Groundbreaking for the new building in the suburb of Glendale began in October of 1965.

The leaders at Reformation Church, many of whom had also relocated to the nearby suburbs, wanted to continue to worship at their original site, but were concerned about their declining membership. These leaders were committed to social justice issues and believed that maintaining a church presence in the community was important. In 1985, they "called" a new pastor, a white male in his late thirties. He was encouraged to pursue strategies that would stabilize church membership, as well as be involved in the needs of the people in the Reformation Church neighborhood. The leaders asked for this specific pastor because he had a measure of success in his previous work in outreach ministries in the Uptown Chicago area. They hoped he could apply his experience to Reformation Church. The decision to hire this new pastor eventually resulted in church leadership which would pursue methods leading to neighborhood betterment and would change a largely white congregation to a racially-mixed one.

In this context, the goal of this chapter is to 1) *discuss* one church's response to urban change and decline, 2) *assess* and *examine* this response in terms of relevance and application to social work practice, and 3) *illuminate* the power religious institutions can have on a neighborhood. The role of the church is especially important in an era where federal and state budgets continue to be slashed and more expectations are being placed on the voluntary sector.

Understanding Urban Change

Urban America has changed dramatically in the last 30 years. Research conducted by Kasarda (1993), Abramson and Tobin (1994) and Massey and Denton (1993) suggest that many American cities have become increasingly segregated in terms of race and income. Such trends have been especially poignant in Milwaukee, a city distinguished by Abramson and Tobin as one of the most racially and economically segregated in the United States. This segregation has resulted in what the journalist, Joel Garreau (1991) has characterized as "edge cities," whereby the more affluent move their families and tax base beyond the city limits to areas that are "self-contained in terms of their social, economic, political, and cultural systems" (p. 14).

Urban communities have also been affected by deindustrialization, whereby family-supporting manufacturing jobs have been eliminated, relocated to outlying areas or moved to other countries (Bluestone & Harrison, 1982). Global restructuring, unemployment, and conservative economic policies (commonly known as supply-side economics, designed to boost profits) have affected all Americans, but especially the urban poor (Rose, 1997).

Various authors such as Murray (1984) and Mead (1986), have gained much public acceptance in their assertion that any aid to the poor only promotes dependence. The media portrayal of urban life as violent, infested

with drugs and filled with gang-bangers contributes to the negative attitudes toward the urban poor. As the affluent become more self-contained,
having minimal contact with the urban poor, it becomes much easier to
objectify the poor and to "blame" them for the city's current social ills.

The History of Urban Change at Reformation Church

The reality of urban change can be seen directly through understanding the history and specific changes in the Reformation Church neighborhood. The Evangelical Lutheran Church of the Reformation, the official
name of the church, was established in 1908. Two former pastors of Reformation characterized the church as a traditional, white, Lutheran Church,
with middle to upper-class membership. Most of the members lived near
the church, owning their homes or renting out the upper half of their duplexes to friends or family members. Most members were employed in various manufacturing or office jobs within the city.

Through the 1950's, Reformation Church maintained a roster of
2000 members and expanded its educational space for 600 Sunday School
children in the congregation. The church appeared poised on a long-
term successful expansion, but the forces of urban change were already
beginning in the Reformation neighborhood. In the mid-1960's, numerous neighborhood homes were demolished as part a proposed freeway
system which never materialized, leaving vacant, open lots. Local businesses and factories began to close or relocate, giving families further
impetus to move to the suburbs and outlying areas.

The Reformation Church Neighborhood

By 1985, the neighborhood had changed dramatically in terms of
racial composition, income level, crime, and home ownership. The congregation dwindled to 150 members, with no children for Sunday School.
The remaining church-goers maintained their membership with Reformation Church, but no longer lived in the immediate neighborhood.
Reformation Church had become a commuter church, having no significant membership from the church neighborhood.

The U.S. Census reports for the census tracts 90, 96, 97, and 98
that surround the Reformation neighborhood reveal marked changes in
the period from 1960 to 1990 (see map). The following reveals these
changes dramatically.

In the 1960's and 1970's, the Reformation Church neighborhood
was virtually all white. By 1990, the neighborhood had become pre-
dominantly African American, with only about 12 percent white resi-

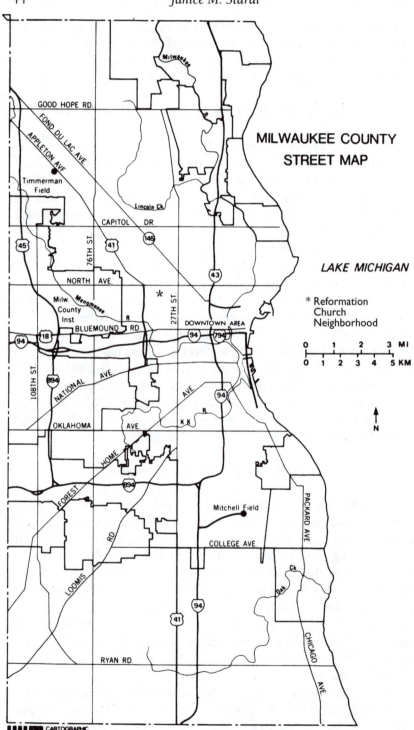

GOOD HOPE RD.

FOND DU LAC AVE.

APPLETON AVE.

Timmerman
Field

Lincoln Ck.

CAPITOL DR.

MILWAUKEE COUNTY
STREET MAP

45

76TH ST.

41

145

43

NORTH AVE.

Menomonee

*

Milw.
County
Inst.

R

27TH ST.

LAKE MICHIGAN

* Reformation
Church
Neighborhood

BLUEMOUND RD.

DOWNTOWN AREA

94

18

94

794

| 0 | 1 | 2 | 3 MI |
| 0 | 1 2 | 3 4 | 5 KM |

108TH ST.

894

NATIONAL AVE.

AVE.

94

N

OKLAHOMA AVE.

K K

R

HOME

894

FOREST

Mitchell Field

PACKARD AVE.

RD.

COLLEGE AVE.

LOOMIS

Ck.

Oak

94

CHICAGO

41

RYAN RD.

AVE.

dents. The percentage of home ownership in the neighborhood changed from an average of 36.9 percent in 1960 to an average of 17.4 percent in 1990. Unoccupied, vacant housing increased from a vacancy rate of 2.7 percent in 1960, to 15.9 percent by 1990. Unemployment for males rose from an average of 3.9 percent in 1960 to 20.3 percent in 1990. The poverty rate rose from 13.8 percent in 1970 to 57.9 percent in 1990.

Data regarding crime in the Reformation neighborhood were difficult to interpret because the Police and Fire Commissions changed reporting procedures in 1980. However, data from 1984 to 1990 document a significant increase in crime in just six years. In 1984, there were 3,302 crimes in the four closest census tracts. By 1990, there were 4,088, a 23.8 percent increase. In 1984, three homicides occurred within the four census tracts. In 1990, 14 homicides occurred (*Milwaukee Fire and Police Commission Report*, 1984, 1990). The area clearly became more violent.

Despite the drastic decline in the neighborhood, it is still one of contrasts and contradictions. Some parts appear to be safe. These areas have rows of wooden frame duplexes and bungalows, typical of Milwaukee working class neighborhoods, with houses facing the city street and alleys behind. Some newly remodeled Habitat for Humanity houses are evident. Other homes are clearly in need of repair, with dilapidated porches, broken windows or screen doors. Within a few blocks of Reformation Church, there are abandoned homes and vacant lots, where homes have either burned down or been demolished.

A pastoral intern who lived next door to the church during her internship gave this researcher the following description:

> You hear shouting outside all the time. You see police throwing people on the ground. You hear shots many nights. When you hear shots, like when you hear a semi- automatic gun, you stay away from the windows. Sometimes the shots are just the teenagers shooting the rats in the alley. You hear screaming every night. Sometimes the screaming is just the teenagers playing around outside.

One of the peer ministers at Reformation described the neighborhood this way:

> I was on 46th Street first, then I moved. Then I got shot up in my house. It wasn't for me. My house was mistaken for the wrong house. There was a bullet laying at my baby's head. I was so scared, so I moved from there. That was 1985. Then I moved to 34th Street. I wanted to get out of the neighborhood, but it's getting bad all over.

A Holistic and Integrated Approach

Visitors coming to the church see a well built, large, white, stone structure. Carved depictions of Martin Luther and words from his "Here I Stand" speech during the time of the Reformation are prominent on the outside of the building. The outside brick of the church is free from graffiti typical of many other neighborhood buildings. There are glass windows on the lower side of the church walls. The glass windows are remarkable for they are some of the few glass windows in the neighborhood that are neither broken nor covered with iron bars. The sanctuary of the church, which occupies a smaller part of the building and seats about 300 to 400 people, reflects an earlier elegance. The church is built in the style of the old German Lutheran Church, with wood ceiling tiles, and dark, thick wood beams on the ceilings and sides. One side of the church is framed with intricately stained glass windows.

This picture of elegance contrasts with other areas of the church which need refurbishing. Furniture is comfortable, but worn. The inside of the church is a labyrinth of rooms, offices and classrooms, with a winding back stairs that connects its three levels. The quietness of the sanctuary contrasts with the activity and chaos which marks visiting areas and hallways.

Church members, community people, and strangers frequent the church during the week. On Sundays and during the week, there are contrasts in the people coming to the church, in terms of race, class, and physical and cognitive abilities. Some of the visitors come to assist and participate in church activities or to socialize. Others request, and sometimes demand, immediate help in the form of food, bus tickets, or other crises assistance. There is both an aura of safety, because most visitors are greeted warmly by staff and community people, and of caution because at times tempers flare and verbal confrontations occur. The violence of the streets is never far away.

Reformation Church's distinctiveness results from these contrasts, as well as its philosophy of what it means to do neighborhood outreach, or as the pastor would say, "to be church." According to the pastor "being church" means developing an integrated, holistic ministry, not one of providing various independent programs. Separating the various methods of Reformation Church outreach ministry is difficult because just like the chaos and the friendly greetings, the methods are interwoven and are affected by each other.

It is difficult to separate the various methods used by Reformation Church for neighborhood betterment, but defining the undergirding philosophy of this work is not. This philosophy is of special interest to social work because it parallels that of Jane Addams' time and her work in the settlement house movement a century ago. For example, the pastor and his family reside in the immediate neighborhood. The outreach methods directed by the pastor attempt to connect individual and community problems to collective action, and are directed at changing public policy. Like the social workers at Hull House, direct aid is provided, but used in the context of supporting individual empowerment or change.

Some social workers may also relate to the overarching values shared by the pastor and the members of Reformation Church, which are a deep faith in God and in the value and dignity of every individual. Biblical scripture is interpreted from the perspective of the poor and the marginalized, referred to in the Roman Catholic tradition as the "preferential option for the poor." Whereas some religious traditions draw a dichotomy between the spiritual and secular, the holistic ministry at Reformation rejects any dichotomy between these two spheres.

The overall philosophy of the pastor of Reformation Church is summarized well in a statement written in the church's monthly newsletter (*The Gleanings*, July-August 1991):

> Hopefully, Reformation does not minister *in* nor *to* the neighborhood, *but with the people!* In this approach, the community and congregation are partners. At times, through town hall meetings, the people of the neighborhood instruct the church. The people of the community, no matter how poor, are seen as people of worth and dignity who have potential and much to offer. Reformation needs to continually join with the people of the neighborhood as they discern and define and live out the kind of community they want.

Community Building

The methods used in Reformation's outreach ministries are well integrated, but the most distinctive feature and the one that supports the overall life of the church is that of "building community." The pastor explains that this community building means developing interdependent relationships among various church members and then extending these relationships to other people who live in the neighborhood. When questioning people at Reformation regarding their church, one of the most frequent comment is "we build community here; everyone is welcome and accepted."

During visits to the church it becomes easy to observe what the pastor means by developing community. During Sunday church services no separation is made between members and nonmembers. Both groups participate equally throughout the service, which includes receiving Holy Communion, which has some restrictions in many Lutheran Churches. Non-alcoholic wine is used for this sacrament, demonstrating concern for those in the community who may be struggling with alcoholism.

Children are encouraged to attend church services, regardless of whether they are accompanied by an adult. Volunteers serve a breakfast to the neighborhood children prior to the beginning of services. The young children sit with each other in the front pews or choose to sit with a favorite adult attending services. Sometimes babies or young children end up in the arms of various adults throughout the service. Early in the service, all children are invited to the altar for a special message. The teenagers, who sit in the back of the church, also participate in this weekly ritual.

In the summer, about 40 to 50 children who attend church services participate in the summer work program — raking, painting, and cleaning up trash at various neighborhood locations. The children spend about four mornings a week, for six weeks of work, earning $210 for the summer. They are supervised by adult members from Reformation, who live in the neighborhood and are usually African American. The summer program also includes field trips, and efforts directed at developing individual skills and building self-esteem.

The children demonstrate their connectedness to Reformation Church by convincing their mothers, and sometimes fathers or extended family members, to attend church with them. In contrast to the tradition of adults bringing their children to church, many adults in the neighborhood are brought to the church through their children.

Church members serve as greeters and stand outside of the church on the sidewalk to invite passersby to church, during both warm and cold weather. Midway through the service, the whole congregation is involved in the "passing of the peace," a ritual of greeting where the 150-200 people attending the service stand and move around to shake hands or hug anyone who is in attendance that Sunday. The "passing of the peace" usually lasts about 10 minutes. Likewise, after services, refreshments of cookies and juice are served to further encourage fellowship. With both the outward show of hospitality and the neighborhood grapevine, people begin to learn that Reformation Church is a place they will be welcomed.

This effort at building community is replicated throughout the week. The pastor calls the activities that occur regularly as "givens," activities scheduled on a regular, predictable basis to which community people can come without having to follow a church schedule. This is especially important to community people experiencing crises. When in crisis they may have to temporarily drop out of the various activities, but can then easily re-enter activities when their lives re-stabilize. Some of these events occur weekly, others occur on a monthly or twice a month basis. For example, community Bible studies occur on Tuesday and Thursday mornings at ten o'clock. Education night and gospel choir are scheduled every Wednesday night. Friday nights are reserved for an evening community meal. Other activities include house churches (small groups meeting in private homes for personal faith sharing and support), self-esteem classes, and game nights.

In addition to the givens, members and neighborhood people frequently come to the church during the week for casual visiting. The church has a small gathering room where people visit or wait to talk to the pastor. Through such informal and formal gatherings at the church, community people develop strong relationships with their neighbors and begin to form a positive connection to the church. During most days of the week and on Sundays, the church is a place of activity and one of the few safe places for visiting.

In this context of community, a source of support is available. For example, when one mother's house was firebombed and burned down, another member of Reformation "took in" the mother and her three children for three months, until she was able to find new accommodations.

Reciprocal Giving and the Peer Ministers

People in the community use the church frequently as a source of assistance, asking the pastor for free food, bus tickets, short-term loans, and sometimes counseling in solving personal or family problems. People are usually supplied with help if the church has adequate resources at the time. However, the pastor suggests that the person asking for help also be asked how he or she can contribute their talents or skills to the church.

This process of reciprocal giving serves a threefold purpose. First, it prevents the church from being seen as only a place for a "hand-out." Secondly, it begins to build a connection between the help seeker and the church. Thirdly, it underscores the reality that the help-seeker has something of value and worth to contribute. If the person requesting help expresses an interest in reciprocating, the minister will inquire about the person's talents or areas of interest, or if the person has no specific interest, the minister will invite the person to experiment with various activities. These activities could include: answering the church office phone, preparing rooms for meetings, monitoring and greeting visitors to the church, attending community social action meetings, or visiting the elderly in nursing homes.

The role of the "peer minister" has been developed through the process of reciprocal giving. A peer minister is someone from the community who has agreed to "volunteer" to do work at the church on a consistent basis with some of the various tasks detailed above. The presence of the peer ministers, usually African Americans who reside in the neighborhood, helps to build a stronger linkage and deeper trust between the church and the people in the community. Peer ministers frequently accompany the pastor or the parish nurse on initial home visits. The family visited is more receptive to the pastor or nurse because of the presence and familiarity of the peer minister.

In exchange for the services of the peer ministers, the pastor provides support to them in pursuing personal goals, such as developing leadership skills, becoming effective in dealing with family problems, obtaining additional education, or acquiring employment. In addition to the supportive counseling to achieve goals, the peer ministers also receive a cash allotment of forty dollars a week.

This linkage with the community has become quite important as many of the children who come to Reformation know who the peer ministers are. One peer minister explains that many of the children come to them for help with problems in their homes. She said, "they see us at church or they know our phone numbers and they call us if they need us."

In some cases, the needs of the person asking for help at Reformation are so complicated and entrenched, or the person is so overwhelmed that direct aid, referral to other agencies, or crisis help is not sufficient. In these instances, the pastor, church staff member, or peer minister engage in what they call, "walking with the poor," working intensely with that person. Instead of referring that person to a community resource, they accompany the person to the agency, helping them to fill out forms, preparing for meetings, and attending meetings with them. In "walking with the poor," the support person continues his or her involvement until the person seeking help has either resolved the problem or finally obtained the confidence, skills, or advocacy needed to overcome the previous barriers to accessing help.

Entering Into Coalitions

The pastor maintains the primary leadership role within the church, but involvement of the peer ministers and other church members is essential. Likewise, coalition-building with both people and organizations within and outside the Reformation Church neighborhood is an essential tool for the pastor's accomplishment of neighborhood outreach.

Participating in coalitions is important for Reformation in order to share information, collaborate on strategic planning, plan collective action, and share in a spirit of solidarity. Some of the coalitions the pastors and Reformation members have been involved in include: Northside Strategy, a group of ten central city Lutheran Churches; a pastor's group from the neighborhood Black Churches; and Milwaukee Inner City Congregation Allied for Hope (MICAH), a church-based social justice group.

Additionally, the pastor has developed relationships with the neighborhood librarian, the teachers and principal of the nearby high school, and some of the remaining local business people. These relationships have afforded mutual support, an exchange of resources, and facilitated people coming to Reformation Church for spiritual or material help.

Collective Action and Community Empowerment

Ernesto Cortez (1993), a faith-based community organizer and writer, provides insight regarding the legitimacy of the church's role in developing community, necessary in order to move toward collective action. He does this by referring to the Latin root word of religion, "re-legare," which means "to bind together that which is disconnected," (p. 303).

Hanna and Robinson (1994) elaborate further by providing a definition of community that explains how Reformation's nurturing of community can lead to collective action. They explain:

> When speaking of community we refer to a specific population defined in terms of geographic location, demographic characteristics, or group commonality, who share a degree of relationship with each other, as well as some experiences of self-interest which can be addressed on a collective basis (p. xii).

Reformation Church has used community building to initiate collective action in confronting the problem of drug houses in their neighborhood. In 1994, the congregation and its neighbors identified twenty-three suspected drug houses and made a map of the location of these houses. In conjunction with these efforts, the pastor worked with members from MICAH, eight area churches, the city housing authority, the media, and local politicians to raise public awareness of the drug houses. On Good Friday, the church coalition sponsored a neighborhood march including 200 marchers. As a result of this collaborative work and collective action, ten of the twenty-three identified drug houses were closed by the police within three months. Five continued under investigation. Twelve others were investigated, but drug activity was not substantiated. Although not all the alleged drug houses were closed, one neighborhood person said, "that at least her block was no longer controlled by the dealers and gangs." She said, "Before that time, we couldn't even go out." Members and neighbors shared a problem, addressed it together and garnered the satisfaction of tangible improvements.

Bridging Race and Class Barriers

Reformation Church is one of the few urban places where people of various classes, races, or abilities can be seen coming together. On Sunday morning, it is not unusual to see a black teenager help an elderly white woman down the church steps, or to observe a well-dressed, middle-income person sitting next to someone whose mental illness is apparent from the person's constant rocking motion, or to see the random hugging during the "passing of the peace."

The peer ministers sometimes talk about the neighborhood pressure they feel from other African Americans who criticize them for "having a white pastor." During a community Bible study, one African American male in his mid thirties, who had suffered from both severe depression and drug use, talked specifically about this criticism. "I don't care what they say," he said. "I don't care what color my pastor is, just that he is honest and is there for me." This testimonial was even more significant to those in the group who knew that he and the pastor had had numerous counseling sessions, some of which were very confrontative, but which eventually led to this man achieving two years of sobriety and control over his depression.

The bridge between race and class has also been built by the pastor's frequent guest preaching at various suburban churches at Sunday morning services. Reformation's pastor preaches an animated, revivalist style sermon, inviting suburban members to become partners in Reformation's urban ministry either through financial gifts or through personal visits to the church. The suburban members who respond to the invitation for a personal visit, usually express surprise at how openly they are welcomed. They also gain a new impression of the neighborhood from that of being a dangerous, alienating place to one where people in the community are poor, but working hard to make a difference in their community.

Other suburban members still too frightened to venture into Milwaukee's central city, respond to the pastor's request for financial help to support Reformation's direct aid to community people. In 1994, "suburban partners" contributed $70,000 to Reformation's overall church budget of $264,950. The invitation to become partners with Reformation helps to bridge the gap between class and race, as well as having the pragmatic effect of comprising over one quarter of the annual Reformation budget. Without this assistance, much of the direct aid, summer work programs, and money for the peer ministers would be impossible.

Implications for Social Work

The strategies utilized by Reformation Church have broad and varied implications for social work. The outreach work carried out at Reformation clearly parallels the generalist model of social work practice. The generalist social worker must intervene in individual difficulties, but also work collaboratively and collectively in confronting community problems. The social worker needs to know when referrals are not enough and when someone must "walk with the poor" until the problem is resolved or the client has gained the competence to resolve the concern.

Social workers need to develop stronger coalitions and discover new allies in dealing with urban problems. Just as "politics creates strange bedfellows," social workers need to forge new alliances with agencies, businesses and other professionals who share concern about the urban poor. Churches should also be included in these alliances, both in terms of providing meeting places and support, and in joining with social workers in advocating for social justice.

Like the work being done at Reformation Church, social workers need to find ways to develop community for their clients. This is especially important in an era of alienation, where people have become isolated and are in great need of mutual support. Social workers need to discern their clients' strengths and find ways in which help-seeking can be both empowering and rejuvenating for both social workers and clients alike.

Finally, social workers need to reclaim their own professional heritage, which includes solidarity with the poor, collective action as a force for social change, and religious roots. This heritage can sustain social workers in the face of today's tremendous challenges and support the social work value of actively working toward social justice.

References

Abramson, Alan J., and Tobin, Mitchell S. (1990). *The Changing Geography of Metropolitan Opportunity: The Segregation of the Poor in U.S. Metropolitan Areas, 1970 to 1990.* Washington D.C. Fannie Mae Annual Housing Conference.

Bluestone, Barry & Harrison, Bennett. (1982). *The Deindustrialization of America.* New York: Basic Books.

Cortez, Ernesto. (1993). Reweaving the Fabric: The Iron Rule and the IAF Strategy for Power and Politics. In Henry Cisneros (Ed.), *Interwoven Destinies.* New York: W.W. Norton Co.

Garreau, Joel. (1991). *Edge Cities: Life on the New Frontier*. New York: Doubleday.

Hanna, Mark G., & Robinson, Buddy. (1994). *Strategies of Community Empowerment*. New York: Edwin Mellen Press.

Kasarda, John D. (1993). Cities as Places Where People Live and Work: Urban Change and Neighborhood Distress. In Henry Cisneros (Ed.), *Interwoven Destinies*. New York: W.W. Norton Co.

Massey, Douglas S., & Denton, Nance A. (1993). *American Apartheid: Segregation and the Making of the Underclass*. Cambridge, Massachusetts: Harvard University Press.

Mead, Lawrence. (1986). *Beyond Entitlement*. New York: The Free Press.

Milwaukee Fire and Police Commission Research Services. *City of Milwaukee 1990 Crime Report*. City of Milwaukee, 1990.

Milwaukee Fire and Police Commission. *Crime in the City of Milwaukee 1984*. City of Milwaukee, 1984.

Murray, Charles. (1984). *Losing Ground: American Social Policy 1950-1980*. New York: Simon and Schuster.

Rose, Nancy. (1997). The Future Economic Landscape: Implications for Social Work Practice and Education. In *Social Work in the 21st Century*. CA: Pine Forge Press.

U.S. Department of Commerce. *Census Population and Housing, Census Tracts: Milwaukee*. Washington D.C.: U.S. Government Printing Office, 1973, 1983, 1993.

CHAPTER 5

SOCIAL WORK IN ACTION: INTEGRATING PEOPLE WITH MENTAL RETARDATION INTO LOCAL CHURCHES AND COMMUNITIES OF FAITH

Rick Chamiec - Case

Many individuals from various walks of life attach significant value and meaning to membership and participation in a local church or community of faith. There are a number of reasons for this. A community of faith, as the term suggests, often provides a **community**:

- which through its corporate life of worship and service assists persons to learn about, love, serve, honor, and enjoy God, whom they believe to be worthy of their ultimate commitment and devotion.
- to which a person feels that he/she "belongs" as a valued member.
- with which a person can identify and which helps him/her form a sense of identity.
- through which a person can reach out to others, enabling him/her to live out his/her shared beliefs and values by "giving back" to those in need.

Unfortunately, people with disabilities like mental retardation are notably under-represented in most faith communities (ANCOR, 1995). As a result, many people with mental retardation miss out on a rich opportunity to participate in a community group which could add significant value and meaning to their lives.

The under-representation of people with mental retardation in many local churches and communities of faith is caused by a number of factors. First of all, up until the past couple of decades, the majority of people with disabilities were placed in self-contained institutional settings outside the mainstream of local society. Many people in institutions lived their entire lives within the walls of that institution.

Yet even progress in assisting individuals with mental retardation to return to community settings in recent years has not done a great deal to reverse this unfortunate under-representation Due to the many decades of institutionalization, there is a very limited history of successful interactions, experiences, and relationships shared between people with disabilities and members of local communities of faith from which to learn and upon which to build. Often people with disabilities and members of communities of faith are just not sure how to relate in a healthy, meaningful way.

In addition, many of the activities and events which occur in communities of faith assume that all participants have a number of skills or abilities which people with mental retardation might not have. As a result, people with disabilities often feel excluded from many of these activities or events. For example, most adult education classes and Bible studies presuppose a participant's ability to read, talk fluently, and reason abstractly:

> . . . in most churches, religious education still means reading,
> writing, and rote memorization of Bible stories along with group
> discussion where participation requires a certain level of verbal fluency. (Webb-Mitchell, p. 32)

Also, most sermons or homilies are presented to reach individuals presumed to have at least a high school education. As such, forums and activities which occur in communities of faith are largely inaccessible or overwhelming to a person with mental retardation.

Lastly, there are often logistical barriers which block the participation of individuals with disabilities like mental retardation in communities of faith. For example, since many people with disabilities don't drive (and alternate forms of public transportation often don't run regularly on weekends), transportation to and from communities of faith can prove to be a significant obstacle. In addition, many worship services and group meetings are conducted in rooms which cannot be reached without climbing up or down a set of stairs. For individuals who might have limited mobility (the prevalance of physical disabilities in persons with mental retardation is significantly higher than in the general population), this can create an almost insurmountable barrier. Compared to many businesses and community organizations, churches have been slow to overcome a wide range of barriers which often prevent full participation of people with disabilities:

If supermarkets and bars are more accessible then altars, then we must all bear the shame. . . . Justice and love will triumph only when segregating walls are knocked down and the barriers of architecture, communication and attitudes are removed. Only then will people with disabilities become full participants in the celebrations and obligations of their faith. (Anderson, p. 44)

For a social worker providing services for people with mental retardation, this situation is one which almost literally cries out for the development of a potent social work intervention. In most cases, this reaction will be felt even more strongly by the Christian social worker, who can strongly empathize with any person who is prevented from full access and participation in a local church or community of faith.

This chapter will outline one Christian social worker's proposed approach addressing this significant issue, and in doing so, illustrate a number of key social worker roles, techniques, and perspectives which play a critical role in this intervention. Specifically, this chapter will describe an approach I have developed called the "Faith Connections Model." This model has been developed from a strengths/competence social work perspective, and calls upon a social worker to fulfill a variety of social work roles in its implementation. A sampling of these social work roles will include: consultant/facilitator, case manager/service broker, advocate, and teacher/trainer. In addition, this chapter will outline several ways in which key Christian beliefs and values play a critical role in the development and implementation of the "Faith Connections Model."

The Faith Connections Model

Simply put, the "Faith Connections Model" is a social work intervention which attempts to match the strengths, preferences, and stated desires of a person with mental retardation with a local church or community of faith. It takes seriously the many barriers which prevent fuller church inclusion described above, and develops strategies to overcome identified barriers to provide the target person with the opportunity to participate and/or become a member in a community of faith of his/her choice.

The 3 key stages of the "Faith Connections Model" are:
1. Exploring the Spiritual Dimension within an Overall Assessment Process
2. Community of Faith Development
3. Community of Faith Coaching

Stage 1: Exploring the Spiritual Dimension within an Overall Assessment Process:

Following the "Faith Connections Model," a target person's interdisciplinary team, facilitated by the social worker, seeks to define the individual's most significant strengths, gifts, interests, preferences, dreams, and capacities in all areas of his/her life (Mount, 1995). Unfortunately, while often looking at the physical, cognitive, emotional, and social dimensions of the person's life, many times assessments of persons with mental retardation do not include an exploration of the person's spiritual or religious dimension. It is a priority focus of the "Faith Connections Model" to include a rich spiritual component in the overall assessment process.

Important to this approach, the spiritual/religious component of the assessment process should, among other things, gather the type of information which allows the team to draw a picture of the type of community of faith (and specific faith community activities) in which the target person would like to become a participating member. It is critical that the social worker assist the team to focus primarily on what the target person can do well - **not** just on what he/she can't - and thus what he/she can bring to the community of faith.

Because of the target person's disability (not to mention the somewhat elusive task of identifying aspects of a person's "spirituality" in general), the spiritual component of this assessment requires more than simply asking the team to fill out a checklist during a hastily thrown-together team meeting. The social worker has to take the time to talk directly with the target person, as well as his/her family, friends, residential support staff (if applicable), and others who know the person well. In addition, the social worker may have to explore a number of creative approaches (role playing exercises, random observations of the person in selected activities, etc.) to help the team better understand the target person's deepest spiritual strengths, gifts, interests, preferences, dreams and capacities! Key areas to explore in the spiritual component of the overall assessment may include (but are not limited to): a. beliefs about God; b. spiritual/religious practices and traditions; c. beliefs about right and wrong; d life satisfaction assessment; e. values inventory; f. assessment of relationship with God and overall religious experience; and g. evaluation of spiritual mentors/"heroes."

It is also important to gather information regarding the target person's (or family's) current connections or prior experiences with local communities of faith. Often a great deal can be learned by reviewing what worked (as well as what didn't work) in any prior experiences for the target person.

Stage 2. Community of Faith Development:

While a good overall assessment helps to identify a person's strengths, needs, and preferences, simply gathering information is never a goal in and of itself. In stage 2 of the "Faith Connections Model," the social worker analyzes the results of (especially the spiritual component of) the assessment process and uses this information to seek a match between the strengths/preferences of the target person and the needs, culture, and resources of a selected local church or community of faith

However, before a social worker can begin to find such a match for a target person, he/she must first develop a pool of communities of faith which are potentially interested in and willing to support these types of connections. The social worker will often start by contacting local communities of faith and asking to meet with the appropriate clergy, staff, or lay leaders to present the "Faith Connections Model." In addition, it is often helpful for the social worker to participate in some of the activities or programs which are an important part of that community's life. Of course, it is equally important for the social worker to have contact with local communities of faith even when not specifically doing community of faith development. Some examples of regular contact might include: supporting church fund-raisers, co-sponsoring seminars and trainings with local communities of faith, etc.

Having identified a rich pool of communities of faith that seem genuinely interested in and committed to welcoming people with disabilities, the social worker begins community of faith development with the target person to select a few faith communities from that pool that he/she thinks might have potential as a match for that particular person. It is important to note that in seeking a match, the social worker may in some cases need to look beyond the boundaries of that person's familiar denomination or faith tradition.

Next the social worker facilitates some times for the target person (and other people important in the target person's life) to visit the selected communities of faith and optimally to join in on some of the activities which the target person has identified as important/desirable to him/her. It is often worthwhile for the team to plan out and structure even these brief initial visits. The more positive the initial impressions (for both the target person and the community of faith), the more likely that a positive connection will be made. From here, in most cases, the target person and important people in his/her life are able to decide which of the selected communities of faith (if any) seems to "fit" best. In general, the most reliable predictor of success is when all involved agree that the community of faith has the capacity and commitment to provide the support needed for the person to participate in that community.

Planning Supports

Once the target person (with the assistance of his/her family and/ or other important people in his/her life) has indicated which community of faith he/she would like to focus on, the next step is for the social worker to convene the team to begin developing a plan of supports to help the target person integrate into the life of that community of faith.

The types of supports a person will benefit from generally vary from person to person, and can range from relatively minimal, informal supports to much more intensive, formal ones. However, one of the critical areas to include is an emphasis on the supports needed to assist the target person to make meaningful social connections within the community of faith. Without question, making meaning social connections is usually far and away the most significant factor contributing to a long term connection.

For clarity's sake, a support plan should include a listing of the specific supports which will be offered to the target person, the individual(s) who will provide each of the listed supports, and the approximate time frame(s) for implementing and then fading each of these supports. It is equally important to develop a support plan that neither over nor under-estimates the supports the target person might benefit from, and one that can be quickly and easily adjusted if necessary.

It is also critical that the person(s) who will provide each of the supports is familiar with the specific activities the person will participate in, and is enthusiastic about his/her role as a support provider. Most of the time the best candidates to provide supports are well-established and well-known members of that community of faith. However, there might be times when the support needed will have to be provided by a person(s) who is not a member of the community of faith. This is more likely to occur when a special level of expertise is needed that cannot be found within the community of faith (including examples such as interpreters, special educators, clinical specialists, etc.). In these cases the social worker is instrumental in helping the team locate and work with these individuals with special expertise.

Stage 3. Community of Faith Coaching:

Once the team has developed a support plan, the most critical stage of the process still remains - implementing the plan! The key element in implementing the support plan is the social worker's selection and training of a member of the community of faith to become the "community of faith coach." The "community of faith coach" (as the name implies) is the person who coordinates, assists, encourages, and provides direction for the various persons providing the supports identified in the support plan.

It is important that the "community of faith coach" is well respected by the other members of the community of faith, and has a thorough knowledge of both the strengths, needs, and preferences of the target person as well as culture, activities, and resources of the community of faith. He/she becomes the "inside" person who both provides on-going support to the other members of the community of faith, as well as maintaining communication with the social worker and team members to let them know how the target person is doing and when any additional assistance might be needed.

Often a member of the clergy or a committed lay leader is able to provide the name(s) of an individual(s) who has the potential to become a quality "community of faith coach." However, simply finding a willing and able candidate is only a small part of the job. It is up to the social worker to provide the hands-on training needed to equip him/her to fulfill this critical role.

The social worker needs to instill in the "community of faith coach" the following characteristics (among others):

- consistent use of a positive approach and frequent reinforcement.
- quickness to recognize and celebrate (even small signs of) progress.
- bias toward problem solving rather than blame-fixing.

In the end, a wisely selected and well-trained "community of faith coach" is the key to supporting the target person's connection with the community of faith on a long-term basis.

The Model at Work: Some Illustrations of the Faith Connections Model

Dave is a 52-year old man with mental retardation who has been living in a group home in a midwestern state for the past 17 years. He shares this house with four other individuals of varying ages with similar disabilities. Dave and his four housemates work together on a production unit in a day services program in the town in which they live. Dave gets along fairly well with most of his housemates, but doesn't seem particularly close to any of them. He appears to enjoy interacting the most with the staff members who work in the group home. Unfortunately, the turnover rate of staff is almost 50% each year, with few staff members staying more than a couple of years.

Dave has no family members who are currently active in his life. In fact, his social worker has not even been able to trace where Dave was born or where (or with whom) he grew up. At the same time, Dave from time to time talks about the members of his family that he remembers including his grandmother, his aunt and uncle, as well as several foster families. Often when he talks about his childhood years, he refers to some of the churches he attended when he was younger, and still remembers many gospel hymns from his youth. He doesn't have many possessions, but he does have a cassette player, and spends much of his leisure time listening to (and singing along with) a collection of gospel hymns and spirituals he has collected through the years.

During the last 15 years in his group home, Dave has only occasionally attended church, generally when the staff members who were working on Sundays wanted to get out of the house for a few hours. However, even when he and his housemates were taken to church, they would usually end up going to the denomination or community of faith with which the staff member on duty on any particular week felt most comfortable. When a new social worker, Joan, began working for the organization, she requested to be allowed to implement the "Faith Connections Model" approach for people who seemed interested in participating in a local church or community of faith. When Joan was given the okay, she met with agency staff members, who suggested that Dave would be a good person to work with in this capacity. When Joan approached Dave, he responded enthusiastically to her offer, so she set up a team meeting to begin.

Stage 1

Joan worked with Dave and his team to define Dave's greatest strengths, gifts, interests, preferences, dreams, and capacities in all areas of his life, including a strong focus on the spiritual dimension of his life. Joan called a number of team meetings and set up several one-on-one discussions with Dave and the staff who knew Dave best to find out more about what was important to Dave. Joan and the team discovered that Dave had many things he wanted to do, and much to contribute to others that in his current life situation he was not able to contribute. A number of important themes emerged from the assessment process. Some of these the major included the following:

- Dave was an exceptionally friendly and patient person.
- Dave greatly enjoyed spending time with children.
- Dave loved singing, and had a strong voice that others liked to listen to.
- Dave wanted to spend more time with people who didn't live at his group home, or work in his production group.
- Dave didn't enjoy attending the churches his staff often took

him to as much as the churches he remembered attending when he was younger where the "people weren't afraid to dance and move around" when they worshipped.

- Dave had a strong faith in God (in spite of some very difficult times during his life), which he enjoyed sharing with others around him.

Stage 2

Joan focused on these themes as she began exploring for possible "matches" with the needs, cultures, and resources of several local communities of faith with whom she had spoken previously. After calling contacts from several promising congregations, presented Dave with a list of 3-4 communities of faith which she felt would be worth his exploring in person. She arranged for Dave and some of his favorite group home staff to visit these selected communities of faith during times when there were activities going on that she felt Dave might especially enjoy. Some of these identified activities included:

- Joining a congregation for an informal Sunday evening hymn sing.
- Helping out with games and serving refreshments at a church's children's Halloween party.
- Attending a church's annual fall picnic.
- Participating in a church's Sunday morning service in which the congregation's style of worship included lively singing, dancing, and plenty of "moving around."

Contacts from a couple of the churches called Dave at his group home before he visited, and most of the church contacts spoke to several of the members of the congregations, asking them to go out of their way to help Dave feel at home when he visited.

While most of the visits went fairly well, there was one church in particular that Dave seemed especially excited about. Fortunately, this church seemed equally eager to have Dave become more involved with them, and it was not long before more and more of Dave's visits were ending up scheduled for this church.

Planning Supports

Once it became clear that Dave was most drawn to this one church (the Memorial Baptist Church), Joan brought his team together with her contact from Memorial Baptist (Bob, who had agreed to be the "community of faith coach") to begin developing a plan of supports to assist Dave to integrate into the life of that community on a (hopefully) long-term basis. Because Dave had gotten off to such a good start at Memorial Baptist, he and his team did not feel that a large number of formal supports would be needed. However, they came up with a few important supports that they felt would be helpful for at least the first 6 months as Dave explored becoming a regular participant/member rather than just a visitor at Memorial Baptist. These supports included the following:

- Developing a pool of 3-4 families living near Dave's group home who could alternate giving him rides to and from worship services and other community of faith events. Dave in exchange agreed to wash each of their cars 1 time per month during the spring, summer, and fall seasons.
- Assigning a fellow tenor in the church choir (Dave wanted to sing in the church choir, and was also a tenor) to be Dave's mentor and to help him learn the weekly choir selections (especially the words to the songs), introduce him to the other members of the choir, "hang out" with him at choir rehearsals, etc.
- Arranging for Dave to assist Baptist Memorial's Youth Group Leader. This would include attending and helping out with youth group activities, making periodic phone calls to families notifying them of upcoming events, etc.

Within several weeks, with the pastor's assistance, Bob had recruited volunteers to provide each of these 3 supports. All of these volunteers had been members of the church for at least a year (except for one of the families which would be helping out with the transportation, and which had just joined Memorial Baptist 4 months ago).

Stage 3

It is worth mentioning that the speed with which volunteers were recruited to implement this support plan owed much of its success to the time Joan invested in training Bob as the "community of faith coach." During the first few months after implementing the support plan, Bob was encouraged to spend time each week observing the interactions between Dave and the other members of the community of faith. In addition, Bob called each of the support persons every other week to find out how things were going, and routinely talked with Joan to provide her with regular updates. Any time there were potentially significant issues, Joan would call the team together (which now included Bob) to either revise the support plan and/or make any other adjustments that might be needed.

After a little less than a year, the team was able to discontinue two of the formal supports, as they were replaced over time by more natu-rally-occurring sources. The exception was the transportation support, which the community of faith coach needed to continue to monitor and coordinate on an on-going basis. After attending Baptist Memorial for over a year, Dave became a member of the congregation, participating in a wide array of church activities several times a week. Most impor-tantly, Dave consistently expressed strong satisfaction with his new friends in the congregation, and with the important role he felt he played at Baptist Memorial. Dave is an example of a person who, with the proper supports, was able to make a meaningful connection with a local community of faith on a long-term basis.

Key Social Work Perspectives and Roles Inherent in the Faith Connections Model

As is hopefully evident from this case study, the "Faith Connec-tions Model" has been strongly influenced by a social work orientation and calls upon the social worker to fulfill a variety of social work roles in its implementation. This section of the chapter will highlight the reliance of the "Faith Connections Model" on the strengths/competency social work perspective, and outline four traditional social work roles which this model requires the social worker to assume.

Strengths/Competency Perspective

The strengths/competency perspective, which has become increas-ingly prominent in the field of social work in recent years (Miley, 1995), maintains that the best way to serve clients (taken as either an indi-vidual or a larger system) is to help them discover and build on their strengths, as opposed to identifying and trying to "fix" their weaknesses:

> Adopting a strengths perspective influences the way that social workers view client systems and involve them in the change process. Focusing on clients' strengths leads to an empower-ing approach that promotes clients' competence rather than working to erase their deficits. . . Strengths-oriented social workers believe that the strengths of all client systems - indi-vidual, interpersonal, familial, organizational, and societal - are resources to initiate, energize, and sustain change processes. (Miley, pp. 62-63).

This strengths/competency perspective is clearly a central emphasis of the "Faith Connections Model." First of all, in stage 1, the focus of the assessment process led by the social worker is on identifying the target person's most significant strengths and competencies in all areas of his/her life (including the spiritual dimension).

In addition, in stage 2, the social worker is called upon to analyze the results of (especially the spiritual component of) the assessment process and use this information to seek a match or fit between the **strengths/preferences** of the target person and the needs, culture, and resources of a selected local community of faith. In fact, one of the priorities in seeking this match is to identify a niche within the community of faith which the target person is able to fill due to the strengths he/she brings with him/her to apply to the applicable area.

In summary, the primary focus of the "Faith Connections Model" is to recognize, reinforce, and build on the target person's strengths and competencies to enable him/her to make a positive, valued, on-going contribution within that community of faith.

Key Social Work Roles

Effective social work practice requires that a social worker assume a variety of different roles and functions when implementing any number of social work interventions. Traditional social work roles include, among others, services broker/case manager, consultant/facilitator, teacher/trainer, and client advocate (Haynes & Holmes, 1994; Miley, 1995). The "Faith Connections Model" actively calls upon the social worker to assume a number of these traditional social work roles.

A. The Role of Case Manager/Service Broker

One of the important roles of the social worker is that of a broker of services or case manager. In many instances, a social worker's client does not know where or how to make (and maintain) connections with services or supports that he/she might need or from which he/she could benefit. A case manager is responsible to see that

> ...the client is (1) connected to the appropriate service provider(s) and that (2) appropriate services are actually being received... (T)heir primary roles and functions are to (1) identify the appropriate service providers, (2) link clients with those providers, (3) continue to coordinate services as needs change, and (4) continually monitor progress. (Haynes & Holmes, p. 287)

The "Faith Connections Model" relies upon the social worker to assume the role of case manager/service broker in at least two ways. First of all, in stage 2, the social worker serves as a broker to help connect his/her client with a community of faith from a pool of faith communities that he/she has recruited to support these types of connection. Secondly, once a match has been established, the social worker plays a key role in following along/monitoring the success of the match to help the client maintain this connection on a long-term basis.

B. The Role of Consultant/Facilitator

Another of the traditional roles of the social worker is that of a consultant/facilitator. Consultants/facilitators are responsible to work together with clients (as well as significant people within a client's system) to gather critical information and develop plans to help clients (at various levels) meet their identified service goals:

> As a function of social work, consultancy refers to social workers and clients conferring and deliberating together to develop plans for change.... Consultancy acknowledges that both social workers and clients systems bring information and resources, actual and potential, which are vital for resolving the issue at hand.   Through consultancy, social workers seek to find solutions for challenges in social functioning with clients systems at all levels including individuals, families, groups, organizations, and communities. (Miley, pp. 16-17)

The "Faith Connections Model" relies upon the social worker to assume the role of consultant/facilitator in a number of ways. In stage 1, the social worker assists the client's team to work together to develop a rich initial client assessment (with an appropriate emphasis on the spiritual dimension). Then in stage 2, the social worker facilitates the team development of the support plan which defines the supports needed to overcome any barriers that might prevent the client from being fully integrated into the identified community of faith. Lastly, the social worker facilitates the team process of using feedback from the client and/or community of faith coach to make any needed adjustments to the support plan as the client begins to participate in community of faith on a regular basis.

C. The Role of Teacher/Trainer

One more of the traditional roles of the social worker is that of a teacher or trainer. A teacher/trainer develops an array of strategies to communicate key information and promote the acquisition of critical skills to their clients as well as those individuals/groups who support their clients:

> As teachers, social workers use learning strategies to promote skill development and enhance the information base of client systems.... Trainers provide instruction to... formal groups and organizations. (Miley, pp. 23-24)

The "Faith Connections Model" relies upon the social worker to assume the role of teacher/trainer in a number of ways. First of all, in stages 1 and 2, the social worker trains team members to define a target person's most significant strengths, interests, preferences, and dreams, and then to develop support plans to assist target persons to meet their aspirations. Secondly, under the "Faith Connections Model", the social worker is called upon to provide hands-on training for the community of faith coach, who in turn is instrumental in offering on-going direction and assistance to the supporting members of the community of faith.

D. The Role of Advocate

Yet one more of the traditional roles of the social worker is that of being an advocate for his/her clients. An advocate is one who speaks or acts to bring about change on behalf of or for the benefit of another:

> ...(t)he advocate is committed to ensuring that service delivery systems are responsive to clients' needs, and that clients receive all the benefits and services to which they are rightfully entitled.... (C)ase managers can and do engage in advocacy on behalf of specific clients who are not being served appropriately. (Haynes & Holmes, pp. 289-90)

The community of faith model relies upon the social worker to assume the role of advocate in one very important way. When developing a pool of communities of faith to participate in a "Faith Connections" project, the social worker advocates on behalf of persons with mental retardation as he/she reminds churches of their responsibility to welcome and support persons with disabilities in the life of their congregation - especially if persons with mental retardation are under-represented within that community of faith. This advocacy, of course, continues as the social worker assists with efforts to help target persons integrate into the on-going life of the community of faith on a regular basis.

The Contribution of Key Christian Beliefs/Values to the Faith Connections Model

In this last section I will outline several ways in which Christian beliefs and values have played a key role in the development of the "Faith Connections Model."

First of all, stage 1 of the "Faith Connections Model" stresses the importance of including a rich spiritual component within the overall assessment of the target person with mental retardation. This emphasis is driven by the Judeo-Christian belief that all persons are made in the image of God (Genesis 1), and as a result are spiritual/religious, as well as physical, cognitive, emotional and social beings. It is important to note that the "Faith Connections Model" does not attempt to introduce this spiritual/religious component as separate or distinct from the overall assessment process. Rather, it advocates that the spiritual/religious dimension not be excluded (as is often the case), but instead allowed to play its rightful role within the context of the development of an overall assessment of a person with mental retardation.

Secondly, the "Faith Connections Model" focuses on assisting persons with disabilities like mental retardation to become integrated into local churches and communities of faith. This emphasis reflects the Christian belief that significant value, meaning, and life satisfaction are associated with the spiritual growth and development which occur with and in a local church community. This is not intended to imply that facilitating participation and membership in a community of faith should be the sole or even primary focus of social work interventions for people with mental retardation. Rather, the "Faith Connections Model" argues that this critical focus (frequently neglected for people with disabilities) should be among those considered when addressing a target person's overall needs and service preferences.

Lastly, the case for churches and communities of faith to support the "Faith Connections Model" is strengthened by an appeal to the metaphor (found in Christian scripture) of the "Body of Christ" to support its case that communities of faith are strengthened as the diversity of its members is expanded:

> The body is a unit, though it is made up of many parts; and though all its parts are many, they form one body. So it is with Christ.... But in fact God has arranged the parts in the body, every one of them, just as he wanted them to be. If they were all one part, where would the body be? As it is, there are many parts, but one body. The eye cannot say to the hand, "I don't

need you!" And the head cannot say to the feet, " I don't need you!" On the contrary, those parts of the body that seem to be weaker are indispensable, and the parts that we think are less honorable we treat with special honor. (Selected verses from I Corinthians 12, New International Version)

This appeal is clearly consistent with the social work emphasis on the importance of diversity within all structures in a society.

In conclusion, it is worth noting that the "Faith Connections Model" represents an approach to a significant social work issue that highlights the cohesiveness of certain key social work and Christian values. While it has not been my experience that one will always find such a tight "fit" between current professional social work perspectives and Christian beliefs/values, the "Faith Connections Model" illustrates at least one case where such integration is alive and well!

References

ANCHOR - American Network of Community Options and Resources. *LINKS*, (1995). Volume XX, No. 1, p. 29 cites a 1994 survey of people with disabilities conducted by the Louis Harris polling firm.

Anderson, Robert C. (1994). A Comprehensive Look at Disability Laws and the Religious Community. *Exceptional Parent*, December, 43-44.

Faith Group Resources. (1994). *Exceptional Parent*, December, 38-39.

Gaventa, Bill. (1994). Religious Participation for All. *Exceptional Parent*, December, 22-25.

Haynes, Karen & Holmes, Karen. (1994). *Invitation to Social Work*. New York: Longman.

Hornstein, Becca. (1994). A Jewish Education for Every Child. *Exceptional Parent*, December, 29-30.

Miley, Karla Krogsrud, O'Melia, Michael, & Dubois, Brenda L. (1995). *Generalist Social Work Practice: An Empowering Approach*. Boston: Allyn and Bacon.

Mount, Beth. (1995). *Capacity Works: Finding Windows for Change Using Personal Futures Planning*. New York: Graphic Futures.

Webb-Mitchell, Brett. (1994). Toward a More Inclusive Protestant Sunday School: Making Religious Education Accessible to All. *Exceptional Parent*, December, 31-33.

CHAPTER 6

DIVERSITY: AN EXAMINATION OF THE CHURCH AND SOCIAL WORK

Lon Johnston

The weekend of October 11-13, 1996, I visited Washington, D.C., to participate in activities related to the display of the AIDS memorial quilt. In many different ways this weekend impacted my life far beyond anything I could have predicted or expected. Walking among the 40,000 quilt squares and watching the thousands of others who had come to see the quilt, I was reminded of how truly diverse God's creation really is. However, it was the interfaith service held at the National Cathedral on Sunday evening that forced me to re-examine how narrowly I had defined God and how limited I had become in understanding God. This service was entitled "The Journey Home: An Interfaith Service of Prayer and Healing." I entered the cathedral feeling very much alone. I had spent much of the weekend visiting my brother's quilt panel and grieving his death from AIDS in 1987, and I hoped to experience some kind of healing as I joined all of these other strangers for worship. From the call to worship by drum and chant by the Little River Drum to the call to prayer by the blowing of the shofar and the ringing of the Tibetan bowls, from the reading of the Baghavad Gita and of the Torah to the anthem sung by the Washington Gay Men's Chorus, from the New Testament and Buddhist readings to the anthem offered by the Voices of Inspiration of the Metropolitan African Methodist Episcopal Church, I was struck by the diversity of people gathered to participate in worshiping God.

One of the worship leaders asked us to look around us—he asked us to take a very good look at all the people seated in this great cathedral. As we looked into the eyes of strangers, the worship leader described what he was seeing: Christian, Jew, Muslim, Buddhist, male, female, gay, straight, African-American, white, Hispanic, Native American, Asian American. After he had finished his description, he reminded us that this was what heaven would look like. God's diverse creation would be gathered there. As I began to notice the multifaceted people gathered that Sunday evening, I felt a connection to the people around me. The loneliness I had brought to the service began to fade. The gender, race or ethnicity, religion or creed, or sexual orientation of the person did not matter; the important thing was that we were all symbolic of God's heterogeneous creation. As the service ended, hands joined throughout the cathedral, voices raised together in singing "We Shall Overcome," and individuals connected as the whole of God's diverse creation. All differences were set aside, and we experienced the joy and peace of belonging to the family of God.

   This is a message that might be uncomfortable to some people who want to define God very narrowly and who refuse to believe that God is an inclusive God. The temptation to limit God's interaction with his creatures is one I believe Christians must avoid, not only within the religious world, but also within the secular social work profession. Many people, from both the secular and religious worlds, believe that theology and social work are incompatible, and emphasis is often placed on choosing one or the other. People in both worlds want to build walls that separate and divide rather than bridges that connect and support. However, there are many areas where theology and social work are very much in agreement, and there are other areas where tensions exist.

   Some people may wonder why Christianity and social work need to have this dialogue in the first place. Why does it matter if tensions and suspicions exist between the two? Loewenberg (1988) gave one of the best answers to this question when he said:

> The religious belief (or lack of belief) of a chemist does not mean anything to the molecules, atoms, or electrons that he explores. An architect's religious beliefs (or lack of beliefs) does not affect the design of a building that he drafts. Or will the accountant who regularly attends church prepare one sort of profit/loss statement and his agnostic colleague another? But the religious beliefs of social workers may have meaning and relevance for those with whom they interact. And these religious beliefs (or lack of them) may influence what they do as practitioners. (p. 81)

   Loewenberg is exactly right. If a social worker has no appreciation or understanding of the diversity of God's creation, then his or her practice will be influenced by that lack of inclusivity. On the other hand, to have such an understanding and appreciation will mean that a social worker views the gospel message as a message of inclusion, and his or her practice will be one based upon an acceptance and appreciation of all people as they are. The practice will be inclusive, just as the Bible is an inclusive book. To state this another way, the practice will be built on common grace. To view the Bible as being exclusive is to seriously misunderstand the message of God. Peter J. Gomes (1996) said:

...people beyond the little world of primitive Jewish Christianity see themselves and their story included in God's activity. When in John's gospel (John 10:16) Jesus says, 'And I have other sheep, that are not of this fold; I must bring them also, and they will heed my voice. So there shall be one flock, one shepherd,' this is a great mandate for inclusivity which these 'other sheep' recognize. As Jesus himself included among his own companions winebibbers, prostitutes, men and women of low degree, people who by who they were, by what they did, or from where they were excluded, so too does the Bible claim these very people as its own.

It is one of the unbecoming but unavoidable ironies of Christianity that Gentile Christians, who were excluded from the Jewish churches and who in time of the Roman persecution were themselves excluded from all hope in life, should themselves become the arch practitioners of exclusion. Even centuries of Christian exclusion, however, extending into our very own day, cannot diminish the inclusive mandate of the Bible, and the particular words of Jesus when he says, 'Come until me, all ye that labor and are heavy ladden and I will give you rest.' What Roman Catholic social theory teaches as the church's 'preferential option for the poor,' to the annoyance of Christians rich in the things of this world, is the same principle that extends the hospitality of the Bible, indeed preferential hospitality, to those who have in face been previously and deliberately excluded. So the Bible's inclusivity is claimed by the poor, the discriminated against, persons of color, homosexuals, women, and all persons beyond the conventional definitions of Western civilization. (pp. 22-23)

The Bible, comprised of the Hebrew and Christian scriptures, serves as the foundation for Christianity, and as Gomes has emphasized, those scriptures are inclusive. Social work is built upon professional values, and those values are also inclusive. It is sad that the secular social work profession only sees the exclusivity of organized religion, and it is equally distressing that organized religion views the inclusivity of professional social work as a threat to all that is sacred. There are differences between Christianity and professional social work that cannot be overlooked; however, these differences should not overshadow the large areas of common ground shared by them.

This chapter will focus on three areas of diversity: gender, sexual orientation, and multi- culturalism. The tensions and similarities that exist between the Christian church and social work will be examined in each of these areas.

Gender

Some of the earliest words recorded in the Hebrew Bible are found in the creation story (Genesis 1:27) where God is described as creating man "in his own image, in the image of God he created him; male and female he created them" (Revised Standard Version). Male interpretations of the Genesis story, often place the blame on Eve more than on Adam for bringing sin into this world, and such an interpretation reinforces the most divisive issue between men and women: power. Wallis (1995) said:

> As punishment women have been assigned a subordinate role to men...the control of women becomes a central male priority and has been the dominant characteristic of patriarchy (the subordination of women to men) from the earliest times....It is a structure of domination....In male dominated societies, the imbalance of power between women and men is deliberate—it is a system of both control and exploitation. As long as the differential of power between the genders is so great, various forms of violence and abuse will continue. When women earn only two-thirds the pay of men for the same job, when they are subject to sexual harassment on those jobs, when key social and religious institutions still refuse to grant half the population full dignity and equality, or when women must also bear the disproportionate weight of responsibility for child rearing, the power imbalance persists. (pp. 123-4)

The imbalance of power and the resulting inequality between women and men is an area where Christianity and social work should be able to stand united. Where would most churches be today if it were not for the women who are the majority of members, direct and staff most programs, give leadership and service in Christian education and social ministry, and influence and shape the moral and religious values of the homes (Gomes, 1996)?

When reading the Christian scriptures, especially the Gospels, it is important to remember these books "were all composed by men, or groups of men, and the new faith to which they testified was one which had risen from the male-oriented religion of Judaism. The readers and hearers of the Gospel...still were not part of a world in which females had equal rights and responsibilities with men" (Clark & Richardson, 1977, p. 32). However, a careful reading of the Christian scriptures reveals "quite a different picture from that which most people have of the sheltered, dependent Palestinian women of the first century" (Tucker & Liefeld, 1987, p. 20). We are told that women often traveled with Jesus, and the early church attracted many types of women, including those of high status. It is also clear that women held positions of importance within the first century church. Phoebe fulfilled the role of deaconess, Prisca was a prominent woman in the Roman congregation, and Mary took a great risk for Paul (Stark, 1996, p. 27). These women are examples of early Christians who somehow broke through the imbalance of power in the patriarchal society of that day.

Women have had the same influence upon and involvement in the social work profession. Where would the profession be without the persistent efforts of Mary Richmond in establishing some standards for professional education? The profession's commitment to the poor was demonstrated on a daily basis by Jane Addams and her female colleagues at Hull House (Morales & Sheafor, 1995). What about the everyday efforts of female social workers who visit abusive homes, comfort dying persons and their families, explain to children why their parents are divorcing, find safe places for elderly persons to live after being discharged from nursing homes, and listen to teenagers who feel threatened in their school environment?

Females comprise the majority of members of both the church and the social work profession. However, women have experienced oppression and exclusion in both these institutions as men have traditionally served in the roles of pastor, priest, deacon, and elder in the church, and men have been employed in the roles of supervisor and administrator in the social work profession. As stated earlier, the issue of unequal power between women and men in the church and in the profession cannot be denied.

It is more than ironic that women are found in such large numbers in the Christian church and social work while experiencing unequal access to power and position. A careful reading of scripture reveals Jesus' belief in the equality of all persons. While bound by the social mores of his time, Jesus did not discriminate in his treatment of women; in fact, his actions elevated women from second-class citizenship to positions of equality and honor. Just as Jesus modeled the way the church should relate to women, the Code of Ethics of the social work profession clearly states that all people are to be treated with dignity and respect (*NASW News*, 1996). There is to be no discrimination within the profession. All persons are to be viewed as equals, but unfortunately this is not always the case.

Several studies (Williams, Ho, & Fielder, 1974; Knapman, 1977; Sutton, 1982; York, Henley, & Gamble, 1987) found that male social workers tend to receive higher salaries than female social workers, and, in spite of the profession's statements to the contrary, this discrepancy continued throughout the 70's and 80's. Huber and Orlando (1995) describe similar inequities today. The question must be asked why a profession that prides itself upon its commitment to equality allows such an injustice to continue. A similar question can be asked of the church. If the Christian scripture is the basis for all that the church is supposed to do and be, then why do women continue to experience oppression, injustice, and inequality within the church? Again, the answer comes back to the issue of power. For equality and justice to occur within the social work profession and the Christian church, men have to be willing to share leadership roles at the risk of losing positions of influence and power.

These issues of power and influence have caused women to be hurt by the church, an institution that should be a healing, redeeming place for all people. Several years ago my wife and I joined a church that was very male dominated. Every time the pastor introduced us he covered my educational background and my present teaching position. Although my wife had a master's degree and was a highly accomplished professional in her own right, this pastor never acknowledged more than her name. Time after time this event repeated itself until one night, after my wife was left feeling discounted and invisible, she turned to me and said, "I never want to come back to this church again." I supported her decision, and we looked for another place to worship where women were seen as equals in God's creation. Sadly, this is not an isolated situation. Women experience these actions again and again in churches throughout this nation. Rather than being a safe, affirming place, some churches continue to oppress the majority of their members by such actions.

In light of this example, it is important to note that large numbers of men are supportive of the efforts of women to achieve equality. As noted by Tolman, Mowry, Jones, and Brekke (1986):

> The women's movement has raised men's consciousness about gender in two different...ways. Challenges to traditional sex roles by feminists have freed men to become more aware of the restrictions imposed by traditional male sex roles. In addition, consciousness of how men oppress women has grown from their relationships with women who confront their sexist behavior. (p. 63)

Men employed in the social work profession can utilize the principles developed by Tolman, et al. (1986) as they attempt to support and encourage the efforts of women seeking gender equality. The principles are:

1. **Develop a Contextual, Historical Understanding of Women's Experience.**

   Without the contextual and historical understanding, men are unable to comprehend the oppression that women have experienced. The ultimate goal is the attainment of empathy.

2. **Men Must Be Responsible for Themselves and for Other Men.**

   For men to continue to rely upon women for consciousness raising, "amounts to continued oppression of women by men....What is required is for men to assume responsibility for their own part in sexist injustice, both individually and collectively."

3. **Redefine Masculinity.**

   As men evaluate what they gain and what they lose with the ending of male dominance, they will necessarily be required to begin the process of redefining what it means to be male.

4. **Accept Women's Scrutiny Without Making Women Responsible.**

   Obviously many men support and encourage gender equality, but men must realize that their efforts will be closely watched by women because of the long history of oppression and dominance of women by men.

5. **Support the Efforts of Women Without Interfering.**

   Men need to understand that women must "define themselves and develop their own power base." Men must be careful that their supportive actions do not "confound or co-opt women's efforts."

6. **Struggle Against Racism and Sexism.**

   According to Tolman, et al. (1986), "Men must be sensitive to the ways in which issues of race and class influence commitment to gender equality. It is a mistake to assume that men, regardless of race and class, have the same resources or responsibilities for promoting an end to male dominance."

7. **Overcome Homophobia and Heterosexism.**

   As men fight to end prejudice and discrimination of gay men, they will discover new ways of relating to all men as equals. Some suggest this is a necessary first step for men in overcoming the dominance of women. Unless men can relate to other men as equals, they stand little chance of relating to women as equals.

8. **Work Against Male Violence in All Its Forms.**

   Tolman, et al. (1986) indicate it is important that "...men actively confront how their own attitudes and behavior support violence, and not place all the blame for violence on the perpetrators of violent crimes."

9. **Do Not Set Up a False Dichotomy: Take Responsibility for Sexism.**

   Men need to understand that their responsibility to address sexism does not end because they believe in and give support to gender equality. Men also have a responsibility to address the sexism that exists in the male-dominated society in which they live.

10. **Act at the Individual, Interpersonal, and Organizational Levels.**

    Not only must men address gender equality at the individual level, but they must also confront sexism that is pervasive in all systems of society.

11. **Attend to Process and Product.**

    If men are to truly make progress in supporting the goal of gender equality, they must be conscious of the ways they gather and organize themselves to address gender inequality. It is easy to fall back into old patterns that lead to continued female oppression even while developing ways to end that oppression.

It is important to note that while Tolman's suggestions are aimed at men, many women within the church and the social work profession have been socialized to believe in the sexist ideologies that permeate male-dominated American culture. The above suggestions can also be utilized by women who want to challenge their own thoughts and behaviors.

Sexual Orientation

While gender diversity continues to divide the Christian church and the social work profession today, it is probably safe to say the issue of sexual orientation creates the most heated debates between these two institutions. Heterosexual Christians can be found who support and work for the inclusion of people whose sexual orientation is different from theirs, and heterosexual Christians can also be found who describe homosexuality as an abomination and believe that homosexuals are not Christians. It is sad to say that similar views exist within the social work profession, a profession grounded in values and ethics of inclusiveness.

Today's religious climate has raised questions in the minds of many people regarding the ability of Christian social workers to openly and honestly address issues of inclusivity and diversity. There are some good reasons for these questions. At the 1997 annual meeting of the Southern Baptist Convention, messengers adopted a resolution to refrain from patronizing any movies produced by or theme parks operated by the Walt Disney Company due to the company's policy of providing health insurance to same sex partners of employees. Southern Baptists join the Assemblies of God, Presbyterian Church in America and American Family Association, among other groups, in boycotting Disney (Caldwell, 1997). In a recent survey of people who identified themselves as belonging to the Religious Right, Allen (1996) found that 78 percent of the respondents would prefer not to have homosexuals as neighbors. Is it any wonder that questions are raised as to whether Christian social workers will be able to uphold the values and ethics of the profession?

One way to answer this question is to note that there are diverse views within mainline Christian denominations regarding sexual orientation. Many religious groups, such as those mentioned above maintain that homosexuality is an abomination, while others, such as some Presbyterians and United Methodists, are conducting ongoing dialogues on the issue. The United Church of Christ even allows the ordination of gays and lesbians as ministers (Swindler, 1993).

It will not be an easy task, but the Christian church and the social work profession must work together to overcome the effects of **heterosexism**. The word "heterosexism" has been purposefully used rather than the more common word "homophobia." According to Mollenkott (1994, p. 145), "It is too easy for people to interpret a phobia as a morbid personal matter. A phobia can be someone else's private abnormality. To speak about heterosexism, however, bears witness that the basic phenomenon is public, institutionalized prejudice about gay, bisexual, and lesbian people throughout this society."

Where does this heterosexism come from? One source is the misuse of the Bible. Hays (1994) states:

> In terms of emphasis, it (homosexuality) is a minor concern, in contrast, for example, to economic injustice. What the Bible does say should be heeded carefully, but any ethic that intends to be biblical will seek to get the accents in the right places. Would that the passion presently being expended in the church over the question of homosexuality were devoted instead to urging the wealthy to share with the poor! Some of the most urgent champions of 'biblical morality' on sexual matters become strangely equivocal when the discussion turns to the New Testament's teachings about possessions. (p. 5)

According to Gomes (1996, p. 149), people tend to turn to the following six "select texts from the Old and New Testament...in seeking the Bible's teaching on homosexuality:"

1. Genesis 1–2	The Creation Story
2. Genesis 19:1–9	Sodom and Gomorrah, with the parallel passages of Judges 19 and Ezekiel 16:46–56
3. Leviticus 18:22 and 20:13	The Holiness Code
4. Romans 1:26–27	Regarded as the most significant of Saint Paul's views
5. I Corinthians 6:9	Pauline lists of vices
6. I Timothy 1–10	Pauline lists of vices

Noticeably absent from this list of scriptures are any references from the Synoptic Gospels (Matthew, Mark, Luke and John.) Most people look to these Biblical books when they desire to know what Jesus Christ had to say about specific issues of his day. According to Furnish (1994):

> Although these traditions include teachings on a number of specific topics, the matter of 'homosexual' relationships or practice is not among them....This silence of the Jesus traditions about same-sex practices does not mean that Jesus had nothing to say on the subject. It does suggest, however, that Jesus had nothing distinctive to say about it, and that 'homosexuality' was not a matter of special concern within the church that preserved and applied his sayings. (p. 23)

If the Synoptic Gospels contain no record of Jesus Christ addressing homosexuality and the entire Hebrew and Christian scriptures contain only six references to sexual orientation, an important question must be asked. Why does the church use the issue of homosexuality to divide and separate people instead of focusing on the biblical reality that all people are created in the image of God, and, thus all are joined together as part of that wonderful creation? Alexander & Preston (1996) describe what too often occurs within the church:

> Every Sunday morning, mainline Christian congregations across this country welcome into their fold new baptized Christians, children of God. Within the liturgy, these congregations pledge their undying support to accept, love, forgive, and nurture this person in the faith. Yet the church honors this covenant selectively. For what was supposed to be a means of unconditional love, grace, and justice becomes a conditional covenant for les-

bian and gay Christians—a compromise ending in silence, oppression, and judgment. It is this church that obstructs God's grace and leads gay and lesbians to doubt that they are children of God. (p. xiii)

The sad fact is that the church is not alone in accepting people selectively. The social work profession must also shoulder some of this blame. Newman, White, and Stock-Linski (1995), in a panel presentation, indicated there is conflicting data related to student attitudes on sexual orientation. They cite several studies that describe the existence of homophobic attitudes among social work students. These attitudes exist they feel because data indicate that large numbers of social work programs have in the past made little effort to include curriculum content on sexual orientation. However, Black, Oles and Moore (1996) administered the Index of Homophobia to 233 social work majors and found that these students scored in the low-grade non-homophobic to the low-grade homophobic range, with students becoming less homophobic as they progressed through their social work studies.

What is the result of the church and the social work profession selectively accepting people based upon sexual orientation? The result is heterosexism, and the outcomes can be devastating to homosexual persons. One way heterosexism is exhibited is that people fail to see homosexuals as people. Schmidt (1995, p. 37) said, "These are people with faces, people with names, often Christian people, and...we must never lose sight of their individual struggles, their individual pain, their faces. If we neglect faces, we neglect the gospel." When we neglect faces, we also neglect people, and that neglect leads to situations such as the following.

A homosexual Christian, responding to an article in *The Other Side*, a Christian magazine, wrote:

> Less than two months ago I was told by a sincere Christian (!) counselor that it would be 'better' to 'repent and die,' even if I had to kill myself, than to go on living and relating to others as a homosexual. (A friend of mine, told something similar by a well-intentioned priest, did just that)

> All I can do is pray that somewhere, someday, someone with compassion will begin the long, slow process of uncovering, discovery, and reconciliation of all who know Jesus Christ as Lord and Savior—both gay and straight.

Probably the most extreme example of Christians refusing to see homosexuals as people with faces and names can be found by visiting the web site of the Westboro Baptist Church of Topeka, Kansas. The address is www.godhatesfags.com. One of the questions posed at this web site is, "Why do we preach hate (of homosexuals)?" The response is, "Because the Bible preaches hate....What you need to hear is that God hates homosexual people, and that your chance of going to heaven is nonexistent unless you repent." Also located at this web site are pictures of members of the Westboro Baptist Church picketing funerals of persons who have died from AIDS. Members of the congregation can be seen standing in front of graves holding signs that say such things as "GOD HATES FAGS," "AIDS CURES FAGS," "THANK GOD FOR AIDS," "NO TEARS FOR QUEERS," "FAGS BURN IN HELL," and "GOD GAVE FAGS UP."

The face of Nicloas Ray West of Tyler, Texas, can not be forgotten. Nicloas was "brutally murdered for being gay. His torturers filled with the hate and poison of bigotry and their own estrangement shot him more times than could be counted by the coroner" (Alexander & Preston, 1994). Another face belongs to Bob (not his real name) who posted an email on the Internet describing his rejection by his family when they discovered he was gay. As a teenager he was kicked out of his home. Over twenty years later Bob does not even know where his parents are. A common friend talked with Bob's sister who said that his parents destroyed any evidence that Bob had ever existed—all pictures, personal belongs, etc.—and his parents tell people they only have two children: Bob's brother and sister.

How can people who call themselves Christians suggest to homosexuals that they are better off dead? How can people who call themselves Christians demonstrate at the funeral of persons who have died from AIDS? How can people murder someone for being gay? How can families turn their backs on their children? For many people, these are difficult questions to answer. Social workers try to answer these questions by looking to the profession's Code of Ethics and responding to all persons with dignity and respect, advocating for protection from hate crimes for homosexuals, and modeling the acceptance of all people as persons of worth. (*NASW News*, 1996, p. 1-4) This is not an easy task, but social workers belong to a profession that prizes the inclusion of all people. Christians who have committed themselves to following Jesus Christ also ought to believe in the inclusion of all.

As uncomfortable as it may be for some people, gay and lesbian issues are not going away. In fact, I believe that equal rights for gay and lesbian persons is the next civil rights battle to be fought in this country—in fact, we are already in the midst of this struggle. Gay and lesbian people deserve protection from losing their jobs simply because of their sexual orientation. Gay and lesbian people deserve the right to have access to a partner who is hospitalized, just as any family member would. Gay and lesbian people deserve the right to worship in **ANY** church without fear of rejection and condemnation. Gay and lesbian people deserve the right to live lives of integrity rather than becoming dehumanized as the victims of hate crimes. These are not any special rights. These are simply rights that are extended to **ALL** other persons—gay and lesbian persons should be included, not excluded. The Christian faith is very clear about who our neighbor is and how we are to treat that neighbor, and the social work profession is just as clear about relating to all person with respect and dignity. There is considerable common ground between the church and the social work profession, and this common ground can provide a foundation upon which the church and the profession can work together for the inclusion of gay and lesbian people in all spheres of society.

The organization known as P-FLAG (Parents and Friends of Lesbians and Gays) has identified ten specific acts people can do if they really want to make the world a better place for homosexuals. In discussing this list, Alexander and Preston (1996, p. 95) say, "You and I may not be able to do all of them yet, but we can pick at least one that we **can** do and start there." Some acts may very well cause value conflicts for some Christian social workers. However, all Christian social workers should be able to commit themselves to performing at least one item from the following list. Making that commitment would mean another step has been taken toward ending oppression and discrimination for gay and lesbian people. The ten acts are (P-FLAG, 1993):

1. Become a member of P-FLAG (or any other support group) and join with thousands of people from all walks of life, working to end discrimination against gays and lesbians.
2. Teach your children that being gay or lesbian is another means of expressing love.
3. If one of your family is gay or lesbian, be sure to let them know you love them just the way they are.
4. Don't tell anti-gay jokes. You just perpetuate the stereotypes about gays and lesbians.
5. Read our P-FLAG literature and find out more about what it is really like to be lesbian or gay in our society.
6. Be open with others about having lesbian or gay friends or family. Secrecy breeds shame.
7. If you overhear someone making an anti-gay comment, let them know you don't agree or approve.

8. Write Congress to protest any anti-gay legislation as you become aware of it.
9. Encourage open and honest discussion of gay and lesbian issues in your home, workplace, and church.
10. Stand with those who believe that discrimination against anyone is a crime against humanity—take a stand with P-FLAG.

Multiculturalism

While the dialogue between the Christian church and the social work profession regarding gender and sexual orientation is fairly recent, both of these groups have been addressing issues of race and ethnicity for many years. Certainly most mainline denominations have moved away from the days of segregated congregations and into a more inclusive environment. From its very founding as a profession, social work has also advocated for the equality of all persons, an end to oppressive acts, and social justice for all. However, it is important to note that areas of agreement and tension exist between the church and social work in relationship to race and ethnicity, or, as more currently referred to as issues of multiculturalism. Freeman (1996, p. 10) describes multiculturalism as two sides of one coin when she says, "Recognizing the universality of the human condition is one side of the coin of multiculturalism, and acknowledging and appreciating the unique culture and contributions of each ethnic group in this pluralistic society is the other side."

The results from a survey conducted by the National Opinion Research Center at the University of Chicago raise some questions regarding the openness to multiculturalism by Christians, specifically the group that has become known as the Religious Right. This survey found that "the Religious Right is 'deeply divided' from other Americans on a number of social issues..." (Allen, 1996). For example, fifty percent of the respondents said they would not vote for a Moslem for president and fourteen percent would not vote for a Jew. Fifty-four percent of the respondents said they would not want to have an atheist as a neighbor, and seventy-five percent said they would not vote for an atheist for president, even if "the candidate were otherwise well qualified."

How do these views impact Christians in the social work profession? Inference can be made that atheists, Moslems, Jews, and people from other minority groups might legitimately question a Christian social worker's ability to effectively provide assistance in a diverse and pluralistic society. Many people, unfortunately, assume that all Christians are equally intolerant. The Religious Right would argue they are not intolerant, but "from their faith comes....reluctance to accept as equal the beliefs and customs of others....it is not that they are intolerant, but they deem tolerance as a lesser value than Christian morality" (Allen, 1996). With Christian morality being more important than tolerance, the Religious Right is facing days ahead when their intolerance will be sorely tested. According to Gould (1996, p. 29), "The 1990 census shows that the racial and ethnic composition of the American population has changed more dramatically in the past decade than at any time in the 20th century, with nearly one in every four Americans identifying themselves as black, Hispanic, Asian...or American Indian." While the Religious Right is focusing on "Christian morality" as opposed to tolerance, the social work profession takes a different position regarding this trend. Gould (1996, p. 29) said, "...these trends certainly underscore the need for the social work profession to speak out publicly, to urge a societal commitment to the values of racial, ethnic, and cultural diversity—values that have been recognized as being part of the profession's 'system of ethics.'"

It is important to note that many Christian denominations support multiculturalism, but it is difficult to overcome the church's long history of intolerance toward people of other races and cultures. As with gender and sexual orientation, the Bible has been used by the white American majority (often Christians) to justify oppressive relationships with people who belong to a different racial or ethnic minority group, particularly African-Americans. According to Gomes (1996), in the summer of 1995 the Southern Baptist Convention publicly repented "for the role it had played in the justification of slavery and in the maintenance of a culture of racism in the United States." This repentance raises an important question:

> It is abundanently clear that the Southern Baptists rejected neither the faith nor the Bible of their mothers and fathers, but they have certainly changed their minds as to what scripture says and to what scriptures means....How is the moral consensus changed without changing the contents of the Bible? (p. 86)

The question needs to asked again: How is the moral consensus changed without changing the contents of the Bible? Will the views of the Religious Right someday change while still affirming the truth of scripture? There are no easy answers to these questions, but they must be given thoughtful attention in light of the fact that the United States is becoming a more heterogenous society. Not only must the church respond to the challenges this heterogeneous society presents, but the social work profession must also make adjustment (Kropf & Issac, 1992).

Breckenridge and Breckenridge (1995, p. 72) have identified several ways for the church to become more culturally aware without compromising its religious beliefs. They state: "It is not so much that we have to change our culture as that we must simply accept the culture of others. To accomplish such openness means that we do not insist on cultural sameness, but that we expand our ability to hear, see, and learn from other groups." This means that the church and the social work profession must change from thinking of society as a melting pot, "a metaphor that suggested that the United States was a country composed of many different ethnic groups, who had all somehow become blended or assimilated into 'Americans'" (Clark, 1994, p.3).

The idea of the melting pot has been replaced by another metaphor, that of the "tossed salad," a concept that according to Clark (1994) implies:

> that although many different groups live in the United States and may, indeed, consider themselves Americans, each also retains its own ethnic and cultural character and that this retention is both possible and desirable. Proponents of the tossed salad view believe that assimilation can be balanced with the preservation of identity; for them, the ideal is not for the elimination of differences but for an increased awareness of and respect for cultural and ethnic diversity. (p. 3)

There are adjustments that social workers and the Christian church can make in order to respond to this heterogeneous—tossed salad—society. One of the most important tasks is for individual social workers to work on becoming anti-racist. According to Wicker (1986, p. 37), "Racism can be unintentional and naively perpetuated by frontline workers because it is so institutionalized that we often do not notice it....we must be prepared to...have the courage to push ourselves, our co-workers, and our administrators to struggle effectively against racism. Passive acceptance of racist attitudes—even ones created by others—ensures the perpetuation of a racist system."

Wicker (1986) has identified a variety of ways social workers can work on their personal racism and has made suggestions that will enable social workers "to scrutinize their racism concerning citizens of a different color." These include:

Personal Work:
1. Form non-hierarchical peer supervision groups at work to discuss basic definitions of racism and prejudice, then use a variety of...techniques...to help one another look at prejudice and racism in clinical work with people of color.

2. Read literature and nonfiction written by people of color to educate ourselves about people who are different and who live in
   different cultures.
3. Attend multicultural events....Support multicultural events in
   your community. Feel what it is like to be in the minority.
4. Attend "unlearning racism" workshops.

Working With Clients:
1. Ask the client how he or she feels about working with you.
2. Are you aware of and do you have information about the client's
   cultural heritage?
3. Ask yourself about your assumptions, hidden or blatant, about
   this client.
4. Be clear on how racism affects clients' lives on a daily basis. If
   you are a member of another minority group—gay, female, Jewish—try to identify the oppression of racism with the kind of
   oppression you have dealt with on a daily basis.
5. Interrupt racism in the therapeutic setting.....Interrupting internalized oppression— defined here as the oppressed taking
   on stereotyped views that the oppressor holds about them—
   with clients of color is essential.
6. Encourage clients to get involved in anti-racist organizations as
   a constructive way to deal with feelings of hopelessness and
   powerlessness.

The Christian church can also employ many of these same tasks.
Breckenridge and Breckenridge (1995) support many of the tasks just
described when they say:

> Christians must be willing to relinquish desire for societal con-
> trol and let those who wish otherwise follow their own life
> path. This is very difficult, but we are reaching a point in our
> society where the church must decide whether its role is to be
> servant or conqueror.... For this reason, we argue that the criti-
> cal place to begin is...with our feelings. We must develop a
> sensitivity which will recognize not only the rights of others,
> but also the presence of inferior feelings within ourselves. A
> large part of the answer is simply imitating Christ. (p. 253)

Imitating Christ! What a simple answer, and yet what a complex
task for most Christians and social workers to do. It is hard to imagine
Jesus Christ stating that he would not want to live next door to an atheist, Moslem, or homosexual. Since Jesus was a Jew it is even harder to

imagine that he would exclude them as neighbors. So, why do Christian social workers struggle in their ability to imitate Christ when confronting multiculturalism? This is a very important question to ponder, and as answers are found, new and exciting ways of relating to God's diverse creation will begin to appear.

Summary

Issues raised in this chapter may have made some readers uncomfortable. Thinking about diversity issues related to gender, sexual orientation, and multiculturalism often stir value conflicts in the best of social workers. What are we to do with these conflicts? As indicated through this chapter, the Code of Ethics of the social work profession must be adhered to with all clients. However, adhering to the Code is sometimes easier said than done.

It is hoped that as social workers grow and mature, the church, as well as the profession, will be impacted in such a way that both of these great institutions become models of inclusion for the rest of society. Striving to reach this goal of inclusivity will benefit all of God's diverse and beautiful creation. There is only one way to start the process, and that is through imitating Jesus Christ. What does imitating Christ mean? I believe it means that we stand in the doors of our offices, arms opened wide, saying "Welcome; anyone who walks through these doors is accepted as a person of worth and dignity. Your race, ethnicity, gender, or sexual orientation takes nothing away from your personhood." Imitating Christ means that we also stand in the doors of our churches, arms opened wide, and offer the very same inclusive welcome to any who enters. Sometimes we may stand alone. That is allright. Jesus Christ often stood alone when he challenged the mores and oppression of his day. Other times we may be joined by people who share our commitment. No matter the number who join us, we must take the stand.

I believe those of us who gathered at the National Cathedral that October day were there not only to worship but to also take a stand. I'm convinced that Jesus stood with us, and had he been physically present there in the Cathedral he would have assured us all "Yes, this **is** what heaven looks like!" As Christians and social workers, let us live to spread that message of good news, inclusion, and grace.

References

Alexander, M.B. & Preston, J. (1996). *We Were Baptized Too: Claiming God's Grace for Lesbians and Gays.* Louisville, KY: Westminster John Knox Press.

Allen, B. (1996, October 2). Religious Right, America Deeply Divided. *The Baptist Standard,* p. 12.

Black, B., Oles, T., & Moore, L. (1996). Homophobia among students in social work programs. *Journal of Baccalaureate Social Work, 2,* 13-41.

Breckenridge, J. & Breckenridge, L. (1995). *What Color Is Your God?: Multicultural Education in the Church.* Wheaton, IL: Victor Books.

Caldwell, D.K. (1997, June 19). Baptists vote to boycott Disney Co. *The Dallas Morning News.,* p. 1A.

Clark, E. & Richardson, H. (1977). *Women and Religion: A Feminist Sourcebook of Christian Thought.* New York: Harper & Row.

Clark, I.L. (1994). *Writing About Diversity: An Argument Reader and Guide.* Fort Worth, TX: Harcourt, Brace & Company.

The National Association of Social Workers Code of Ethics. (1995, November). *NASW News, 41(10),* 17-20.

Edwards, A. (1996). Practitioner and client value conflict: Suggested guidelines for social work practice. *Social Work and Christianity, 23,* 28-38.

Freeman, E.M. (1996). I Am A Human Being. In Ewalt, P.L., Freeman, E.M., Kirk, S.A., & Poole, D.L. (Eds.), *Multicultural Issues in Social Work.* Washington, D.C.: NASW Press.

Furnish, V.P. (1994). The Bible and Homosexuality: Reading the Texts in Context. In J.S. Siker (Ed.), *Homosexuality in the Church: Both Sides of the Debate* (pp.18-35). Louisville, KY: Westminster John Knox Press.

Gomes, P.J. (1996). *The Good Book: Reading The Bible With Mind and Heart.* New York: William Morrow and Company.

Goodstein, L. (1996, June 13). Baptist Group Plans Boycott of Disney Company: Firm is Denounced for Policies on Gays. *Washington Post.*

Gould, K.H. (1996). The Misconstruing of Multiculturalism: The Stanford Debate and Social Work. In Ewalt, P.L., Freeman, E.M., Kirk, S.A., & Poole, D.L. (Eds), *Multicultural Issues in Social Work.* Washington, D.C.: NASW Press.

Hays, R. (1994). Awaiting the Redemption of Our Bodies: The Witness of Scripture Concerning Homosexuality. In J.S. Siker (Ed.), *Homosexuality in the Church: Both Sides of the Debate.* Louisville, KY: Westminster John Knox Press.

Huber, R. & Orlando, B.P. (1995). Persisting gender differences in social workers' incomes: Does the profession really care? *Social Work,* 40, 585-591.

Knapman, S.K. (1977). Sex discrimination in family agencies. *Social Work, 22,* 461-465.

Kropf, N.P. & Issac, A.R. (1992). Cultural Diversity and Social Work Practice: An Overview.In Harrison, D.F., Wodarski, J.S., & Thyer, B.A. (Eds.), *Cultural Diversity and Social Work Practice.* Springfield, IL: Charles C. Thomas.

Loewenberg, F.M. (1988). *Religion And Social Work Practice In Contemporary American Society.* New York: Columbia University Press.

Mollenkott, V.R. (1994). Overcoming Heterosexism—To Benefit Everyone. In J.S. Siker (Ed.), *Homosexuality in the Church: Both Sides of the Debate.* Louisville, KY: Westminster John Knox Press

Morales, A.T. & Sheafor, B.W. (1995). *Social Work: A Profession of Many Faces.* Boston: Allyn and Bacon.

Newman, B.S., White, J., & Strock-Linski, D. (October, 1995). *Populations at Risk: An Integrated Approach to Curriculum Building.* Panel presentation at the meeting of Baccalaureate Program Directors, Nashville, TN.

Parents and Friends of Lesbians and Gays. (1993). *Ten Simple Things You Can Do To Make A Difference.* [Brochure].

Scanzoni, L.D. & Mollenkott, V.R. (1994). *Is The Homosexual My Neighbor: A Positive Christian Response.* San Francisco: Harper.

Schmidt. T.E. (1995). *Straight & Narrow?: Compassion & Clarity in the Homosexuality Debate.* Downers Grove, IL: InterVarsity Press.

Stark, R. (1996). *The Rise of Christianity: A Sociologist Reconsiders History.* Princeton, NJ: Princeton University Press.

Sutton, J.A. (1982). Sex discrimination among social workers. *Social Work, 27,* 211-217.

Swindler, A. (1993). *Homosexuality and World Religions.* Valley Forge, Pennsylvania: Trinity Press International.

Tolman, R.M., Mowry, D.D., Jones, L.E., & Brekke, J. (1986). Developing a Profeminist Commitment Among Men in Social Work. In Van Den Bergh, N. & Cooper, L. (Eds.), *Feminist Visions for Social Work.* Silver Spring, MD: NASW Press.

Tucker, R.A. & Liefeld, W. (1987). *Daughters of the Church.* Grand Rapids, MI: Academie.

Wallis, J. (1995). *The Soul of Politics: Beyond "Religious Right" And "Secular Left".* San Diego: Harcourt Brace and Company.

Wicker, D.G. (1986). Combating Racism in Practice and in the Classroom.. In Van Den Bergh, N. & Cooper, L. (Eds.), *Feminist Visions for Social Work..* Silver Spring, MD: NASW Press.

Williams, M., Ho, L., & Fiedler, L. (1974). Career patterns: More grist for women's liberation. *Social Work, 19,* 466-466.

York, R.O., Henley, H.C., & Gamble, D.N. (1987). Sexual discrimination in social work: Is it salary or advancement? *Social Work, 32,* 50-55.

CHAPTER 7

CALLING: A SPIRITUALITY MODEL FOR SOCIAL WORK PRACTICE

Beryl Hugen

In making a career choice, many Christian students find the social work profession a good fit with their religious faith. Or at least at first glance it appears so. For example, as part of the application process for the social work program I teach in, students are asked to explain why they have chosen social work as a major. What motivates them to enter this field of study? Some answer the question by relating past experiences with social work services or role models who were social workers, but almost all describe a moderate or fairly strong religious impulse to serve people and society.

Many specifically relate their faith to their choice of social work—stating something like this: In being loved by God, they in turn wish to share some of this love with those who are poor or hurting or are in need of help of some kind. Some of these students believe that to be a Christian in social work they must work in an agency under religious auspices, whereas others plan to work in programs that do not have a specific religious base or affiliation, but are part of the larger community of governmental social welfare responses to those in need. Despite these differences, almost all are interested in finding ways to integrate their faith and their newly chosen field of study.

But it doesn't take long in their social work studies for these students to begin to recognize the complex tensions between their religious faith, agency auspices, and the secular values of the social work profession. This discovery is not surprising; social work is, after all, a secular profession. At times, students find the profession very critical of religion, even suspicious of anyone who claims to have religious motives for helping others.

This feeling is understandable, for in the last thirty to forty years, the social work profession has simply ignored religious insights and accepted the principle of separating the sacred and secular. Religion came to be seen as having no particular insight to offer or relevance for everyday professional practice. Because of this attitude, the recent professional literature does not offer much help to students in thinking through the relationship of religious faith and professional practice. It is ironic that social work, which claims as its unique focus the "whole person" in the whole environment, has for so long neglected the religious dimension of life.

Not only do students continue to come to the profession with religious motivations, but the roots of social work are largely grounded in religious faith (Devine, 1939). Social work originated and came of age under the inspiration of the Judeo-Christian traditions and the philanthropic and service motivation of religious people. As Leiby (1985) indicates, the Christian biblical command to love God and to love one's neighbor as oneself was directly translated into a sense of moral responsibility for social service. As the social work profession secularized in the 20th century, these earlier religious rationales and models for service were replaced by doctrines of natural rights, utilitarianism, and humanistic ideology.

Dealing with human need apart from religious motives and methods is actually a very recent development in the history of charity and philanthropy. The notion of a secular profession focused on responding to human suffering would have struck many of our professional ancestors as quite inconsistent and confusing. Many of them were religiously motivated and expressed their faith by means of social work as a vocation, a calling from God to serve their brothers and sisters who were in need. With their perception of social work as a calling, a vocation, they formalized a link between their religious faith and social work practice.

What is meant by viewing social work as a calling? Several recent articles have addressed this "old fashioned" concept of calling or vocation, sensing its power and value for current social work practice (Gustafson,1982; Reamer, 1992). However, these writers essentially have attempted to take the religious concept of calling and use it in a secular fashion. They have done so in order to provide a moral purpose for the profession—to counteract what they perceive to be the focus on self-interest inherent in the social work profession which has become increasingly professionalized, specialized and bureaucratic.

My intent in this chapter is to explain, or more accurately to reintroduce, the religious model of calling as used by Christian social workers, past and present, in linking Christian faith and professional social work practice. Both its attractiveness and shortcomings as a model will be addressed. My purpose is not only to help social workers and the profession understand or correct misunderstandings related to this model, but also help social workers better understand the broader issues related to the spirituality of social work practice, in that other religious models and spiritual traditions address many of the same integration of faith and practice questions. Also, reintroducing the model of calling will lead us to see the significance of how the perspectives and writings of our religiously motivated social work ancestors—of which there are many— -can contribute to the profession's current discussions regarding spirituality and social work practice.

Religion, Faith, and Spirituality

Before discussing the model of calling, it is helpful to define what is meant by the terms spirituality, religion, belief and faith. The profession has long struggled with this definitional dilemma. The dilemma has focused on how to reintroduce religious or spiritual concerns into a profession which has expanded beyond specific sectarian settings and ideologies to now include diverse sources of knowledge, values and skills, and how to respond to the needs of a much more spiritually diverse clientele. Addressing this dilemma, Siporin (1985) and Brower (1984) advocated for an understanding of spirituality that includes a wide diversity of religious and non-religious expressions, with such an inclusive understanding of spirituality encouraging social workers to reflect upon their clients both within and outside of particular institutional religious settings and ideologies.

From this beginning, Canda (1988a, 1988b) further developed a concept of spirituality for social work that incorporates insights from diverse religious and philosophical perspectives. He identifies three content components to spirituality—values, beliefs and practice issues— "all serving the central dynamic of a person's search for a sense of meaning and purpose, developed in the context of interdependent relationships between self, other people, the nonhuman world, and the ground of being itself" (Canda, 1988a, p. 43).

In the same vein, the work of James Fowler, known more for his model of faith development, is particularly instructive. Fowler (1981) states that to understand the "human quest for relation to transcendence," the key phenomenon to examine is not religion or belief but faith (p. 14). According to Fowler, who draws upon the ideas of religionist Wilfred Smith, *religions* are "cumulative traditions," which represent the expressions of faith of people in the past (p. 9). Included in a cumulative tradition are such elements as "texts of scripture, oral traditions, music, creeds, theologies," and so forth. *Belief* refers to "the holding of certain ideas" or "assent to a set of propositions" (p. 13). *Faith* differs from both religion and belief. Fowler describes faith as a commitment, "an alignment of the will...in accordance with a vision of transcendent value and power, one's ultimate concern" (p. 14). One commits oneself to that which is known or acknowledged and lives loyally, with life and character being shaped by that commitment. Defined in this way, faith is believed to be a universal feature of human living, recognizably similar everywhere, and in all major religious traditions.

What does faith consist of then? Fowler describes three components of what he calls the contents of faith. The first he terms *centers of value*, the "causes, concerns, or persons that consciously or unconsciously have the greatest worth to us." These are what we worship, things that "give our lives meaning" (p. 277). The second component of faith is described as our *images of power*, "the power with which we align ourselves to sustain us in the midst of life's contingencies" (p. 277): these powers need not necessarily be supernatural or transcendent. Finally, faith is comprised of "the *master stories* that we tell ourselves and by which we interpret and respond to the events that impinge upon our lives." Essentially, our master stories reveal what we believe to be the fundamental truths, "the central premises of [our] sense of life's meaning" (p. 277).

In discussing spirituality and faith, Fowler and Canda both emphasize its pervasive, all encompassing nature in an individual's life. Faith or spirituality is not a separate dimension of life or compartmentalized specialty, but rather an orientation of the total person. Accordingly, the three components of faith—centers of value, images of power, and master stories (Fowler, 1981) - and spirituality—values, beliefs, and practices (Canda, 1988) - exert "structuring power" in our lives, shaping our characters and actions in the world, including our work. Faith and spirituality are defined here as the essence of religion. Faith and spirituality take on a Christian religious meaning when the centers of value, images of power, and master stories of one's faith, the central dynamic of one's search for a sense of meaning and purpose, are grounded in the creeds, texts of scripture, and theology etc. of the Christian tradition. I will attempt to present the Christian religious concept of calling within these more inclusive frameworks of spirituality and faith.

Calling in Action

Perhaps the best way to develop an understanding of the religious concept of calling is to start with an illustration. Robert Coles, in his book *The Call to Service* (1993), tells of a six year old black girl who initiated school desegregation in the South in the early 1960's. Tessie, a first grader, each day facing an angry and threatening mob, was escorted by federal marshals to school. The mob almost always greeted her with a litany of obscenities. Tessie's maternal grandmother, Martha, was the family member who usually got Tessie up and off to school each morning.

Coles reports that one day Tessie was reluctant to go to school—claiming to feeling tired, having slipped and fallen while playing in a nearby back yard, and having a difficult time with a current substitute teacher. Tessie suggested to her grandmother that she might stay home that day. Her grandmother replied that that would be fine if Tessie truly wasn't well, but if she was more discouraged than sick, that was quite another matter. She goes on to say:

"It's no picnic, child—I know that, Tessie—going to that school. Lord Almighty, if I could just go with you, and stop there in front of that building, and call all those people to my side, and read to them from the Bible, and tell them, remind them that He's up there, Jesus, watching over all of us—it don't matter who you are and what your skin color is. But I stay here, and you go—and your momma and your daddy, they have to leave the house so early in the morning that it's only Saturdays and Sundays that they see you before the sun hits the middle of its traveling for the day. So I'm not the one to tell you that you should go, because here I am, and I'll be watching television and eating or cleaning things up while you're walking by those folks. But I'll tell you, you're doing them a great favor; you're doing them a service, a big service."

"You see, my child, you have to help the good Lord with His world! He puts us here—and He calls us to help Him out. You belong in that McDonogh School, and there will be a day when everyone knows that, even those poor folks—Lord, I pray for them!—those poor, poor folks who are out there shouting their heads off at you. You're one of the Lord's people; He's put His Hand on you. He's given a call to you, a call to service—in His name! There's all those people out there on the street." (p. 3-4)

Later Coles questions Tessie whether she understood what her grandmother meant by "how you should be of service to those people out there on the street." She replied:

"If you just keep your eyes on what you're supposed to be doing, then you'll get there—to where you want to go. The marshals say, 'Don't look at them; just walk with your head up high, and you're looking straight ahead.' My granny says that there's God, He's looking too, and I should remember that it's a help to Him to do this, what I'm doing; and if you serve Him, then that's important. So I keep trying." (p. 4-5)

The heart of what Tessie had learned was that for her, service meant serving, and not only on behalf of those she knew and liked or wanted to like. Service meant an alliance with the Lord Himself for the benefit of people who were obviously unfriendly. Service was not an avocation or something done to fulfill a psychological need, not even an action that would earn her any great reward. She had connected a moment in her life with a larger ideal, and in so doing had learned to regard herself as a servant, as a person called to serve. It was a rationale for a life, a pronouncement with enormous moral and emotional significance for Tessie and her grandmother. This call was nurtured by the larger black community, her pastor, family, and the biblical values of love and justice—the stories of exile and return, of suffering and redemption—the view of the powerful as suspect and the lowly as destined to sit close to God, in His Kingdom.

Coles himself recounts how ill-prepared professionally he was to understand this family and their sense of calling:

> "I don't believe I could have understood Tessie and her family's capacity to live as they did, do as they did for so long, against such great odds, had I not begun to hear what *they* were saying and meaning, what *they* intended others to know about their reasons and values—as opposed to the motivations and reactions and "mechanisms of defense" I attributed to them. Not that there wasn't much to be learned by a psychoanalytic approach. Tessie and her companions, like human beings everywhere (including those who study or treat other human beings), most certainly did demonstrate fearfulness and anxiety; she also tried to subdue those developments by not acknowledging them, for instance, or by belittling their significance. Mostly, though, she clung hard to a way of thinking in which she was *not* a victim, *not* in need of "help" but someone picked by fate to live out the Christian tradition in her life. "I'm trying to think of the way Jesus would want me to think," she told me one evening. When I asked how she thought Jesus wanted her to think, she replied, "I guess of others, and not myself, I'm here to help the others." (p. 26)

Calling: The Meaning of Work

For some Christians, like Tessie and her grandmother, connecting one's work to the divine intentions for human life gives another dimension to the meaning and purpose of one's work and life. Certainly adequate pay, financial stability, social status and a sense of personal fulfillment remain significant criteria in choosing a career, but they are not the central motivation. The central motivation is the means by which one's Christian religious tradition has tied one's work and faith together, this concept of vocation, or calling.

Martin Luther originally formulated the notion of vocation or calling largely in reaction to the prevailing attitude toward work in medieval society. Medieval thinkers devalued work. They believed that in and of itself, work had little or no spiritual significance. They held, like the Greeks earlier, to the idea that the highest form of life, the form in which humans can realize their noblest potential, is the contemplative life of the mind. By thinking, we liken ourselves to God. Work was thus a hindrance to an individual's relation to God, which could be cultivated only in the leisure of contemplation. Because peasant serfs did most of the work in medieval society, and because the earthly character of their occupations prevented them from participating directly in the religious life, they received grace through the church by means of the sacraments.

Not only the life of productive work, but also the practical or active life, consisting of doing good to one's neighbor, was viewed by many medievals as an impediment to the true goals of the religious life. The activity given precedence was always the contemplative life. An early church father, St. Augustine (1950) wrote: "the obligations of charity make us undertake virtuous activity, but if no one lays this burden upon us, we should give ourselves over in leisure to study and contemplation" (p. 19). The need for the active or charitable life was temporary, whereas contemplation of God was eternal.

Luther's concept of vocation or calling fits neatly within the compass of this thought since he draws a basic theological distinction between the kingdom of heaven and the kingdom of earth. To the kingdom of heaven belongs our relationship to God, which is to be based on faith; to the kingdom of earth belongs our relationship to our neighbor, which is to be based on love. A vocation, properly speaking, is the call to love my neighbor that comes to me through the duties attached to my social place or *station* within the earthly kingdom. A station in this life may be a matter of paid employment, but it need not be. Luther's idea of station is wide enough to include being a wife or a husband, a mother or a father, a judge or politician, as well as a baker, truck driver, farmer or social worker. Thus, the call to love one's neighbor goes out to all in general. All of these callings represent specific and concrete ways of serving my neighbor, as I am commanded to do by God Himself.

What do we accomplish when we discharge the duties of our stations in life, when we heed the call of God to serve our neighbor in our daily tasks? Luther believed the order of stations in the kingdom of earth has been instituted by God Himself as His way of seeing to it that the needs of humanity are met on a day-by-day basis. Through the human pursuit of vocations across the array of earthly stations, the hungry are fed, the naked are clothed, the sick are healed, the ignorant are enlightened, and the weak are protected. That is, by working we actually participate in God's providence for the human race. Through our work, people are brought under His providential care. Far from being of little or no account, work is charged with religious significance. As we pray each morning for our daily bread, people are already busy at work in the bakeries.

Luther conceived of work as a way of serving others. He never recommended it as either the road to self-fulfillment or a tool for self-aggrandizement. We, of course, find it natural to assess the attractiveness of a particular job on the basis of what it can do for us. But Luther saw quite clearly that work will always involve a degree of self-sacrifice for the sake of others, just as Christ sacrificed himself for the sake of others.

During the time of Luther, and for many centuries preceding him, people thought of human society to be stable, static, and as incapable of change, as the order of nature itself. Shortly after Luther's time, however, European civilization underwent a dramatic transformation under the combined influence of a rapidly expanding market economy, accelerated urbanization, technological innovation, and vast political reorganization. In the face of these astounding changes on all fronts of social life, people soon saw that the structure of human society is itself in part a product of human activity, changeable and affected by sin. Once people recognized this fact, it became clear, in turn, that to the degree human activity is motivated by sinful desires and worldly ambitions, the society thus produced is also likely to be structurally unsound and in need of reform. For example, an economy based upon greed and a government based on the arbitrary use of power stand in just as much need of repentance as the individuals who are a part of them. For this reason, other reformers insisted that not only the human heart, but also human society must be reformed in accordance with the Word of God. The emergent vision of the Christian life at the dawn of modern social work practice, then, required not only that people obey God in their callings, but that the callings themselves be aligned with the will of God.

Calling Within Social Work

Although historically there have been many models of spirituality in social work, the calling model perhaps has been the most prominent, or at least the most extensively referred to in the social work literature. In fact, in the very early years, it was the dominant model. This dominance is certainly related to the fact that Protestantism was the dominant religious form at the time. Many early social workers in their writings refer to the relationship of their spirituality and social work within this calling model. Their response is not surprising, since many of them grew up in devoted religious families, many had theological training, and still others were very active as lay people in their churches. All found in their spiritual experiences something which gave impetus, meaning, and value to their work of service.

The following examples illustrate the prominence of the calling model and how it has been articulated and practiced by a variety of different leaders within the profession.

Edward Devine, a leader in the Charity Organization Society and the first director of one of the first schools of social work, records in his book *When Social Work Was Young* (1939) the early experiences in social work education and summarizes these experiences as follows:

> "The real start towards the professional education of social workers as such was made in 1898, when the Society launched its summer school of philanthropy with thirty students enrolled....
>
> For several years this summer school gathered from all parts of the country a substantial number of promising candidates, and a brilliant corps of instructors, who for one day, or sometimes for an entire week, expounded and discussed the fundamentals of the slowly emerging profession. Jane Addams, Mary Richmond, Zilpha Smith, Mrs. Glendower Evans, Graham Taylor, Jeffrey Brackett, John M. Glenn, Mary Willcox Brown, before and also after she became Mrs. John M. Glenn, James B. Reynolds, Mary Simkhovitch-a full roster of the lecturers in the school would be like a list of the notables in the National Conference of Social Work. Certainly no religious gathering could have a deeper consecration to that ideal of learning how to do justly, and to love mercy, and to walk humbly, which Micah described as being all that is required of us." (p. 125-6)

He ends the book by stating that in his opinion the spirit of social work finds its power, value, and purpose from the biblical Sermon on the Mount.

Richard Cabot (1927) addressed the model of calling more specifically in an article entitled "The Inter-Relation of Social Work and the Spiritual Life." He writes:

"religion is the consciousness of a world purpose to which we are allied...when I speak of the purpose being a personality, I speak of the person of God of whom we are children... I think it makes absolutely all the difference in social work to know this fact of our alliance with forces greater than ourselves. If a person wants to find himself and be somebody he has got to find his particular place in the universal plan. In social work, we are trying to help people find themselves, find their places and enjoy them. The chief end of man is to glorify God and to enjoy Him forever." (p. 212)

Cabot also articulated several spiritual powers applicable to social work practice that come to those who hold this faith: courage, humility and the ability to stand by people. He goes on to explain that the goal of social work is to:

"maintain and to improve the channels of understanding both within each person and between persons, and through these channels to favor the entrance of God's powers for the benefit of the individuals....

Unblocking channels is what social workers do. The sort of unblocking that I have in mind is that between capital and labor, between races, or between the members of a family who think they hate each other....

Spiritual diagnosis, I suppose, means nothing more than the glimpse of the central purpose of the person, unique and re-lated to the total parts of the world. Spiritual treatment, I sup-pose, is the attempt to open channels, the channels I have been speaking of, so as to favor the working of the world purpose. In this way social workers participate in the providence of God." (p. 215-16)

Perhaps the most prominent example of the power and dominance of the calling model is illustrated in Owen R. Lovejoy's presidential address to the National Conference of Social Work in 1920, entitled "The Faith of a Social Worker." In the speech he attempts to draw upon the foundations of faith of the members in order to aid in their approach to discussions during the Conference and to help create a real basis for unity. He begins by first disclaiming any intention of committing the Conference to any specific creed of social service. His desire, rather, is to discover "some of the those underlying principles which bind people together."

He states that all social workers have a philosophy of life, a faith, a "basic enthusiasm," and those who act on this faith can choose to:

"regard this as a sacred ministry and claim their commission as the ancient prophet claimed his when he said: "The Lord hath anointed me to preach good tidings to the meek, to bind up the broken hearted, to proclaim liberty to the captives, the opening of prison to them that are bound, to give a garland for ashes, the oil of joy for mourning, the garment of praise for the spirit of heaviness." Certainly this is not a slight task to which we are called, but the expression of a joyful faith carried with cheerfulness to those in the world most in need of it...a field of service based on the conviction that men are warranted in working for something corresponding to a divine order "on earth as it is in heaven." (p. 209)

He warns those "who look upon the visible institutions connected with their religion as the essential embodiment of faith," recognizing such a sectarian position frequently leads to imposing one's own values on others and proselytizing—similar issues we face today. He ends the address stating that the secret of their usefulness as social workers is found in the following litany.

God is a Father,
Man is a brother,
Life is a mission and not a career;
Dominion is service,
Its scepter is gladness,
The least is the greatest,
Saving is dying,
Giving is living,
Life is eternal and love is its crown. (p. 211)

It is difficult to imagine an address on such a topic being given today. Such was the significance of spirituality and the calling model in the social work profession at that time.

The calling model's chief apologist, however, was Ernest Johnson, a prolific writer and interpreter of Protestant religion and the social work profession. His writings detail the principles which he hoped would govern efforts to bring Protestantism to bear through the social work profession in meeting human needs. Recognizing that Protestantism had a majority position and influence in the culture, he strongly advocated, with some exceptions, for a pattern of social work based on the calling model. The result was to minimize the operation and control of agencies and social welfare enterprises by churches or religious groups and maximize Protestant participation in non-sectarian agencies.

Later in life he recognized that Protestantism, particularly when its pre-eminent position was beginning to wane, would never obtain complete cultural dominance or create an approximation to the ideal of a Christian society—the Corpus Christianum. The result, he lamented, would be only a partial transformation of the culture—and regrettably, a partial accommodation on the part of Protestantism to the culture. But despite this limitation, he still believed the Protestant pattern or model of influencing social work enterprises and social movements "indirectly" (through the means of one's calling or vocation) was essentially sound. Johnson (1946) states:

> "It [the calling model] affords the most effective channel through which our churches, in the midst of a religiously heterogeneous population, can bring to bear their testimony through community endeavor and make their impact on a secular culture. This means, however, a recovery of the sense of lay Christian vocation, which has been so largely lost. The major Protestant contribution to social work can be made, I believe, through the consciously Christian activities of persons engaged in non-sectarian enterprises and movements. In the existing situation in America a revival of a sectarian, possessive attitude toward social work would be definitely reactionary....
>
> In a word, then, we need to devise our social strategy in the light of our Protestant history, with its emphasis on freedom, and in the light of our cultural situation, which puts a premium on vocational work as Christian testimony. We can make our best contribution without seeking to enhance Protestant prestige, seeking rather to influence contemporary life and to meet human need through the activities of those whose lives have been kindled at our altars and nourished in our fellowship." (p. 2-4)

As Johnson relates, the calling model has not always functioned as intended. Already in 1893, one leader of the new social work profession, responding to the widening gap between religion and the emerging influence of scientific models in social work, characterized social work as "a revolutionary turning of thought in our society from a religious service to God to a secular service to humanity" (Huntington, 1893). Along this line of thought, Protestant theologian Reinhold Niebuhr (1932) grappled with the practical consequences of the calling model for social work. With three-fourths of social workers then functioning under secular auspices, many had become "inclined to disregard religion." This development he regarded as a significant loss for social work—"destroying or remaining oblivious to powerful resources and losing the insights religion provided in keeping wholesome attitudes toward individuals" and "preserving the sanity and health in the social worker's own outlook upon life" (p. 9). He believed social workers needed, therefore, a renewed sense of vocation or calling. In addition, this loss of calling partially contributes to what church historian Martin Marty (1980) later referred to as "godless social service," or the migration (privatization) of faith or spirituality from social work.

Conclusion

Because of our distance from the thoughts and assumptions of our predecessors in social work and perhaps from the language of spirituality itself, efforts regarding such historical reflections as these may seem awkward and archaic. The goal is not, however, to recreate the past, but rather to identify the models of spirituality that guided our social work ancestors and then to find ways to translate and apply the spirit of these models to our present situation.

This model of calling offers significant insight into current discussions relating spirituality and professional social work practice. Within this calling model, religious faith is not the private possession of an individual, but is grounded in tradition and divine revelation, permeating the whole of life, connecting public and private spheres, and linking the individual with the community. The model also places professional techniques and methods in the context of larger goals and values that give life meaning and purpose for both clients and practitioners.

Historically, religiously motivated persons and groups found their faith propelling them into actions of concern for others, especially the poor and the vulnerable in society. These social workers have affirmed in a variety of ways their shared belief that the faith dimension of life leads to a transcendence of individualism, and to a commitment to others—to social work practice motivated by a calling to a life of service.

The model presented is helpful to social workers from the Christian faith tradition, but also to others who seek to acquire a better understanding of the meaning and effects of spirituality in their own and their clients' lives. A social worker's own cultivation of spirituality is a crucial preparation for the competent application of knowledge and skills in practice. The model is particularly helpful in taking into account the distinctive values, sources of power and master stories of one particular religious and cultural tradition, Christianity—represented by many persons like Tessie and her grandmother whom social workers daily encounter in practice, as well as by many social workers themselves.

Although the model does not resolve the tensions and conflicts which exist between the Christian spiritual tradition and the current largely secular profession, it does provide a beginning framework for integrating Christian spirituality and social work at both the personal and professional levels. The profession's roots are significantly tied to this particular model of spiritual/professional integration, and many social workers as well as clients continue to define their lives, personally and professionally, in the context of this Christian-based spiritual call to service. The Christian values of love, justice, and kindness; its stories related to the poor, the vulnerable, and those of liberation from oppression; and its emphasis on self-sacrifice, are the "passion of the old time social workers" that many find attractive and wish to bring back—albeit in a form more adaptable to a more diverse clientele and changed environment (Constable, 1983; Gustafson, 1982; Reamer, 1992; Siporin, 1982, 1985; Specht & Courtney, 1994).

References

Augustine, Saint. (1950). *City of God*. XIX, 19, New York: Modern Library.

Brower, Irene. (1984). *The 4th Ear of the Spiritual-Sensitive Social Worker*. Ph.D. diss., Union for Experimenting Colleges and Universities.

Cabot, Richard C. (1927). The Inter-Relation of Social Work and the Spiritual Life. *The Family*, 8(7), 211-217.

Canda, Edward R. (1988a). Conceptualizing Spirituality for Social Work: Insights from Diverse Perspectives. *Social Thought*, Winter, 30-46.

Canda, Edward R. (1988b). Spirituality, Religious Diversity and Social Work Practice. *Social Casework*, April, 238-247.

Coles, Robert. (1993). *The Call of Service*. New York: Houghton Mifflin Company.

Constable, Robert. (1983). Religion, Values and Social Work Practice. *Social Thought*, 9, 29-41.

Devine, Edward T. (1939). *When Social Work Was Young*. New York: Macmillan Company.

Fowler, James W. (1981). *Stages of Faith*. San Francisco: Harper and Row.

Gustafson, James M. (1982). Professions as "Callings." *Social Service Review*, December, 105-515.

Huntington, James. (1893). Philanthropy and Morality. In Addams, Jane, (Ed.), *Philanthropy and Social Congress*, New York: Crowell.

Johnson, Ernest F. (1946). The Pattern and Philosophy of Protestant Social Work. *Church Conference of Social Work*, Buffalo, New York.

Leiby, James. (1985). Moral Foundations of Social Welfare and Social Work: A Historical View. *Social Work*, 30(4), 323-330.

Lovejoy, Owen R. (1920). The Faith of a Social Worker. *The Survey*, May, 208-211.

Marty, Martin E. (1980). Social Service: Godly and Godless. *Social Service Review*, 54, 463-481.

Niebuhr, Reinhold. (1932). *The Contribution of Religion to Social Work*. New York: Columbia University Press.

Reamer, Frederic G. (1992). Social Work and the Public Good: Calling or Career? In Reid, Nelson P. & Philip R. Popple (Eds.), *The Moral Purposes of Social Work*, (11-33), Chicago: Nelson-Hall.

Specht, Harry & Courtney, Mark. (1994). *Unfaithful Angels*. New York: The Free Press.

Siporin, Max. (1982). Moral Philosophy in Social Work Today. *Social Service Review*, December, 516-538.

Siporin, Max. (1983). Morality and Immorality in Working with Clients. *Social Thought*, Fall, 10-41.

Siporin, Max. (1985). Current Social Work Perspectives on Clinical Practice. *Clinical Social Work Journal*, 13, 198-217.

CHAPTER 8

THE RELATIONSHIP BETWEEN BELIEFS AND VALUES IN SOCIAL WORK PRACTICE: WORLDVIEWS MAKE A DIFFERENCE

David A. Sherwood

In some circles (including some Christian ones) it is fashionable to say that what we believe is not all that important. What we do is what really counts. I strongly disagree. The relationship between what we think and what we do is complex and it is certainly not a simple straight line, but it is profound. Social work values, practice theories, assessments, intervention decisions, and action strategies are all shaped by our worldview assumptions and our beliefs.

I believe that a Christian worldview will provide an interpretive framework which will solidly support and inform commonly held social work values such as the inherent value of every person regardless of personal characteristics, self-determination and personally responsible freedom of choice, and responsibility for the common good, including help for the poor and oppressed. And it will challenge other values and theories such as might makes right, exploitation of the weak by the strong, and extreme moral relativism. In contrast, many other worldviews, including materialism, empiricism, and postmodern subjectivism lead to other interpretations of the "facts."

Worldviews Help Us Interpret Reality

What is a "Worldview?"

Worldviews give faith-based answers to a set of ultimate and grounding questions. Everyone operates on the basis of some worldview or faith-based understanding of the universe and persons— examined, or unexamined, implicit or explicit, simplistic or sophisticated. One way or another, we develop functional assumptions which help us to sort through and make some sort of sense out of our experience. And every person's worldview will always have a faith-based component (even belief in an exclusively material universe takes faith). This does not mean worldviews are necessarily irrational, unconcerned with "facts," or impervious to critique and change (though they unfortunately might be). It matters greatly how conscious, reflective, considered, or informed our worldviews are. The most objectivity we can achieve is to be critically aware of our worldview and how it affects our interpretations of "the facts." It is far better to be aware, intentional, and informed regarding our worldview than to naively think we are (or anyone else is) objective or neutral or to be self-righteously led by our biases which we may think are simply self-evident truth.

These worldviews affect our approach to social work practice, how we understand and help people. What is the nature of persons—biochemical machines, evolutionary products, immortal souls, all of the above? What constitutes valid knowledge—scientific empiricism only, "intuitive" discernment, spiritual guidance (if so, what kind)? What kinds of social work theories and practice methods are legitimate? What are appropriate values and goals—what is healthy, functional, optimal, the good?

To put it another way, we all form stories that answer life's biggest questions. As I become a Christian, I connect my personal story to a much bigger story that frames my answers to these big questions. Middleton and Walsh (1995, p. 11) summarize the questions this way:

1. Where are we? What is the nature of the reality in which we find ourselves?
2. Who are we? What is the nature and task of human beings?
3. What's wrong? How do we understand and account for evil and brokenness?
4. What's the remedy? How do we find a path through our brokenness to wholeness?

Interpreting the Facts

"Facts" have no meaning apart from an interpretive framework. "Facts" are harder to come by than we often think, but even when we have some "facts" in our possession, they have no power to tell us what they mean or what we should do.

That human beings die is a fact. That I am going to die would seem to be a reliable prediction based on what I can see. In fact, the capacity to put those observations and projections together is one of the ways we have come to describe or define human consciousness. But what do these "facts" mean and what effect should they have on my life? One worldview might tell me that life emerged randomly in a meaningless universe and is of no particular value beyond the subjective feelings I may experience from moment to moment. Another worldview might tell me that somehow biological survival of life forms is of value and that I only have value to the extent that I contribute to that biological parade (with the corollary that survival proves fitness). Another worldview might tell me that life is a gift from a loving and just Creator and that it transcends biological existence, that death is not the end of the story. Different worldviews lend different meanings to the same "facts."

The major initial contribution of a Christian worldview to an understanding of social work values and ethical practice is not unique, contrasting, or one of conflicting values, but rather a solid foundation for the basic values that social workers claim and often take for granted (Holmes, 1984; Sherwood, 1993). Subsequently, a Christian worldview will shape how those basic values are understood and how they interact with one another. For example, justice will be understood in the light of God's manifest concern for the poor and oppressed, so it can never be only a procedurally "fair" protection of individual liberty and the right to acquire, hold, and transfer property (Lebacqz, 1986; Mott, 1982; Wolterstorff, 1983).

The Interaction of Feeling, Thinking, and Behavior

Persons are complex living ecological systems—to use a helpful conceptual model common in social work—systems of systems, if you will. Systems within our bodies and outside us as well interact in dynamic relationships with each other. For example, it is impossible to meaningfully separate our thinking, feeling, and behavior from each other and from the systems we experience outside ourselves, yet we quite properly think of ourselves as separate individuals. The lines of influence run in all directions. What we believe affects what we experience, including how we define our feelings. For example, does an experience I might have of being alone, in and of itself, *make* me feel lonely, or rejected, or exhilarated by freedom, for that matter? Someone trips me, but was it accidental or intentional? I have had sex with only one woman (my wife Carol) in over fifty years of life. How does this "make" me feel? Are my feelings not also a result of what I tell myself about the meaning of my experience? But it works the other way too.

All this makes us persons harder to predict. And it certainly makes it harder to assign neat, direct, and one-way lines of causality. The biblical worldview picture is that God has granted us (at great cost) the dignity and terror of contributing to causality ourselves through our own purposes, choices, and actions. We have used this freedom to our hurt, but this also means that we are not mechanistically determined and that significant change is always possible. And change can come from many directions—thinking, emotions, behavior, experience. We are especially (compared to other creatures) both gifted and cursed by our ability to think about ourselves and the world. We can form purposes and act in the direction of those purposes. Our beliefs about the nature of the world, other persons, and ourselves interact in a fundamental way with how we perceive reality, how we define our own identity, and how we act.

If this is true in our personal lives, it is equally true as we try to understand and help our clients in social work practice. And it is no less true for clients themselves. What we believe about the nature of the world, the nature of persons, and the nature of the human situation is at least as important as the sheer facts of the circumstances we experience.

Worldviews Help Construct Our Understanding of Values

Cut Flowers: Can Values Be Sustained Without Faith?

One significant manifestation of the notion that beliefs aren't all that important is the fallacy of our age which assumes that fundamental moral values can be justified and sustained apart from their ideological (ultimately theological) foundation. Take, for example, the fundamental Christian and social work belief that all human beings have intrinsic dignity and value.

Elton Trueblood, the Quaker philosopher, once described ours as a "cut-flower" generation. He was suggesting that, as it is possible to cut a rose from the bush, put it in a vase, and admire its fresh loveliness and fragrance for a short while, it is possible to maintain the dignity and value of every human life while denying the existence or significance of God as the source of that value. But the cut rose is already dead, regardless of the deceptive beauty which lingers for awhile. Even uncut, "The grass withers, and the flower falls, but the Word of the Lord endures forever" (I Peter 1:24-25).

Many in our generation, including many social workers, are trying to hold onto values—such as the irreducible dignity and worth of the individual—while denying the only basis on which such a value can ultimately stand. We should be glad they try to hold onto the value, but we should understand how shaky such a foundation is. A secular generation can live off its moral capital only so long before the impertinent questions (Why should we?) can no longer be ignored.

Doesn't Everybody "Just Know" That
Persons Have Dignity and Value?

But doesn't everybody "just know" that human beings have intrinsic value? You don't have to believe in God, do you? In fact, according to some, so-called believers in God have been among the worst offenders against the value and dignity of all persons (sadly true, in some cases). After all, a lot of folks, from secular humanists to rocket scientists to New Age witches to rock stars, have declared themselves as defenders of the value of the individual. Isn't the worth of the person just natural, or at least rational and logically required? The plain answer is, "No, it's *not* just natural or rational or something everyone just knows."

I received a striking wake-up call in regard to this particular truth a number of years ago when I was a freshman at Indiana University. I think the story is worth telling here. I can't help dating myself—it was in the spring of 1960, the time the Civil Rights movement was clearly emerging. We were hearing of lunch room sit-ins and Freedom Riders on buses. Through an older friend of mine from my home town I wound up spending the evening at the Student Commons talking with my friend and someone he had met, a graduate student from Iran named Ali. I was quite impressed. My friend Maurice told me his father was some sort of advisor to the Shah (the ruling despot at that point in Iran's history).

The conversation turned to the events happening in the South, to the ideas of racial integration, brotherhood, and social justice. Ali was frankly puzzled and amused that Maurice and I, and at least some other Americans, seemed to think civil rights were worth pursuing. But given that, he found it particularly hard to understand what he thought was the wishy-washy way the thing was being handled. "I don't know why you want to do it," he said," but if it's so important, why don't you just do it? If I were President of the United States and I wanted integration, I would do it in a week!" "How?" we asked. "Simple. I would just put a soldier with a machine gun on every street corner and say 'Integrate.' If they didn't, I would shoot them." (Believable enough, as the history of Iran has shown)

Naive freshman that I was, I just couldn't believe he was really saying that. Surely he was putting us on. You couldn't just do that to people. At least not if you were moral! The conversation-debate- argument went on to explore what he really did believe about the innate dignity and value of the individual human life and social responsibility. You don't just kill inconvenient people, do you? I would say things like, "Surely you believe that society has a moral responsibility to care for the widows and orphans, the elderly, the disabled, the emotionally disturbed." Incredibly (to me at the time), Ali's basic response was not to give an inch but to question *my* beliefs and values instead. "Society has no such moral responsibility," he said. "On the contrary. You keep talking about reason and morality. I'll tell you what is immoral. The rational person would say that the truly *immoral* thing is to take resources away from the strong and productive to give to the weak and useless. Useless members of society such as the disabled and mentally retarded should be eliminated, not maintained." He would prefer that the methods be "humane," but he really did mean eliminated.

It finally sunk into my freshman mind that what we were disagreeing about was not facts or logic, but the belief systems we were using to interpret or assign meaning to the facts. If I were to accept his assumptions about the nature of the universe (e.g. that there is no God—Ali was a thoroughly secular man; he had left Islam behind—that the material universe is the extent of reality, that self-preservation is the only given motive and goal), then his logic was flawless and honest. As far as he was concerned, the only thing of importance left to discuss would be the most effective means to gain and keep power and the most expedient way to use it.

In this encounter I was shaken loose from my naive assumption that "everybody knows" the individual person has innate dignity and value. I understood more clearly that unless you believed in the Creator, the notion that all persons are equal is, indeed, *not* self-evident. The Nazi policies of eugenics and the "final solution" to the "Jewish problem" make a kind of grimly honest (almost inevitable) sense if you believe in the materialist worldview.

The "Is-Ought" Dilemma

Not long afterward I was to encounter this truth much more cogently expressed in the writings of C. S. Lewis. In *The Abolition of Man* (1947) he points out that both the religious and the secular walk by faith if they try to move from descriptive observations of fact to any sort of value statement or ethical imperative. He says "From propositions about fact alone no *practical* conclusion can ever be drawn. 'This will preserve society' [let's assume this is a factually true statement] cannot lead to 'Do this' [a moral and practical injunction] except by the mediation of 'Society ought to be preserved' [a value statement]" (p. 43). "Society ought to be preserved" is a moral imperative which no amount of facts alone can prove or disprove. Even the idea of "knowing facts" involves basic assumptions (or faith) about the nature of the universe and human beings. The secular person (social worker?) tries to cloak faith by substituting words like natural, necessary, progressive, scientific, rational, or functional for "good," but the question always remains— For what end? and Why? And the answer to this question always smuggles in values from somewhere else besides the facts.

Even the resort to instincts such as self-preservation can tell us nothing about what we (or others) *ought* to do. Lewis (1947, p. 49) says:

We grasp at useless words: we call it the "basic," or "fundamental," or "primal," or "deepest" instinct. It is of no avail. Either these words conceal a value judgment passed *upon* the instinct and therefore not derivable *from* it, or else they merely record its felt intensity, the frequency of its operation, and its wide distribution. If the former, the whole attempt to base value upon instinct has been abandoned: if the latter, these observations about the quantitative aspects of a psychological event lead to no practical conclusion. It is the old dilemma. Either the premise is already concealed an imperative or the conclusion remains merely in the indicative.

This is called the "Is-Ought" dilemma. Facts, even when attainable, never have any practical or moral implications until they are interpreted through the grid of some sort of value assumptions. "Is" does not lead to "Ought" in any way that has moral bindingness, obligation, or authority until its relationship to relevant values is understood. And you can't get the values directly from the "Is." It always comes down to the question—what is the source and authority of the "Ought" that is claimed or implied?

The social work Code of Ethics refers to values such as the inherent value of every person, the importance of social justice, and the obligation to fight against oppression. It is a fair question to ask where those values come from and what gives them moral authority and obligation.

A Shaky Consensus: "Sexual Abuse" or "Intergenerational Sexual Experience?"

For an example of the "Is-Ought Dilemma," is child sexual abuse a fact or a myth? Or what is the nature of the abuse? Child sexual abuse is an example of an area where there may seem to be more of a consensus in values than there actually is. In any event, it illustrates how it is impossible to get values from facts alone. Some intervening concept of "the good" always has to come into play.

Fact: Some adults have sexual relations with children. But so what? What is the practical or moral significance of this fact? Is this something we should be happy or angry about? Is this good or bad? Sometimes good and sometimes bad? Should we be encouraging or discouraging the practice? Even if we could uncover facts about the consequences of the experience on children, we would still need a value framework to help us discern the meaning or practical implications of those facts. And to have moral obligation beyond our own subjective preferences or biases, this value framework must have some grounding outside ourselves. What constitutes negative consequences? And even if we could agree certain consequences were indeed negative, the question would remain as to what exactly was the cause.

In the last few years there has been a tremendous outpouring of attention to issues of child sexual abuse and its effects on adult survivors. I must say that this is long overdue and much needed. And even among completely secular social workers, psychologists, and other therapists there currently appears to be a high degree of consensus about the moral wrong of adult sexual activity with children and the enormity of its negative consequences on the child at the time and in later life. As a Christian I am encouraged, especially when I recall the self-described "radical Freudian" professor I had in my master's in social work program who described in glowingly approving terms high levels of sexual intimacy between children and each other and children and adults as "freeing and liberating" (that was the early 1970's).

However, if I look more closely at the worldview faith underlying much of the discussion of sexual abuse and its effects, the result is not quite so comforting to me as a Christian. The moral problem tends not to be defined in terms of a well-rounded biblical view of sexuality and God's creative design and purpose or an understanding of the problem of sin. Rather, it tends to be based on a more rationalistic and individualistic model of power and a model of justice which pins its faith on reason. Sexual abuse grows out of an inequity in power which a person rationally "ought not" exploit. Why not, one might ask.

But what if we take away the coercive element and get rid of the repressive "body-negative" ideas about sexual feelings? What if much or all of the negative effects of non-coercive sexual activity between adults and children is the result of the misguided and distorted social attitudes which are passed on to children and adults? Defenders of non-exploitive sexual activity between adults and children can (and do) argue that any negative consequences are purely a result of sex-negative social learning and attitudes. Representatives of a hypothetical group such as P.A.L. (Pedophiles Are Lovers!) would argue that what needs to be changed is not the intergenerational sexual behavior, but the sexually repressive social values and behavior which teach children the negative responses. These values are seen as the oppressive culprits. Then, the argument might go, should we not bend our efforts to eradicating these repressive sexual values and attitudes rather than condemning potentially innocent acts of sexual pleasure? Indeed, why not, if the only problem is exploitation of power?

You should also note that this argument in favor of intergenerational sexual behavior is not exclusively scientific, objective, or based only on "facts." It has to make faith assumptions about the nature of persons, the nature of sexuality, the nature of health, and the nature of values. By the same token, my condemnation of adult sexual activity with children is based on faith assumptions about the nature of persons, sexuality, health, and values informed by my Christian worldview. It is never just "facts" alone which determine our perceptions, conclusions, and behavior.

Right now, it happens to be a "fact" that a fairly large consensus exists, even among secular social scientists and mental health professionals, that adult sexual activity with children is "bad" and that it leads quite regularly to negative consequences. Right now you could almost say this is something "everyone knows." But it would be a serious mistake to become complacent about this or to conclude that worldview beliefs and faith are not so important after all.

First, not everyone agrees. Although I invented the hypothetical group P.A.L. (Pedophiles Are Lovers), it represents real people and groups that do exist. The tip of this iceberg may be appearing in the professional literature where it is becoming more acceptable and common to see the "facts" reinterpreted. In preparing bibliography for a course on sexual issues in helping, I ran across a very interesting little shift in terminology in some of the professional literature. One article was entitled "Counterpoints: Intergenerational sexual experience or child sexual abuse" (Malz, 1989). A companion article was titled "Intergenerational sexual contact: A continuum model of participants and experiences" (Nelson, 1989). Words do make a difference.

Second, we shouldn't take too much comfort from the apparent agreement. It is sometimes built on a fragile foundation that could easily come apart. The fact that Christians find themselves in wholehearted agreement with many secular helping professionals, for example, that sexual activity between adults (usually male) and children (usually female) is exploitive and wrong may represent a temporary congruence on issues and strategy, much more so than fundamental agreement on the nature of persons and sexuality.

But back to the "Is-Ought" dilemma. The fact that some adults have sexual contact with children, by itself, tells us *nothing* about what, if anything, should be done about it. The facts can never answer those questions. The only way those questions can ever be answered is if we interpret the facts in terms of our faith, whatever that faith is. What is the nature of the world? What is the nature of persons? What is the meaning of sex? What constitutes health? What is the nature of justice? And most important—why should I care anyway?

Worldviews Help Define the Nature and Value of Persons

So—Worldviews Have Consequences

Your basic faith about the nature of the universe has consequences (and everyone, as we have seen, has some sort of faith). Faith is consequential to you personally and the content of the faith is consequential. If it isn't *true* that Christ has been raised, my faith is worthless (I Cor. 15:14). And if it's *true* that Christ has been raised, but I put my faith in Baal or the free market or the earth goddess (big in New England these days) or Karl Marx (not so big these days) or human reason, then *that* has consequences, to me and to others. What are we going to *trust*, bottom-line?

In I Corinthians 15, the apostle Paul said something about the importance of what we believe about the nature of the world, the *content* of our faith. He said, "Now if Christ is proclaimed as raised from the dead, how can some of you say there is no resurrection of the dead? If there is no resurrection of the dead, then Christ has not been raised; and if Christ has not been raised, then our proclamation has been in vain and your faith is also in vain . . . If Christ has not been raised, your faith is futile and you are still in your sins . . . If for this life only we have hoped in Christ, we are of all people most to be pitied" (12-14, 17, 19).

I've been a student, a professional social worker, and a teacher of social work long enough to see some major changes in "what everyone knows," in what is assumed or taken for granted. "What everyone knows" is in fact part of the underlying operational *faith* of a culture or subculture—whether it's Americans or teenagers or those who go to college or social workers — or Southern Baptists, for that matter.

When I went to college, logical positivism was king, a version of what C. S. Lewis called "naturalism," a kind of philosophical materialism. It said that the physical world is all there is. Everything is fully explainable by materialistic determinism. Only what can be physically measured or "operationalized" is real (or at least relevantly meaningful). In psychology it was epitomized in B. F. Skinner's behaviorism.

I remember as a somewhat bewildered freshman at Indiana University attending a lecture by a famous visiting philosophy professor (a logical positivist) from Cambridge University (whose name I have forgotten) entitled "The *Impossibility* of any Future Metaphysic" (his take-off on Kant's title "Prologomena to any Future Metaphysic"). I can't say I understood it all at the time, but his main point was that modern people must permanently put away such meaningless and potentially dangerous ideas as spirituality, the supernatural, and any notion of values beyond subjective preferences. We now know, he said, that such language is meaningless (since not empirical) except, perhaps, to express our own subjective feelings.

In a graduate school course in counseling, I had an earnest young behaviorist professor who had, as a good behaviorist, trained (conditioned) himself to avoid all value statements that implied good or bad or anything beyond personal preference. When faced with a situation where someone else might be tempted to make a value statement, whether regarding spaghetti, rock and roll, or adultery, he had an ideologically correct response. He would, with a straight face, say "I find that positively reinforcing" or, "I find that negatively reinforcing." (I don't know what his wife thought about this kind of response) Notice, he was saying "I" (who knows about you or anyone else) "find" (observe a response in myself at this moment; who knows about five minutes from now) "that" (a particular measurable stimulus) "positively reinforcing" (it elicits this particular behavior now and might be predicted to do it again).

Above all, the idea was to be totally scientific, objective, and *value-free*. After all, values were perceived to be purely relative, personal preferences, or (worse) prejudices induced by social learning. And "everyone knew" that the only thing real was physical, measurable, and scientific. If we could only get the "facts" we would know what to do.

But this was, and is, a fundamental fallacy, the "Is-Ought" fallacy we discussed earlier. Even if facts are obtainable, they have no moral power or direction in themselves. If we say they mean something it is because we are interpreting them in the context of some values which are a part of our basic faith about the nature of the world.

Shifting Worldviews: The Emperor Has No Clothes

In the meantime we have seen some rather amazing shifts in "what everyone knows." I am old enough to have vivid memories of the 1960's and the "greening of America" when "everybody knew" that people under 30 were better than people over 30 and that human beings are so innately good all we had to do was to scrape off the social conventions and rules and then peace, love, and total sharing would rule the world. An astounding number of people truly believed that—for a short time.

In the '70s and early '80s "everybody knew" that personal autonomy and affluence are what it is all about. Power and looking out for Number One became the articles of faith, even for helping professionals like social workers. Maximum autonomy was the obvious highest good. Maturity and health were defined in terms of not needing anyone else (and not having any obligation to anyone else either). Fritz Perls "Gestalt Prayer" even got placed on romantic greeting cards:

I do my thing, and you do your thing.
I am not in this world to live up to your expectations.
And you are not in this world to live up to mine.
You are you and I am I,
And if by chance we find each other, it's beautiful.
If not, it can't be helped.

If you care too much, you are enmeshed, undifferentiated, or at the very least co-dependent.

And here we are at the turning of the millennium and, at least for awhile, it looks as though values are in. Time magazine has had cover stories on ethics. Even more amazing, philosophy professors and social workers are not embarrassed to talk about values and even character again. 'Family Values' are avowed by the Republicans and Democrats. The books and articles are rolling off the presses.

But we should not be lulled into a false sense of security with this recovery of values and ethics, even if much of it sounds quite Christian to us. The philosophical paradigm has shifted to the opposite extreme, from the modern faith in the rational and empirical to the postmodern faith in the radically subjective and relative, the impossibility of getting beyond our ideological and cultural horizons. Our culture now despairs of any knowledge beyond the personal narratives we make up for ourselves out of the flotsam of our experience and fragments of disintegrating culture (Middleton & Walsh, 1995). Postmodernism says each person pieces together a personal story through which we make sense out of our lives, but there is no larger story (meta-narrative) which is really true in any meaningful sense and which can bind our personal stories together.

It is remarkable, as we have seen, how rapidly some of these assumptions can shift. The seeming consensus may be only skin-deep. More importantly, unless these values are grounded on something deeper than the currently fashionable paradigm (such as a Christian worldview), we can count on the fact that they will shift, or at least give way when they are seriously challenged. It's amazing how easy it is to see that the emperor has no clothes when a different way of looking is introduced to the scene. Remember both enlightenment empiricism and postmodern subjectivity agree that values have no transcendent source.

What Is a "Person?"

Controversies regarding abortion and euthanasia illustrate the profound consequences of our worldview faith, especially for worldviews which deny that values have any ultimate source. Even more fundamental than the question of when life begins and ends is the question what is a person? What constitutes being a person? What value, if any, is there in being a person? Are persons owed any particular rights, respect, or care? If so, why?

If your worldview says that persons are simply the result of matter plus time plus chance, it would seem that persons have no intrinsic value at all, no matter how they are defined. From a purely materialist point of view, it may be interesting (to us) that the phenomena of human consciousness and agency have emerged which allow us in some measure to transcend simple biological, physical, and social determinism. These qualities might include the ability to be self-aware, to remember and to anticipate, to experience pleasure and pain, to develop caring relationships with others, to have purposes, to develop plans and take deliberate actions with consequences, and to have (at least the illusion of) choice. We may choose to define personhood as incorporating some of these characteristics. And we may even find it positively reinforcing (or not) to be persons. But then what? In this materialist worldview there are no inherent guidelines or limits regarding what we do to persons.

Do such persons have a right to life? Only to the extent it pleases us (whoever has the power) to say so. And what in the world could "right" mean in this context? But what if we do choose to say that persons have a right to life. What degree or quality of our defining characteristics do they have to have before they qualify? How self-conscious and reflective? How capable of choice and action?

It is common for people to argue today that babies aren't persons before they are born (or at least most of the time before they are born) and thus that there is no moral reason for not eliminating defective ones, or even just unwanted or inconvenient ones. And there are already those who argue that babies should not even be declared potential persons until they have lived long enough after birth to be tested and observed to determine their potential for normal growth and development, thus diminishing moral qualms about eliminating wrongful births. After all, what is magic about the birth process? Why not wait for a few hours, days, or weeks after birth to see if this "fetal material" is going to measure up to our standards of personhood? And at any point in life if our personhood fails to develop adequately or gets lost or seriously diminished through accident, illness, mental illness, or age, what then? Was my college acquaintance Ali right? Is it immoral to take resources from the productive and use them to support the unproductive? Do these "fetal products" or no-longer-persons need to be terminated?

A Solid Foundation

If I balk at these suggestions, it is because I have a worldview that gives a different perspective to the idea of what constitutes a person. I may agree, for example, that agency—the capacity to be self-aware, reflective, remember and anticipate, plan, choose, and responsibly act—is a central part of what it means to be a person. But I also believe that this is a gift from our creator God which in some way images God. I believe that our reflection, choice, and action have a divinely given purpose. This purpose is summarized in the ideas of finding and choosing God through grace and faith, of growing up into the image of Jesus Christ, of knowing and enjoying God forever. All of this says that persons have a special value beyond their utility to me (or anyone else) and that they are to be treated with the care and respect befitting their status as gifts from God. Even when something goes wrong.

Having a Christian worldview and knowing what the Bible says about God, the world, and the nature of persons doesn't always give us easy answers to all of our questions, however. And having faith in the resurrection of Jesus Christ doesn't guarantee that we will always be loving or just. But it does give us a foundation of stone to build our house on, a context to try to understand what we encounter that will not shift with every ideological or cultural season. I can assert the dignity and worth of every person based on a solid foundation, not just an irrational preference of my own or a culturally-induced bias that I might happen to have. What "everybody knows" is shifting sand. Even if it happens to be currently stated in the NASW Code of Ethics for social workers.

Some Basic Components of a Christian Worldview

Space does not permit me to develop a detailed discussion of the components of a Christian worldview here, but I would at least like to try to summarize in the most basic and simple terms what I perceive to be quite middle-of-the-road, historically orthodox, and biblical answers to the fundamental worldview questions I posed at the beginning (cf. Middleton & Walsh, 1995). This suggests the Christian worldview that has informed me and has been (I would hope) quite evident in what has been said. This little summary is not the end of reflection and application, but only the beginning.

1. *Where are we?* We are in a universe which was created by an eternal, omnipotent, just, loving, and gracious God. Consequently the universe has built-in meaning, purpose, direction, and values. The fun-

damental values of love and justice have an ultimate source in the nature of God which gives them meaning, authority, and content. The universe is both natural and supernatural.

2. **Who are we?** We are persons created "in the image God" and therefore with intrinsic meaning and value regardless of our personal characteristics or achievements. Persons are both physical and spiritual. Persons have been given the gift of "agency"– in a meaningful sense we have been given both freedom and responsibility. Persons created in the image of God are not just autonomous individuals but are relational–created to be in loving and just community with one another. Persons are objects of God's grace.

3. **What's wrong?** Oppression and injustice are evil, wrong, an affront to the nature and desire of God. Persons are finite and fallen–we are both limited in our capacities and distorted from our ideal purpose because of our selfishness and choice of evil. Our choice of selfishness and evil alienates us from God and from one another and sets up distortion in our perceptions, beliefs, and behavior, but we are not completely blind morally. Our self-centeredness makes us prone to seek solutions to our problems based on ourselves and our own abilities and accomplishments. We can't solve our problems by ourselves, either by denial or our own accomplishments.

4. **What's the remedy?** Stop trying to do it our way and accept the loving grace and provisions for healing that God has provided for us. God calls us to a high moral standard but knows that it is not in our reach to accomplish. God's creative purpose is to bring good even out of evil, to redeem, heal, and grow us up–not by law but by grace. "For by grace you have been saved through faith, and this is not your own doing; it is the gift of God–not the result of works, so that no one may boast. For we are what he has made us, created in Christ Jesus for good works, which God prepared beforehand to be our way of life." (Ephesians 2:8-10)

Why Should I Care? Choosing a Christian Worldview

Moral Obligation and Faith: Materialism Undermines Moral Obligation

To abandon a theological basis of values, built into the universe by God, is ultimately to abandon the basis for any "oughts" in the sense of being morally bound other than for purely subjective or cultural reasons. Normative morality that is just descriptive and cultural (This is what most people in our society tend to do), subjective (This is what I happen to prefer and do or It would be convenient for me if you would do this), or utilitarian (This is what works to achieve certain consequences) has no power of moral *obligation*. Why should I care? On materialist or subjective grounds I "should" do this or that if I happen to feel like it or if I think it will help me get what I want. But this is using the word "should" in a far different and far more amoral sense than we ordinarily mean. It is a far different thing than saying I am *morally obligated or bound* to do it.

Many will argue that reason alone is enough to support moral obligation. This is the argument used by Frederic Reamer in his excellent book on social work ethics, *Ethical dilemmas in social services* (1990), based on Gewirth (*Reason and morality*, 1978). If, for example, I understand that freedom is logically required for human personal action, then this theory says I am logically obligated to support freedom for other persons as I desire it for myself. But I have never been able to buy the argument that reason alone creates any meaningful moral obligation for altruistic behavior. Why *should* I be logical, especially if being logical doesn't appear to work for my personal advantage? Any idea of moral obligation beyond the subjective and personally utilitarian seems to lead inevitably and necessarily to God in some form or to nowhere.

The "Method of Comparative Difficulties"

Although it is logically possible (and quite necessary if you believe in a materialist universe) to believe that values are only subjective preferences or cultural inventions, I have never been able to completely believe that is all our sense of values such as love and justice amounts to. There are, in all honesty, many obstacles in the way of belief in God as the transcendent source of values. But can we believe, when push comes to shove, that all values are either meaningless or totally subjective? Elton Trueblood calls this the "Method of Comparative Difficulties" (1963, p. 73; 1957, p. 13).

It may often be hard to believe in God, but I find it even harder to believe in the alternatives, especially when it comes to values. It's easy enough to say that this or that value is only subjective or culturally relative, but when we get pushed into a corner, most of us find ourselves saying (or at least *feeling*), "No, *that* (say, the Holocaust) is really wrong and it's not just my opinion." (Cf. C. S. Lewis, "Right and Wrong As a Clue to the Meaning of the Universe," *Mere Christianity*, 1948)

Dostoevski expressed the idea that if there is no God, all things are permissible. C. S. Lewis (1947, pp. 77-78) said that "When all that says 'it is good' has been debunked, what says 'I want' remains. It cannot be exploded or 'seen through' because it never had any pretensions." Lust remains after values have been explained away. Values that withstand the explaining away process are the only ones that will do us any good. Lewis concludes *The abolition of man* (1947, p. 91):

You cannot go on "explaining away" for ever: you will find that you have explained explanation itself away. You cannot go on "seeing through" things for ever. The whole point of seeing through something is to see something through it. It is good that the window should be transparent, because the street or garden beyond it is opaque. How if you saw through the garden too? It is no use trying to "see through" first principles. If you see through everything, then everything is transparent. But a wholly transparent world is an invisible world. To "see through" all things is the same as not to see.

Seeing Through a Mirror Dimly: Real Values But Only a Limited, Distorted View

So, I believe in God as the ultimate source and authenticator of values. I believe that real values exist beyond myself. And I believe these values put us under real moral obligation. To believe otherwise, it seems to me, ultimately makes values and moral obligation empty shells, subjective and utilitarian, with no real life or content. It may be true that this is all values are, but I find it very hard to believe. Belief in a value-less world, or one with only "human" (that is to say, purely subjective) values, takes more faith for me than belief in God.

But (and this is very important) this understanding of values as having ultimate truth and deriving from God is a very far cry from believing that I fully comprehend these values and the specific moral obligations they put me under in the face of a particular moral dilemma when these values come into tension with one another and priorities have to be made. Much humility is required here, an appropriate balance. At any given moment, my (or your) understanding of these values and what our moral obligations are is very limited and distorted. In fact our understandings are in many ways subjective, culturally relative, and bounded by the interpretive "language" available to us. And any particular place where I can stand to view a complex reality at best only yields a partial view of the whole. Remember the story of the blind men and the elephant ("It's like a snake," "It's like a wall," "It's like a tree").

We can see, but only dimly. God has given us light but we will only be able to see completely when we meet God face to face (I Cor. 13:8-13). In the meantime we are on a journey. We are pilgrims, but we are not wandering alone and without guidance. We see through a mirror dimly, but there is something to see. There is a garden beyond the window.

Love never ends. But as for prophecies, they will come to an end; as for tongues, they will cease; as for knowledge, it will come to an end. For we know only in part, and we prophesy only in part; but when the complete comes, the partial will come to an end. When I was a child, I spoke like a child, I thought like a child, I reasoned like a child; when I became an adult, I put an end to childish ways. For now we see in a mirror, dimly, but then we will see face to face. Now I know only in part; then I will know fully, even as I have been fully known. And now faith, hope, love abide, these three; and the greatest of these is love. (I Corinthians 13:8-13)

> Now we have received not the spirit of the world, but the Spirit that is from God, so that we may understand the gifts bestowed on us by God. And we speak of these things in words not taught by human wisdom but taught by the Spirit, interpreting spiritual things to those who are spiritual. Those who are unspiritual do not receive the gifts of God's Spirit, for they are foolishness to them, and they are not able to understand them because they are spiritually discerned. Those who are spiritual discern all things, but they are themselves subject to no one else's scrutiny. "For who has known the mind of the Lord so as to instruct him?" But we have the mind of Christ. (I Corinthians 2:12-16)

Now the Lord is the Spirit, and where the Spirit of the Lord is, there is freedom. And all of us, with unveiled faces, seeing the glory of the Lord as though reflected in a mirror, are being transformed into the same image from one degree of glory to another; for this comes from the Lord, the Spirit. (II Corinthians 3:17-18)

References

Gewirth, Alan. (1978). *Reason and morality*. Chicago: University of Chicago Press.

Homes, Arthur. (1984). *Ethics: Approaching moral decisions*. Downers Grove, IL: InterVarsity Press.

Lebacqz, Karen. (1986). *Six theories of justice: Perspectives from philosophical and theological ethics*. Minneapolis, MN: Augsburg Publishing House.

Lewis, C. S. (1947). *The abolition of man*. New York: Macmillan Publishing Company.

Lewis, C. S. (1948). *Mere Christianity*. New York: Macmillan Publishing Company.

Malz, Wendy. (1989). Counterpoints: Intergenerational sexual experience or child sexual abuse. *Journal of Sex Education and Therapy, 15*, 13-15.

Middleton, J. Richard & Walsh, Brian J. (1995). *Truth is stranger than it used to be: Biblical faith in a post-modern age*. Downers Grove, IL: InterVarsity Press.

Mott, Stephen. (1982). *Biblical ethics and social change*. New York: Oxford University Press.

Nelson, J. A. (1989). Intergenerational sexual contact: A continuum model of participants and experiences. *Journal of Sex Education and Therapy*, 15, 3-12.

Reamer, Frederic. (1990). *Ethical dilemmas in social service*. 2nd Ed. New York: Columbia University Press.

Sherwood, David A. (1993). Doing the right thing: Ethical practice in contemporary society. *Social Work and Christianity*, 20(2), 140-159.

Trueblood, David Elton. (1963). *General philosophy*. New York: Harper and Row.

Trueblood, David Elton. (1957). *Philosophy of religion*. New York: Harper and Row.

Wolterstorff, Nicholas. (1983). *When justice and peace embrace*. Grand Rapids, MI: Eerdmans Publishing Company.

CHAPTER 9

BATTLE BETWEEN SIN AND LOVE IN SOCIAL WORK HISTORY

Katherine Amato-von Hemert
Editorial Assistance, Anisa Cottrell

Is it heresy to discuss "sin" and "love" in the context of social work? Most social workers believe it is. This chapter, however, argues that it is impossible to understand the history of social work without understanding the pivotal roles that attitudes toward sin and love played in the founding institutions, actors and actions of American social work. Religiously-trained leaders dominated the pioneer decades of social work (Leiby, 1984). American social work is indebted to two social movements which straddled the launch of the twentieth century: the Charity Organization Society (COS) movement and the Social Settlement movement. Religious ideas influenced both primary threads of historical social work. The COS writings regarding human nature tend to emphasize the role of sin and the need to cultivate morally uplifting habits to combat it. Late nineteenth and early twentieth century Protestantism struggled with the influence of Calvinist Puritanism. Among the most liberal of these Puritans were the Unitarians, who counted among their members social leaders Josephine Shaw Lowell and Joseph Tuckerman. Social Settlement movement writings tend to emphasize the role of love in human relations and focus on the goal of creating an ideal community. Early twentieth century Protestant social gospel theology influenced many Settlement leaders, such as Graham Taylor and Robert Woods. The social work techniques that emerged from both movements are, in revised form, still apparent in contemporary social work. The COS legacy includes the individual-focused work of casework and clinical practice. The Settlement tradition spawned community organizing and group work. Social work technologies from both traditions grew from particular theologies.

The differences and conflicts between the Christian theologies of these two foundational social work movements will be discussed. The Puritan-based theology and the social gospel-based theologies are examined. These beliefs are explicitly and implicitly revealed in the documents written by social activists of the late nineteenth century and early twentieth century. In the 1930's, Protestant social critic and theologian Reinhold Niebuhr critiqued social work. His insights synthesize the schism between the love-based and sin-based competing visions of social work. Listen to the voices of those early social workers who sought to cure personal and social "ills." References to sin, love and justice are unmistakable in them.

Why are these issues relevant to social workers now? They are important because these same divergent understandings of human nature and of God's action in the world operate in the language that modern day social workers use to discuss social problems and to justify practice and policy decisions. By elucidating the theological concepts of "sin" and "love" as held by some of the diverse mothers and fathers of our profession, we can understand better how these same concepts affect our work as social workers today.

Sin

The idea of sin is relevant to the dispute between the Charity Organization Society movement and the Social Settlement movement because one of the hallmark differences between these groups' perspectives arose from their divergent beliefs about sin.

Charity Organization Society Perspective on Sin

The concept of "sin" has been defined in many ways. Sin can be conceptualized as individual, willful acts that are contrary to the will of God. It can also be viewed as a general state of alienation from God. This later perspective focuses less on human action and more on the human state of being. Many of the more liberal COS movement leaders were influenced by a form of Puritan theology which rejected the Calvinist doctrine of predestination.[1] This doctrine of predestination maintained that all people are sinful and thereby bring Divine wrath upon themselves. Some people are saved, not through their own merit but through God's love and mercy. In this way of thinking, everyone "deserves" damnation and salvation occurs through God's mercy. Adamantly against the idea that one can attain salvation through works, "works righteous", adherents of this doctrine believed that a person's eternal fate was sealed with Adam's fall. Viewing sinfulness as an ingrained and intractable personality trait logically results from these beliefs. Many charity leaders, however, felt that people could improve their situation, both on earth and in life after death. Their belief, called "Arminianism," originated during the Protestant Reformation as a reaction to the Calvinist doctrines of original sin and predestination. By embracing Arminianism, C.O.S. leaders affirmed the belief that people, regardless of their environment, could improve their situation, build their character, and work toward salvation through reforming their life.

The sin-related issue for these COS leaders included three significant features — attitudes toward character, attitudes toward salvation and particular images of poverty. Charity Organization leadership believed that people were born morally neutral; they were intrinsically neither good nor bad. They were born with the capacity to shape their own character and thus had a moral obligation to self-improvement. These Puritans trained their attention on habits and disposition. They believed bad habits enslaved the sinner to his/her vices, while good habits protected him/her against temptations. "Once a sinner had started down the path of bad habits, it was nearly impossible for him to return to the path of rectitude." This moral philosophy maintained an implicit tendency "to classify people as 'good' or 'bad'" (Howe, 1988, p. 111). At the same time, consistent with earlier forms of Puritanism, these leaders "judged men on the basis of their disposition rather than their deeds, their character rather than their individual acts. Character was hard to develop and not easy to change" (Howe, 1988, p. 111). Thus, the issue of salvation was of paramount importance. Unlike predestinarian theology, Arminianism contended that individuals had the freedom to work out their own salvation (Howe, 1988, p. 68). The conscience was autonomous and therefore needed to be trained to regulate the passions. Self-mastery was the aim of these training efforts.

> Sin consisted in a breakdown of internal harmony, an abdication by the higher faculties of their dominion over the lower. No longer was sinfulness considered inherent in the human condition; instead, it was an abnormal state of disorder, 'the abuse of a noble nature.' Sin represented a failure to regulate impulses that were not in themselves evil. (Howe, 1988, p. 60-61)

Individuals were charged with the responsibility to foster good habits to protect against sinfulness and to exonerate themselves for sinful actions.

The prevalent attitudes toward poverty of this time were derived from widespread beliefs about the human person and about salvation. Most nineteenth century Americans believed that poverty was the result of sinfulness or laziness. Poverty was viewed as either an act of God's punishment, or as a result of the individual's disposition or habits. The goal of charity was to teach the poor morally uplifting habits which would cause them to love and seek virtue. Tuckerman maintained, "the best resources for improving the condition of the poor are *within themselves*, they often need enlightenment respecting these resources more than alms." Regardless of whether poverty was punishment for sinfulness or the result of the individual's propensities, "the conditions of poverty could lead to sin" so Christians were obligated to help the poor improve their economic condition (Howe, 1988, p. 240).[2] "Charity was intended to reform and uplift the poor, not merely to mitigate their sufferings" (Howe, 1988, p. 239). Indiscriminate almsgiving was considered dangerous because alms were believed to "encourage indolence and wastefulness." Rationally disciplined educational approaches were "intended to be judicious and discriminating, designed to get to the root of problems" (Howe, 1988, p. 240). These perspectives on the individual, sin and poverty resulted in a moralistic charity.

The COS theology of sin provides additional insight into the expectations and hopes of the charity programs designed to serve the poor. Giving to the poor person "a friend not alms" makes sense when it is understood in the context of the belief that individuals needed to foster good habits to stave off sinfulness and to learn the love of virtue. Good habits could be taught within the relationship nurtured between a "friendly visitor" and an impoverished person. The assumption that poverty in some way resulted from sin leads reasonably to the conclusion that the development of virtue would eradicate poverty. This reading of the COS is not especially novel. What is of greater importance is consideration of its long term implications — the COS legacy.

Mary Richmond articulated the theory of social casework within the context of this COS theology.[3] Social casework placed particular importance on service to the individual, on social investigation and on the caseworker-client relationship.[4] All of these techniques assumed that sin plays a pivotal role in human nature. The priority attention given to the individual derived from the COS leaders' Arminian beliefs. Cultivating self-improvement was necessary because salvation resulted from individual effort. Social investigation was the practice of interviewing neighbors, family members and employers of potential service recipients in order to generate a detailed profile of need. This derived both from the rationalism of the theology as well as from the expectation that individuals in need may not necessarily be truthful about the specifics of their situation. One of the staunchest arguments on behalf of organizing the charity societies into COS's was the belief that fraud was rampant and duplication of requests for assistance could be reduced by greater communication among charity organizations.

Finally, the healing relationship between caseworker and client derived from the expectation that moral uplift is best achieved at close quarters. Accountability played an important role in this relationship and was therefore as much an opportunity for the caseworker to monitor and point out client's "bad habits" as well as for the client to learn good ones. These techniques, influenced by an understanding of the individual as a sinful being, have been passed down to contemporary social work (with modifications of course). Social casework's emphasis on service to the individual now holds a dominant position in current clinical social work practice. Its assumptions regarding human nature warrant closer attention; they may illuminate the current debates in the profession between those who seek to assist individuals psychotherapeutically versus those who engage in social reform. This line of inquiry may lead to additional insights when applied to the Social Settlement theology as well. Social Settlement leaders rejected many of these assumptions and created alternative institutions aimed to address social conditions of poverty. As in the case of the COS leaders, Settlement leaders had theological reasons for doing so. Contrary to the COS leaders, these Settlement advocates were more compelled by a theology focused on love rather than on one based on sin. This does not mean, however, that the Settlement leaders held no opinion on sin. The Social Settlement perspective on sin is just more difficult to tease out from within the overall love-focused sensibility.

Social Settlement Movement Perspective on Sin

The social gospel movement was an American religious phenomenon prominent during the early decades of the twentieth century. It aimed to move society toward a vision of justice; toward the incarnation of the "kingdom of God" on Earth. Its adherents focused more on societal reform and less on individual salvation. Social work practice which was influenced by social gospel theology acknowledged the existence of sin but viewed it as embedded within social relations which were subject to political, social and/or economic reform. A person who might have been seen by the COS leaders as "sinful" or in need of character reform was seen through the lens of the social gospel as a person at the mercy of an unjust, sinful society. The social environment caused people to receive fewer choices or to make unwise decisions. It is difficult to find explicit references to sin among Social Settlement writings and social gospel writings regarding social work. This theology's concern centered on issues of love; God's love for humanity, and our consequent love for one another. The individual was understood to be primarily defined by the social group (family, neighborhood, church or synagogue, industrial organization, etc.).

The most explicit shift in theological focus can be seen in the writings of the Anglican couple, Henrietta and Samuel Barnett. Prior to founding England's Toynbee Hall, the Barnetts were active in organized charity efforts. They became disenchanted and critical of the literal, evangelical appeals associated with the Charity Organization Societies. In 1882 Henrietta criticized the C.O.S.'s "materialist" reification of sin and hell and charged that, "religion has been degraded by these teachers until it is difficult to gain the people's ears to hear it" (Barnett, 1895a, p. 91). Within two years, her critique of the COS orientation included stronger appeals to the role love must play in charity and from then on, discussion of love received greater emphasis than attention to sin in all her writings. Her concern shifted to those charity workers who "fear the devil more than they love God; or, in other words, they fear to do harm more than they love to do good" and she claimed "personally, I doubt if anything but love for God will mean social reform" (Barnett, 1895b, p. 213, 219).

Graham Taylor, the founder of the Chicago Commons, a 100 year old social settlement house, is representative of the Social Settlement pioneers. In his first book, *Religion in Social Action* (1913), Taylor referred to sin fewer than one dozen times. If sin was an important dimension of Taylor's understanding of human character, his chapter, "Personality: a Social Product and Force," would refer to it. It does not. This omission is suggestive. In commenting upon the changes in Christian thought of the time, he noted that "the individual and the race are coming to be more inseparable in our consciousness of both sin and salvation" (Taylor, 1913, p. 97). Sin was viewed not as a feature of an individual's character or destiny but as a consequence of environmental influences. Salvation's goal "is more closely brought to bear upon turning the self from sin" (Taylor, 1913, p. 91) in order to train focus upon the promise of the Kingdom on earth. Sin was seen primarily as evil events spawned by evil circumstance.[5] This emphasis on the social leads to the assertion that "more and more men need to be convicted of and turned away from their social, industrial, and political sins, in order to be made conscious of and penitent for their personal sins" (Taylor, 1913, p. 100).

Walter Rauschenbusch, "the acknowledged professorial leader" of the social gospel movement (Marty, 1986, p. 288), spoke of those whom social workers serve as peoples who "have gone astray like lost sheep" (Rauschenbusch, 1912, p. 30). These are not people with sinful natures, they are people who have merely stepped off the path of righteousness. He spoke of the sacrifice and suffering intrinsic to social work's service to humanity with reference to the crucifixion of Jesus, claiming, "without the shedding of blood in some form there has never been cessation of sin"

(Rauschenbusch, 1912, p. 27). Above all, Rauschenbusch focused on the redemptive task and nature of social work (Rauschenbusch, 1912, p. 12-13, 26-27). A measure of the close linkage between social work and social religion at the beginning of this century comes from this text which to late twentieth century ears is quite shocking: "Social workers are in the direct line of apostolic succession. Like the Son of Man they seek and save the lost" (Rauschenbusch, 1912, p. 12). This pattern is consistent throughout the social gospel social work literature. The primary focus is on the social nature of individual life and whatever minimal references to sin that exist are located within this type of context. The concept of "social sin," as reflected in Taylor's statement above, fleetingly appears occasionally, though it is not fully developed. Conceptualizing sin was less important to the development of the Social Settlement movement. Social Settlement leaders emphasized love; something that the COS leaders did to a much lesser degree.

Love

It is also helpful to explore the contrasting perspectives on love found in writings from Charity Organization Society leaders with those found among Social Settlement movement leaders. COS leaders tended to view love as a remedy for evil while Social Settlement leaders discussed love in terms of both its personal expression and social necessity.

Charity Organization Society Perspective on Love

In 1890, Charles Stewart Loch reflected on the first twenty years of England's Charity Organization Society movement. He claimed, the "new movement," was vigorously dedicated to serve the best interests of the State, the stability of which was threatened by the existence of pauperism. "The new charity does not seek material ends, but to create a better social and individual life" (Loch, 1892, p. 6). Of the three forces at work in the new movement—a stronger sense of citizenship, a renewed commitment to remind the rich of their community obligations and a deepening religious consciousness—discussion of the need for a change in religious consciousness took precedence. Loch argued,

> Yet [religious communities'] efforts to improve the general conditions of the life of the poor were often but *feeble and transient*. Their charity was *not allied to any wider conception of citizenship*. It was too often, perhaps, the hopeless push and protest of the saint against the evils of a hopeless world, where he

had no abiding place; and then, *if zeal grew cold, it found a
sufficient expression in a charity from which love had evaporated,
and which was no better than the payment of a toll on the high
road of life* (Loch, 1892, p. 7-8, emphasis added).

Loch criticized the instability of emotionally motivated charity.
Charity motivated by mere sentiment, he claimed, is isolated from the
larger concerns of "citizenship," undependable because "transient," and
when its religious passion "grows cold," it is merely the scattering of
coins among bystanders. The COS intent, therefore, was to improve
upon such efforts by creating scientifically based systems of moral support which express commitment to a higher order of love. This love is a
disciplined one. It demands development of virtuous habits. "The social life implies discipline. This may spring from habits grown almost
instinctively and handed down from the past like heirlooms. . . .Or the
discipline may be newly imposed in order to brace the individual, or the
family, or the nation, to a new endeavor" (Loch, 1904, p. 190).

The love that motivated the COS enterprise assumed moral defect
among the poor had to be uplifted. Reverend D.O. Kellogg, an advocate
of "scientific charity" and organizing charity societies, addressed this
issue in the *Journal of the American Social Science Association* in 1880.

> Defective classes are not a social evil; but pauperism is, and it is
> a sign of moral weakness. The weak and depressed, and *all the
> victims of unsocial habits, need to be awakened to a proper love of
> approbation from their fellow men, to have their hearts kindled* to
> a sympathetic glow by neighborliness and respect; to be quick-
> ened to hope by examples among their associates of courage,
> versatility and self-reliance; to see a world of pleasure and honor
> opened to them in the companionship of the refined and the
> pure-souled. *To these add suitable industrial training; but with-
> out the other this will be of small avail.* (Kellogg, 1880, p.89,
> emphasis added)

"Industrial training" without moral regeneration was considered
ineffective. Love's primary implications are personal rather than social.
The "victims of unsocial habits" needed to learn or re-learn *love of virtue.* Kellogg was not interested in the charity worker's expression of
love, or in charity as such, as an expression of love. Love may have
motivated charitable action but it was primarily a redemptive ideal. As
such, it entailed certain demands. These lead Kellogg to envision a relationship between love and science.

In Kellogg's view, the practice of charity must be scientific, not only to achieve greater effectiveness but because it is required by "the law of love" which is its originating impulse.

> Charity has its laws which can only be detected by a study of past experience. It is, therefore, a science,—the science of social therapeutics. Again, as art is the application of science, *it follows that there can be no true art of charity until its laws are formulated.* Until this is done, benevolence is not much else but quackery, however amiable its motive. Indeed *the true impulse of love cannot rest until it has found its science;* for it cannot stop short of effective methods and sound principles. (Kellogg, 1880, p. 86, emphasis added)

Love in this perspective, motivated not the particular practice of a single or collective group of charity workers—love was an ideal which required articulation and organization It was concerned with issues that can be discovered and formulated as law.

Social Settlement Movement Perspective on Love

A review of settlement leaders' writings reveals liberal use of a theologically influenced language of love.[6] Graham Taylor and Jane Addams are illustrative.[7] Taylor's first book, *Religion in Social Action* (1913), (for which Addams wrote the Introduction), reflects the influence of the social gospel thinkers of the time. Taylor spoke publicly and in print of his "social work" in explicitly theological terms throughout his career. In a 1908 review of the Social Settlement movement Cole stated, "Professor Graham Taylor defines a settlement as a 'Group of Christian people who choose to live where they seem most needed, for the purpose of being all they can to the people with whom they identify themselves, and for all whose interests they will do what they can'" (Cole, 1908, p. 3). After citing a second definition[8] which did not use religious language, Cole concluded that:

> In both of these definitions, brief as they are, the underlying spirit and purpose [of the Social Settlement movement] are emphasized. The spirit is one which may be shared by many who do not call themselves Christians. *It is a spirit of adventurous friendship which the Gospel of Christ has made familiar to the world. From this has arisen the purpose which may be described in a word as service through sharing.* Whatever the social worker may have in character, attainment, or experience, he draws upon in meeting the needs of the less fortunate" with whom he has contact (Cole, 1908, p. 3, emphasis added).

In the late 1930's Taylor spoke of a settlement house colleague as a "shepherdess of sheep without a fold, serving the one flock of the one Shepherd" who when she took "up the arms of *love* and *persuasion,* of *service* and *sacrifice,* she was moved by her *reverence for the sanctity and worth* of every human life, which *her religion told her was created in the image of God and capable of being restored to that image by grace* divine" (Taylor, 1937, p. x, emphasis added). The language of love, grace and sanctity of human life is the context in which the term "service" must be understood. This language is the most consistent thread found among Taylor's major works (Taylor, 1931; Taylor, 1936; Wade, 1964).

Jane Addams, the reformer most often associated with the Social Settlement movement, told the stories of Hull House's visitors to ever larger audiences as her platform became an international one. Even though religious language is less prominent in her work, Addams made clear her motivation and aim with reference to the words of "the Hebrew prophet [who] made three requirements from those who would join the great forward moving procession led by Jehovah. 'To love mercy and at the same time 'to do justly'. . ." (Addams, 1967, p. 69-70). The difficulty of this is great. Addams' solution was to advocate the prophet's third requirement,

> 'to walk humbly with God,' which may mean to walk for many dreary miles beside the lowliest of His creatures, not even in that peace of mind which the company of the humble is popularly supposed to afford, but rather with the pangs and throes to which the poor human understanding is subjected whenever it attempts to comprehend the meaning of life. (Addams, 1967, p. 70)

Creating a place that enabled the poor to mingle with the affluent so that individuals may share their common burdens was one of Addams' primary aims. Interestingly, her writings reveal virtual total silence on the question of individualistic sin or evil. (This is not uncommon among Settlement leaders as demonstrated previously). For Social Settlement leaders, love entailed a socially structured way of being. It was not an antidote to evil.

Sin, Love and Justice

Eminent social critic and theologian Reinhold Niebuhr's work on sin, love and justice as they relate to social work offers a way to bridge the schism between historic social work's emphasis on individual (sin-based) approaches and social (love-based) approaches. In 1928-29 Niebuhr gave a series of six lectures to social workers at the Columbia University School of Social Work. The book that anthologizes these pieces, *The Contribution of Religion to Social Work* (1932), bridges the sin-based theology which motivated the Puritan-oriented social reformers and the love-based social gospel oriented activists. In his lectures, Niebuhr challenged social work to rise above sentimentality, claiming, "social work, in its acceptance of philanthropy as a substitute for real social justice, and for all its scientific pretensions, does not rise very much higher than most sentimental religious generosity" (Niebuhr, 1932, p. 82).

For Niebuhr, the tension between love and sin is complicated and illuminated by his overarching emphasis on social justice. Instead of focusing on either sin or love in an exclusive and individualistic way, Niebuhr urged social work to adopt a more balanced view of human nature and to use its unique position in the community to further the aims of social reform.

> The fact that *social workers so frequently fail to think beyond the present social and economic system, and confine their activities to the task of making human relations more sufferable within terms of an unjust social order, places them in the same category as the religious philanthropists* whose lack of imagination in this respect we have previously deplored. *A great deal of social effort, which prides itself upon its scientific achievements and regards religious philanthropy with ill-concealed contempt, is really very unscientific in its acceptance of given social conditions.* (p. 80, emphasis added)

Niebuhr chastised social work for its piecemeal approach to socially embedded injustice. He believed this approach inevitably resulted from a misguided sentiment of love. Niebuhr charged that social work, "...builds a few houses for the poor, but does not recognize that an adequate housing scheme for the poor can never be initiated within the limits of private enterprise. Every modern society must come, even if slowly, to the recognition that only a state, armed with the right of eminent domain and able to borrow money at low interest rates, can secure ground and build such houses for the poor as they can afford to buy or rent" (*Contribution*, p. 80-81). Therefore he urged upon social work a realist approach to human nature which would issue in advocacy for social justice.

The question of justice is what launched Niebuhr's theology of love. Niebuhr considered love both in personal and social terms, though discussion of love's social implications predominate. Niebuhr's perspective on love is not Romantic. Indeed, his concern for the dangers or potential problems that arise from love dominates his treatment of the concept. This is perhaps the single most important contribution Niebuhr offered social work thought. For Niebuhr, several particular dangers inhere with the conventional philosophies of love. Of primary relevance to social work is the danger of sentimentality. Niebuhr's cautionary remarks to social work in *Contribution* derive from his years of experience ministering in a Detroit parish and working in numerous left-wing political struggles. He worked with social workers both in Detroit as well as after he wrote *Contribution*, when he was professor of social ethics in New York City (Brown, 1992; Phillips, 1957).

Niebuhr underscores four major dangers regarding love. First, romanticized love can quickly degenerate into sentimentality as referred to previously. This theme figures prominently in Niebuhr's critique of liberalism. An additional feature of this critique is that liberalism discredits the transcendent nature of love. Diminishing the province of love as known through relationship with God, eclipses the realistic sin/ love paradox. Love expressed in human relational terms alone disguises the realities of sin because of its "blindness," and because it unduly inflates human capacity. A third danger of a sentimentalized conception of love is that it seduces people into self-righteousness and pride. Niebuhr illustrates this feature of love through extended commentary on the hypocrisies of philanthropy, wherein the selfish can convince themselves of their unselfishness by "giving of their superfluity." Finally, the Christian love ideal is always in danger of betraying its ethical imperative by sinking into social conservatism. In this case, the inherent perfectionism of idealized love restricts critical analysis of political and economic conditions because it potentially tarnishes the ability to express positive emotional responses.[9] It therefore maintains existing unjust economic and power distributions. All of these snares are embedded in the conflictual relation between love and justice, and he believed, commanded additional attention by the social work profession. These ideas were pivotal in the belief systems of the pioneers of social work.

Niebuhr made several recommendations for social workers related to the dangers of sentimentality. First, the unstable, transient nature of the sympathy which motivates a benevolent vocation should be connected with a vision of an ultimate value. Second, the "shrewder insights" of a religion, which understands the human personality to be paradoxically God-like yet finite, can defend against the sentimentality that an idealistic or personalized view of love fosters. Finally, he recommended that the Christian ideal of perfect love is "probably too high for the attainment of any nation" or any group, because groups will not sacrifice themselves to serve the interests of another group. Niebuhr concluded therefore, that groups should aspire to justice rather than to love. Implicitly, this suggests to social workers that they, even though motivated by sympathy, ought to seek justice rather than the impossible specter of an ideal self-sacrificing love.

Niebuhr speaks at length in *Contribution* and elsewhere of the dangers of sentimentality. But is sentimentality dangerous in social work? Three observations of social work trends confirms Niebuhr's hypothesis that sentimentality deteriorates and is therefore problematic for social work. The first observation is that the dual social work tradition from the COS and the Social Settlement movement are not equally represented in current social work practice. The individual-focused practices from the COS movement dominate the profession as evidenced by the debates regarding the "legitimacy" of private practice and the fact that the majority of current National Association of Social Work members do direct practice. Policy advocacy and groupwork, inherited from the Social Settlement pioneers, play minor roles in contemporary social work practice. Secondly, this narrowed focus has also privatized social work practice and its community roles. Social work roles in public welfare agencies are diminishing in all but management positions as incidence of private clinical social work is rising. The profession, rather than taking prominent roles in community advocacy, tends to look inward.

Niebuhr also recommended that social work subordinate its vocational aim to an ultimate ideal. Is this necessary? The risk of *not* having an ultimate guiding principle, implied by Niebuhr, is that an emotional and privatized motivation is not sturdy enough for the profession to weather expectable storms in its contact with the depths of human misery and social injustice. The decades of debate the profession has carried on regarding its identity, mission and values evidence analogous concern. Although the profession has grown (in size and sophistication) through these years of debate, no "ultimate value" has been settled upon. Social work's emotion-based motivation has survived. The problem is also that the debates over identity, mission and values all assume the same fundamentally sentimental presuppositions. Human beings are good. Period. They are finite and capable of great good; due to nature, nurture or some combination. When evil is encountered, the desire to, in language of the Social Settlement tradition, "turn the stray sheep back to the path," becomes the priority, and debate regarding the profession's aim resolves into debate about relative effectiveness of competing technique.[10] In addition, the field's tenacious defense of a principle of self-determination is seemingly due to the inability of the profession to articulate a secularized equivalent "doctrine of sin" to hold in tension with its generous estimation of human possibilities. This necessarily cursory review suggests that the act of debating professional identity may in fact lead the profession away from its intent to articulate its ultimate value, because it is predisposed to an image of human nature that is imbalanced.

Niebuhr's Critique of Social Work:
A Useful Prescription for the Profession?

Niebuhr's theological conception of love is useful to illuminate and critique social work's tradition. *Contribution* was written during the historic period when the social work profession was seeking to synthesize its dual traditions. Niebuhr critiqued both theologies which were at the basis of each strand in the tradition—the COS and the Settlement's. The outcome in the profession was the adoption of the practice from the COS tradition and the philosophy of the Social Settlement movement. This hybrid, while in theory would hold in tension the two conflicting theologies of which each is a product, in practice has given rise to interminable and seemingly irresolvable debate regarding the profession's mission, membership and values.[11] Given the overly positive estimation of human nature and the lack of agreement on an "ultimate" value to serve, the profession remains a conglomeration of factions. Unlike the Social Settlement workers who valued their role as "interpreters" of social conditions, current social workers tend to be embroiled in internal, professional disputes.

How might Niebuhr's insights assist? One resolution comes from paying closer attention to the historical moment in which *Contribution* appeared. As presented above, the theological differences between the COS and Settlement movements up into the post-W.W.I. period can be broadly construed as a conflict between an emphasis on sin and an emphasis on love. According to Niebuhr, sin is inevitable and love is "impossible." Given the tendency in social work to privilege one or the other, and the incumbent problems with this, something is needed to hold these two in fruitful tension. Drawing upon Niebuhr's recommendation, can *justice* serve this mediating function?

Niebuhr's realist approach to the individual in society holds in tension the "paradoxes of religion" (Niebuhr, 1932, p. 67). The primary paradox is the Christian insight that the human is both made in the image of God and is a sinner.

> This emphasis upon the sinfulness of man has been just as strong, in classical religion, as the emphasis upon his Godlikeness. It has *saved religion, at its best, from the sentimentality into*

which modern culture has fallen since the romantic period, with
its reaction to dogma of man's total depravity by its absurd insistence upon the natural goodness of man. The *real religious*
spirit has no illusions about human nature. It knows the heart of
man to be sinful. It is therefore not subject to the cynical disillusion
into which sentimentality degenerates when it comes into contact
with the disappointing facts of human history. (ibid., p. 66, emphasis added)

From this perspective Niebuhr criticized both the classical or orthodox excessive attentiveness to human's sinful nature and the modern or liberal denial of sin. He chastised the likes of the charity organiz-
ers by indicting their moralism as counterproductive. Their excessive
focus on the individual created blindness to the injustices of social conditions. He chastised the likes of the Settlement workers as hopelessly
sentimental and therefore easily disillusioned and embittered. Consequently, Niebuhr urged upon the orthodox a greater measure of the loving forgiveness which the liberals prize as well as attention to social
conditions; and he urged the liberals to greater mindfulness of the realities of sin. Proponents of both theologies easily succumb to self-righteousness. The orthodox charity worker who busily goes about the business of saving others' souls can easily forget the limitations of their own.
The liberal who blithely confesses the sins of their group, from which
they feel emancipated, is easily seduced by "the temptation to be humble
and proud at the same time" (Niebuhr, 1957b, p. 120). Niebuhr com-
mended to social work a moderate position which both acknowledges
the realities of sin and posits human goodness while maintaining in
tension the interaction between the individual and the group. Absent
this, social conditions are not subject to critique, so reform of the struc-
tural causes of impoverishment and injustice is not possible. In sum, he
cautioned social work to guard against the sentimentalism found among
modern liberal religionists.

How might this critique and recommendation inform the understanding of historical social work? The pioneers of both the COS and the Settlement House movement represent poles along the continuum between "Sin"
and "Love". In their attempts to eradicate human sinfulness and express
divine love, respectively, they succumbed to the temptation to ignore the
larger questions of social justice. By bridging the gap between love and sin
with a strong critique of those who ignore social injustice, Niebuhr avoided
the pitfalls of both extremes and oriented the discussion away from individual sin or love and toward the action of the whole. Contemporary social
work would do well to follow his lead.

Notes

[1] Examples include Josephine Shaw Lowell and Joseph Tuckerman. See (Howe, 1988). These Unitarians were among the theological liberals of their day. They rejected the more conservative evangelical "revivalists." Tuckerman believed, for example, that "a Calvinist preacher who went into the slums teaching predestination and depravity did more harm than good" (Howe, 1988, p. 242). Both Calvinist Puritans and Unitarian Puritans were active in public life. Most relevant to social work's tradition is the Unitarian theology, however, it co-existed in a society still very much influenced by Calvinism and undoubtedly in practice reflected these influences (Cole, 1954).

[2] The city itself was also seen as fostering the conditions of sinfulness that led to pauperism. See Paine's 1893 text, "Pauperism in Great Cities: Its Four Chief Causes" for additional detail (Paine, 1964).

[3] She followed Josephine Shaw Lowell's work quite closely.

[4] Richmond uses the term "client" as early as 1917 in her classic text, *Social Diagnosis* (Richmond, 1917).

[5] Taylor offers the text of a letter from a pastor who works on the streets as an example of the impossibility of saving an individual if sinful environments are left untouched. "'Dear Pastor, In the first place, when we try to help a fallen brother, the odds against us are too great. Last night I believe that man was in earnest. When he said, 'I am tired of sin,' he meant it. . . .He went out from God's house, away from those commissioned to do his work. Where could he go but out into the cold, friendless streets of a great city? Then what? . . . .he was to shun the dram shop. He did this. He passed by seven, with the struggle which God only knows. The door of the eighth stood open. It did look warm and comfortable within. So he finally went in. . . Where could I have taken him? Cannot something be done to lessen these odds, to even things up, to give the Lord a fair show with a man who wants to be saved?'" (Taylor, (1913), p. 26).

[6] For an excellent review of the general role the social gospel played in the social settlement movement see: (Carson, 1990).

[7] Taylor is known to current social work students as the founder of the Chicago Commons settlement and the initiator of the social work courses that became institutionalized as the University of Chicago's School of Social Services Administration predecessor institution, the Chicago School of Civics and Philanthropy. Less known is the fact that Taylor was an ordained Protestant minister who accepted his teaching position at the Chicago Theological Seminary on the condition that he be allowed to set up a settlement house.

[8] The second definition is offered by Ada Woolfolk.

[9] One of Niebuhr's illustrations of this is of a good liberal minister in a Kentucky coal mining town who sided against the miners in a labor dispute on the grounds that strikes, because they were assertive, were contrary to Biblical love (Niebuhr, 1957a).

[10] Ehrenreich makes this case regarding social work between 1920 and 1945; see: (Ehrenreich, 1985).

[11] The inclusion of "membership" points to the mid-century debates regarding bachelor degree trained social workers and the earlier debates regarding volunteers and graduate-school trained social workers. See: (Popple, 1983). Specifics regarding the values debate fall beyond the scope of this study. For good summaries, see (Abbott, 1988; Berlin, 1990; Biestek, 1967; Faver, 1986; Gordon, 1965; Heineman, 1981; NASW, 1967; Reid & Popple, 1992; Timms, 1983; Weick, 1991).

References

Abbott, A. A. (1988). *Professional choices: Values at work*. National Association of Social Workers, Inc.

Addams, J. (1967). *Democracy and social ethics* (1902). New York: Macmillan Co.

Barnett, H. R. (1895a). Passionless reformers (1882). In S. A. Barnett & H. R. Barnett (Eds.), *Practicable socialism: Essays on social reform*. London: Longmans, Green & Co.

Barnett, H. R. (1895b). What has the Charity Organization Society to do with social reform? (1884). In S. A. Barnett & H. R. Barnett (Eds.), *Practicable socialism*. London: Longmans, Green & Co.

Berlin, S. B. (1990). Dichotomous and complex thinking. *Social Service Review*, 64(1), 64- 59.

Biestek, F. P. (1967). Problems in identifying social work values. In NASW (Eds.), *Values in social work: A re-examination*. Silver Spring, MD: National Association of Social Workers.

Brown, C. C. (1992). *Niebuhr and his age: Reinhold Niebuhr's prophetic role in the twentieth century*. Philadelphia: Trinity Press International.

Carson, M. J. (1990). *Settlement folk: Social thought and the American settlement movement 1885-1930*. Chicago: University of Chicago Press.

Cole, C. C. (1954). *The social ideals of the northern evangelists 1826-1860*. New York: Columbia University.

Cole, W. I. (1908). *Motives and results of the social settlement movement: Notes on an exhibit installed in the Social Museum of Harvard University*. Cambridge: Harvard University.

Ehrenreich, J. H. (1985). *The altruistic imagination: A history of social work and social policy in the United States*. Ithaca, NY: Cornell University Press.

Faver, C. A. (1986). Religion, research, and social work. *Social Thought*, 12(3), 20-29.

Gladden, W. (1894). *The church and the kingdom*. New York: Revell.

Gordon, W. E. (1965). Knowledge and value: Their distinction and relationship in clarifying social work practice. *Social Work*, 10(3), 32-39.

Heineman, M. B. (1981). The obsolete scientific imperative in social work research. *Social Service Review*, 55(3), 371-396.

Howe, D. W. (1988). *The Unitarian conscience: Harvard moral philosophy 1805-1861*. Middletown, CT: Wesleyan University Press.

Kellogg, D. O., Rev. (1880). The principle and advantage of association in charities. *Journal of Social Science, XII*, 84-90.

Leiby, J. (1984). Charity Organization Reconsidered. *Social Service Review*, (December), 523-538.

Loch, C. S. (1904). If citizens be friends. In C. S. Loch (Ed.), *Methods of social advance: Short studies in social practice by various authors*. London: Macmillan and Company Limited.

Loch, S. C. S. (1892). *Charity organization* (2nd ed.). London: S. Sonnenschein & Co.

Marty, M. E. (1986). *Modern American religion: The irony of it all 1893-1919*. Chicago: The University of Chicago Press.

Mathews, S. (1907). *The church and the changing order.* New York: Macmillan.

NASW (Ed.). (1967). *Values in social work: A re-examination*. Silver Spring, MD: National Association of Social Workers.

Niebuhr, R. (1932). *The contribution of religion to social work.* New York: Columbia University.

Niebuhr, R. (1933). Letter. *Christian Century, 50*(11), 363-364.

Niebuhr, R. (1957a). Religion and class war in Kentucky (1932). In D. B. Robertson (Ed.), *Love and Justice: Selections from the Shorter Writings of Reinhold Niebuhr.* Louisville, KY: Westminster/John Knox Press.

Niebuhr, R. (1957b). The confession of a tired radical (1928). In D. B. Robertson (Ed.), *Love and Justice: Selections from the Shorter Writings of Reinhold Niebuhr.* Louisville, KY: Westminster/John Knox Press.

Phillips, H. B. (1957). *The reminiscences of Reinhold Niebuhr [Microfilmed interview transcripts].* New York: Oral History Research Office Columbia University.

Popple, P. R. (1983). Contexts of practice. In A. Rosenblatt & D. Waldfogel (Eds.), *Handbook of clinical social work.* San Francisco: Jossey-Bass.

Rauschenbusch, W. (1912). *Unto me.* Boston: The Pilgrim Press.

Reid, P. N., & Popple, P. R. (Eds.). (1992). *The moral purposes of social work: The character and intentions of a profession.* Chicago: Nelson-Hall.

Richmond, M. E. (1917). *Social diagnosis.* New York: Russell Sage Foundation.

Taylor, G. (1913). *Religion in social action.* New York: Dodd, Mead and Co.

Taylor, G. (1931). *Pioneering on social frontiers.* Chicago: University of Chicago Press.

Taylor, G. (1936). *Chicago Commons through forty years.* Chicago: Chicago Commons Association.

Taylor, G. (1937). Introduction: Mary McDowell—Citizen. In C. M. Hill (Ed.), *Mary McDowell and municipal housekeeping.* Chicago: Chicago Council of Social Agencies.

Timms, N. (1983). *Social work values: An enquiry.* London: Routledge & Kegan Paul.

Tucker, W. J. (1911). *The function of the church in modern society.* Boston: Houghton, Mifflin.

Wade, L. C. (1964). *Graham Taylor: Pioneer for social justice, 1851-1938.* Chicago: University of Chicago Press.

Weick, A. (1991). The place of science in social work. *Journal of Sociology and Social Welfare, 18*(4), 13-34.

CHAPTER 10

THE POOR WILL NEVER CEASE OUT OF THE LAND? OR THERE WILL BE NO POOR AMONG YOU? A CHRISTIAN PERSPECTIVE ON POVERTY

Beryl Hugen

To advocate for the poor in the context of today's debates on welfare reform is not easy. In fact, it can be quite an intimidating task. But it apparently has always been a difficult and somewhat unpopular task to defend the poor. Daniel Boorstin, in his book *The Creators: A History of Heroes of the Imagination*, on the artistic history of Western civilization, states that with the birth of rhetoric or speech, it became customary in learning the art, to take as a topic the defense of the poor. This was done, he says, because it was considered an excellent, if not the best, test of an orator's skill.

More striking than the difficulty in defending the poor, however, is the implied assumption that there will always be the poor to defend. This too is not a new idea. The writer of Deuteronomy said, "The poor will never cease out of the land." Every Western society since has had within it people who cannot or do not support themselves and are dependent on others for help. While no accurate count of the poor can be made since definitions of poverty vary, probably in most societies the number of all adults who are poor has never fallen below five percent. The estimates of poverty during the Depression of the 1930's—even those that showed fifty percent of the population below the poverty line—do not appear particularly large from a historical or international perspective. In the 1930's America was a phenomenally rich country by world standards. When the Russians viewed the film *The Grapes of Wrath*, they marveled that the Okies had cars. Humorist Will Rogers quipped that the United States was the only nation in history that went to the poorhouse in automobiles.

At certain times the percent of the population living in poverty has been very high, as for instance in the latter days of the Roman Empire, and at present it is probably not much higher or lower than the average over the years. Societies have from time to time launched campaigns to eliminate poverty, the most recent being Lyndon Johnson's "War on

Poverty" in the 1960's. Although small gains were made, the problem persists. Nor, as far as I am aware, has the problem ever been reduced to what might be thought of as its irreducible minimum: those who are handicapped, sick, or victims of disaster.

This chapter attempts to trace historically the motives, principles and values of Christians who have over the centuries, tried to help, support, and sometimes to control or reform this unassimilated group in society. I will not attempt to explain why the poor are poor. The causes of poverty are relevant only when what is perceived as the cause of poverty affects how the poor are treated.

For example, there have been many theological explanations. St. Ambrose thought that inequalities in possessions were a result of the Fall. St. John Chrysostom of the early church believed God permitted poverty so that the well-to-do would have someone to give to, and therefore earn their reward in Heaven. Some Puritans held that the poor were the non-elect, who were deemed an insult to God.

Most common, historically, have been moral explanations. The poor have consistently been accused of laziness and intemperance. John Locke, the philosopher of liberty, wrote in 1696 that the increase of the poor could only be caused by "the relaxation of discipline and the corruption of manners." The Reverend Jerry Falwell alleges that material wealth is God's way of rewarding those who do his will—and presumably, poverty is His way of punishing those who don't. Lack of thrift has often been charged to the poor. Occasionally, the moral onus has rested on the well-to-do, who were seen as exploiting the poor. This can be seen in several early twentieth century "social hymns," such as Walter Russell Bowie's *Holy City Seen of John* and Frank North's *Where Cross the Crowded Ways of Life*, both of which speak of greed. But these are exceptions to the general rule.

There have also been sociological and economic explanations, ranging from the effects of the Enclosure Acts in England, to technological unemployment and economic maladjustments, such as the Depression of the 1930's, and disasters such as the Black Death in the 14th century and the potato famine in Ireland in the 1840's. In the twentieth century there has been some recognition that an economic system that favors the majority of the people may at the same time leave part of the population poor; so, for example, the battle against inflation may increase unemployment or a free market depress wages. But these theories and explanations are only significant for our purposes as people come to believe in them.

I will also not attempt to describe in detail the various mechanisms and institutions humankind has devised to cope with the poor. These programs, mechanisms, and institutions, as well as the laws under which they were developed, generally reflect the Christian motives, values, and principles of helpers. Suffice it to say that in the history of Western civilization from Biblical times to the present day—society has used at least the following mechanisms: the hospice, the allocation of the tithe, settlement laws, overseers of the poor, the workhouse, subsidization of wages, work-relief, less-eligibility, social insurance, public assistance, public provision of certain benefits such as education or health care, graduated taxation, the distribution of surplus commodities, soup kitchens, and mutual aid societies. A complete list would be significantly longer.

Drift and Revival

Crucial to understanding the historical development of Christian responses to poverty is the fact that programs to combat poverty may start with one set of ideals or motives, but gradually become diverted from their original intention without changing too much in form. For example, this is what has happened to Aid to Families with Dependent Children (AFDC) in the United States, for many years the program most people referred to when they thought about welfare. It was originally conceived as a long-term income replacement program, strictly financial, enabling single parents to stay at home with their children. It soon began to take on rehabilitative overtones, requiring that the single parents work if at all possible, and urging recipients to exert every effort to become self-supporting as soon as they could.

This theme of a gradual change in direction or meaning in human institutions, indeed in any principle or motive, though maintaining similar form or language, is one that is central. We possess an almost infinite ability to distort our values and stated principles. Progress in dealing with poverty, therefore, has not always been a continually upward process, with perhaps a plateau or two on the way, or even a series of hills and valleys, but rather a series of new starts and a wandering away from the direction of that start. Progress occurs most often when a new idea is born, or when either a major happening (such as the Reformation, a World War, a great Depression) or some person or theory (the impact of Freudian psychology) forces people to reconsider their assumptions. There is then a return to the original direction and a new direction built upon that one. This is similiar to the role played by the prophets in the Old Testament - to bring the people back to essentials: "What does the Lord require of you, but to do justice, to love kindness, and to walk humbly with your God." Indeed, the Old Testament can be read as a paradigm of this drift and revival process. It is with this process in mind that I will explore the Christian impulse to help the poor.

Why Help?

Societies have given a variety of reasons why human beings are willing to help those who cannot help themselves. There have been societies where the poor and the sick were simply left to starve or die of disease, and at times this has even been suggested, in theory at least, to be desirable, as in the works of the Social Darwinists who thought that in feeding the victims of famine we only contribute to the "population explosion," thus ensuring still greater famine. Socio-biologists ascribe the motive to help to an instinct for the preservation of the species, but always have problems explaining why certain species seem to care for the sick and the wounded, while other species clearly do not. Humanists believe helping the poor is somehow characteristic of humankind as we have evolved as social creatures.

Christians believe that God commands it. There have been in the course of Western history, at least four principles, or conscious motives, upon which Christians have based their efforts for helping the poor and less fortunate.

From the Hebrew world came the ideal of justice, basically a religious concept. It held that every human being, as a child of God, had certain rights to a small part of God's blessings. No person or class of persons had the right to take everything. The entire concept was wider than this—including the use of just weights and measures and prohibiting using one's superior status or power to take advantage of the poor. The writer of Exodus commanded that the fields not be gleaned "so that the poor may eat." Proverbs praises the man "who knows the rights of the poor." The word "rights" is significant—it establishes something that personal judgment cannot deny. Micah puts justice before kindness, as does the Old Testament as a whole. Numerous references to justice are made in the Old Testament, and although all of these do not refer to the poor, the poor were certainly included, often specifically. It is not surprising that many of the strongest advocates for a strictly "rights" program of public assistance have been Jewish.

To the Hebrew ideal of justice, early Christianity added love, or charity—which in its original meaning included the concept of valuing or thinking well of its recipient. Love in its purest form is best described in I Corinthians 13, which emphasizes that love does not insist on its own way and has a capacity to endure. Love's mainspring is responding to God's love. Having been greatly loved by God, Christians could do little else than love in return. They also believed that one must love one's enemies as well as one's friends, and accepted the apostle Paul's statement that "there is now no distinction since all have fallen short of the glory of God."

But early Christianity encountered both the Greek and the Roman world. The Greek's believed persons were self-fulfilled only if they were involved with others. Although this had largely to do with involvement in community affairs, it also referred to helping those in distress. From the Roman world came the idea that those more fortunate had a responsibility, even a duty, to help the poor. This sense of "noblesse oblige" was practiced so assiduously in Rome one writer calculated that in the later days of the Roman Empire 580,000 people were receiving some sort of public subsidy, and only 90,000 were self-sufficient, a ratio of more than six to one (Uhlhorn, 1883).

These four principles—justice, love, self-fulfillment, and responsibility—all arose initially from noble sentiments. All at times and to some extent have been distorted. They also have had to compete with two other principles, both basically good. The first is that one's actions should produce some moral good, the other being the need for order in society. These two principles, in turn, like the original four, have often times been distorted.

The need for order in society was strong in the Middle Ages, but rarely was argued for directly, perhaps because it was simply assumed. During this time the need for order was based on the belief that God had ordained the status quo. As the nineteenth century hymn *All Things Bright and Beautiful* puts it, in a verse rarely sung today, "The rich man in his castle, the poor man at his gate / God made them, high or lowly, and ordered their estate." Christians during this period accepted society as it was, believing it had been ordained as such.

The Directions of Diversion

What has happened, at various times, to these original four principles?

Responsibility to help the poor can very easily become paternalism and colonialism—the "White Man's Burden" or the company town. It can be used to justify intruding into the lives of those for whom one assumes responsibility, usually with the intent of "doing them good." Frequently it has involved an elite who see themselves as morally superior and wiser than the people they wish to help. Often it has been used to exercise social control.

Self-fulfillment through helping others has been perverted in two directions. On the one hand, it often takes the form of the desire for gratitude from the person being helped, or to be loved and thanked by them. On the other hand, it may involve pity for the poor, an emotion that always involves a belief in one's own superior fortune or kindness. It is essentially patronizing and demeaning, less concerned with the real needs of the people it serves than with feeling good about serving. A peculiar turn that self-fulfillment took, quite early in its history, was when self-fulfillment began to mean not feeling good in this world, but earning salvation in the next.

But the principle perverted most was Christian love, or charity, as the debasement of the latter word testifies. The original impulse was apparently comparatively short-lived. It flourished for a while, as we know from the book of Acts, overcoming distinctions of wealth, citizenship, and of slave or free status. It greatly enhanced the status of women. But what was possible in the small closed community of the early church could not be carried out in the world at large and by the time of Constantine "the idea of equalizing social conditions for love's sake had pretty much disappeared" (Troeltsch, 1931, p. 37). Charity or love began to mean doing good by exhorting the poor to greater frugality or morality.

Of the four principles, the one perverted least is that of justice. What perversion has occurred is found in rigid categorizing rules: the failure, that is, to temper justice with mercy. There is considerable debate today on how far commutative justice, that which is owed to persons simply by the fact of their existence or being children of God, should go. Does it include, for instance, the right to a minimum income or to health care? Certainly commutative justice needs to be balanced to some degree by distributive justice, or that which is owed to persons in relation to their contribution to society. The problem has been that for the most part, commutative justice has had to take very much of a back seat to distributive justice.

These four principles, in pure or perverted form, have had periods of either great popularity or little influence. Yet they constitute the basic Christian motives for caring for and helping the poor.

A Historical Look

How have these principles or motives been acted upon in history? In what specific ways have these principles or motives been distorted? What is the Christian record regarding treatment of the poor?

As we have seen, the idea of equalizing social conditions for love's sake did not last long. The early church soon recognized the poor would not "cease from the land" and would need individual assistance. This was accomplished by the giving of alms and by distributing the tithe.

But immediately the question arose: Were these "poor" people really in need? Were not some of them, at least, merely pretending to be poor? And would they spend what was given to them for their support in immoral living? This was then, and is still today, an important question that preoccupies us. Johnny Cash sings of the "Welfare Cadillac." Because there are always a few who abuse any system, we tend to suspect all.

The writers in the early church usually stressed helping the poor even at the risk of assisting some who were undeserving. Clement of Alexandria, at the beginning of the third century, said, "For by being fastidious and setting thyself to try who are fit for thy benevolence, and who are not, it is possible that thou mayest neglect some who are the friends of God." At the end of the fourth century, St. John Chrysostom, wrote, "And yet be we as large hearted as we may, we shall never be able to contribute such love towards man as we stand in need of at the hand of a God that loveth man." On the basis of this theology, Chrysostom asserted that "the poor have only one recommendation: their need. If he be the most perverse of all men, should he lack necessary food, we ought to appease his hunger." He even had empathy for those who asked for alms unnecessarily, recognizing that the poor might be tempted more than the rich. Regarding the moral effect of giving on the recipient, Chrysostom said one could not and should not judge (Uhlhorn, 1883).

Notwithstanding Chrysostom's empathy with the supposed impostor, he was much more concerned with the hardness of heart of the giver than with the effects of his charity. And despite his understanding of the unmerited grace of God, Chrysostom was not free of the belief that man, through his own efforts, could win treasure in heaven. He believed that the poor were "useful" to the rich so that the rich might get rid of their material excess and so win that treasure.

Gradually, love for one's neighbor drifted toward and was superseded by self-love—charity became useful as a means to earn salvation. So strongly was this believed that Augustine warned against the assumption that one might obtain a license to sin through giving alms. This assumption was a major heresy of the medieval church. Yet, in one respect at least, the medieval church protected the poor. Only the church was large enough and universal enough to speak for those who were outside the system. The feudal system, through its reciprocal responsibilities, could be counted on to take care of most people. But it was not structured to care for the sick, the migrant, or the fugitive. It is significant that the three services most typical of the church at that time were the hospital, the hospice, and sanctuary. With the fragmentation of the church following the Reformation, this safeguard was lost and did not appear, in America, at least, until the federal government assumed something of this role in the 1930's.

Toward Judgmentalism

Nothing in the theology of the Reformation in itself should have led to a contempt for the poor, a desire to reform them or make life so miserable for them so that they would reform themselves. But this attitude began to dominate the relationship between rich and poor for the next two centuries or more.

The Reformation theology in which 'works' were totally ineffectual might have dried up the generosity of the rich, but it should not have led to the utter contempt for the poor. All men were sinners— there was now "no distinction,"— nothing a man could do to earn favor with God. This would seem to be a breeding ground for humility and not for sweeping judgments on one's fellows. Yet it proved to be exactly the opposite. Not only were the poor despised, but they were treated as if each one of them had the characteristics of the least worthy.

There have been a number of explanations, both theological and economic, for what happened. Some point to Luther's emphasis on work as a necessity. Yet, Luther did not have in mind the necessity to engage in a gainful occupation at whatever wages are offered. He argued that a worker was fulfilling God's intention as well, or better, than the man given to the contemplative life.

It took the development of the new capitalist economy, however, to translate this involvement in worldly affairs into a demand that the first duty of human beings was to earn their own living. Those among the poor who either could not find work or were too sick to work were the natural victims of this demand. Consequently, those who could not or did not work were naturally seen as inferior or unfit.

But this new evaluation of work was not the sole factor operating. Max Weber (1930) believed that the crux of the matter was found in the doctrine of election and the "absolute duty" of the elect to "consider himself chosen, and to combat all doubts as temptations of the devil, since lack of self-confidence is the result of insufficient faith." This meant one could be sure one was of the elect only if one was actively engaged in doing work. As a corollary, those who did not or could not work showed they were not of the elect. This led to a hatred of those who did not or could not work as being an insult to God. But to look for evidences of election in human behavior was to deny and distort the whole rationale of Calvin's election doctrine. It meant that God chose those who pleased Him through their activities, and led to the identification of worldly success with election. It opened the door to the possibility that it was human beings and not God who determined their election.

The Poor and the Social Order

During the transition period between the end of the feudal system and the full establishment of market economies, most nations developed laws or systems of public relief. In England these were called poor laws. It was a period of great hardship for the poor, many of whom were uprooted from the land and became destitute. The measures set up as public relief were always accompanied by stricter and stricter laws against begging and leaving one's settlement or residence. One could be branded, enslaved, or even executed (on a third offense) for begging. Public relief sprang not so much from compassion for the poor, but primarily to avert public disorder.

In 1601 the Poor Law declared all able-bodied poor must do some kind of work to earn their sustenance; the sustenance itself was provided by the parish—the local unit of administration in England. For some time both church-sponsored charity and public relief co-existed. In many communities, a public overseer of the poor was appointed. By 1750, however, rural poverty began to rise dramatically, driven by an unprecedented occurrence—a permanent surplus in labor in the countryside accompanied by a boom in trade. To meet this great distress and encourage employers to hire more workers, the poor laws were modified to subsidize wages, creating a guaranteed minimum income of sorts. Under this new system a man received relief, even if he was working, if his wages fell below the family subsistence income. With his meager income now guaranteed whatever his wages - and with the added certainty that he could never make more than a guaranteed subsistence income - the laborer had little motivation to satisfy his employer. Conversely, an employer could now obtain labor at minuscule wages; whatever he paid, the subsidy from the poor rates brought the laborer's income up to the guaranteed minimum scale. There was no easy way out of this vicious cycle. Poverty had become very expensive.

The best Christian minds in England at the time grappled with this problem of poverty. The general consensus was to abolish the Poor Laws (wage subsidies and outdoor relief) and replace them with workhouses (indoor relief), guided by the principle of less-eligibility. According to this principle, if the living conditions and assistance rates of persons maintained at public expense were equal to or better than the lowest paid persons maintained at their own expense, calamity would be inevitable. Living conditions and assistance for the poor, therefore, should be made *less* than what the lowest paid *eligible* worker received. Also recommended was to make the conditions of relief so odious, humiliating, and forbidding that one would do anything short of starving to avoid it. When the new Poor Law of 1834 came into being, this was the rule that was followed. The only thing worse than dependency would be death itself. The law of 1834 was the most important piece of social legislation passed in the nineteenth century. The English poor were compelled to be "independent" and were forced into the competitive labor market. They were now free and independent in a new and unheard of way. They were solely responsible for themselves.

When the new law went into effect it was greeted with great anger. No piece of legislation in English history has probably ever been so hated or despised. One of England's greatest writers was on hand to comment on this monumental development. In his novel *Oliver Twist*, Charles Dickens gives a blistering satire on the new Poor Law and the principles that animated it, including the awareness that independence in the scheme of political economy was easily convertible into isolation and abandonment. What was learned, perhaps, was that it is possible to degrade people by caring for them and to degrade people by not caring for them.

Control of Pauperism

The major thrust of welfare policy by the early nineteenth century became, therefore, to control pauperism or dependency. In the public mind, being poor and being a pauper were different. Paupers were characterized by their moral degeneracy, drunkenness, vice, and corruption. They were outcasts, no different than criminals. The dividing line between the poor and the paupers was the ability and willingness to work. Those who could support themselves, but didn't, crossed the line from being poor to being paupers.

The goal of welfare policy was to prevent the poor from crossing that line. The poor were seen as precariously balanced on the brink of moral disaster, and one sure way to tip the balance and send a family downward into pauperism was the indiscriminate giving of aid. Therefore, the public policy was to reform those poor who applied for relief. Incentives for reforming would-be applicants were either a government's denying assistance or making the conditions of accepting relief extremely onerous. The methods used to try to reform the poor and spur them to independence were nearly all negative. Kindness towards them was suspect. It would tempt the poor to be content with their state. To receive relief, a family was required to go to the poorhouse where the humiliating conditions were designed to deter applications for relief. Deterrence was thought to be rehabilitative. This was the nineteenth century's attempt to reform the poor. To help take people out of poverty would not have made sense to this generation, for they truly believed in taking the poverty out of people.

The belief that one can stop people from being or becoming poor by making them miserable is one that persists today. George Gilder (1981), believed by some to have provided the theological justification for the Reagan administration's economics, is quoted as saying that for the poor to succeed and cease to be poor, they "need most of all the spur of their poverty," — hence the "crucial goal should be to restrict the [welfare] system as much as possible, by making it unattractive and even a bit demeaning."

Evangelical Revival

The religious revivals of the middle eighteenth and early nineteenth centuries could have counteracted the rigidities of these capitalist-puritan beliefs, but did not. Because evangelical revivalism emphasized love rather than justice and was essentially individualistic, it did not further an understanding of the plight of the poor. Evangelicalism was not, according to Niebuhr (1932), a true "religion of the disinherited." Although it appealed to all classes, it remained largely middle class. It was selective in its view of sin, emphasizing personal sins such as irreverence and intemperance rather than collective ones such as oppression and injustice. It was also more impressed by the vices to which the poor had succumbed than by the evils to which they had been subjected. The sins of which evangelicals convicted the rich and the poor were very different.

The main impact of the evangelical movement on the rich may have been to restore for a time the prominence of self-fulfillment as a motive for helping others. While not so blatant, perhaps, as in medieval times, the motive is obvious. The philanthropy of the wealthy during the first part of the nineteenth century was the bridge in many cases between their business dealings and their Christian conscience. Throughout the nineteenth century the charitable response of the American people was almost as generous as their pursuit of gain was selfish. Charles Wesley's solution was to get all one can, save all one can, and give all one can.

The two streams of giving and getting converged at the end of the nineteenth century in the gospel of wealth. This doctrine harmonized with the major tenets of individualism, and through the idea of stewardship, endowed individualism with moral sanctity. It was Andrew Carnegie who in word and deed gave the gospel of wealth its classic expression. Believing that enormous differences in the economic conditions of men were normal and beneficial, Carnegie asserted that wealth was a sacred trust to be administered by the person possessing it for the welfare of the community. The aim of the millionaire, he declared, should be to die poor. For all its undoubted romantic appeal the gospel of wealth did not solve or help understand poverty, for Carnegie was not seeking to correct poverty, but to justify wealth. The weakness of the approach lay in its failing to recognize that the suffering the wealthy generously relieved with one hand, was in many instances, but the product of the ills they sowed with the other.

Science and Advice

By the late nineteenth century there was a great deal more interest in the conditions of the poor. This took various forms. One, which was primarily humanitarian but had a strong religious base, consisted largely in the founding of missions in poor neighborhoods. Part of the motive of these missions was a genuine concern to improve the conditions under which the poor were compelled to live and part was a desire to reform the character of the poor. Many social welfare organizations of this period had their origin in religious missions of this form.

Alongside these was another form, the scientific Association for Improving the Condition of the Poor, with its concept of "friendly visiting." They operated with a conviction that what the poor needed was the "influence" (primarily moral advice) of the visitor and not material relief. Part of this feeling was religious, that spiritual things were much more important than material. Principles of the society were put forward as, "FIRST, the moral elevation of the poor; and SECOND, ...the relief of their necessities" (Brown, 1855).

Jesus' use of Deuteronomy 8:3, or rather the partial statement, "Man does not live by bread alone," was often quoted in support of the primacy of intangible services, as if Jesus was condemning bread, despite his asking for it in the Lord's Prayer. To elevate intangible services over the practical is poor theology, but it became the primary attitude of helpers during this period.

As social conditions for the poor worsened under the impact of the Industrial Revolution and America also had to contend with a vast influx of immigrants, social reformers turned to Charity Organization Societies (COS). In many ways these organizations continued what the Association for Improving the Condition of the Poor had done, favoring friendly visits over material relief. In fact, the detection of fraud is listed as the Society's first function, ahead of the adequate relief of the honest poor (Gurteen, 1882).

Applicants for assistance who could pass the rigid examinations of the COS agents were certified as worthy and referred to a cooperating agency for the relief of their needs. Thus, when prospective contributors to the New York COS asked how much of their donation would go to the poor, the director was able to answer proudly, "Not one cent." It saw as the principal cause of pauperism the "misdirected charity of benevolent people" (Gurteen, 1882, p. 170).

Birth of Social Work

It did not take long before America, with its tradition of individual responsibility and its belief in technology, carried the scientific claims of the Charity Organization Society to their logical conclusion and developed a new science, that of social casework.

The person most responsible for developing this new "science" of social casework was Mary E. Richmond. She had been a Charity Organization Society worker; in fact, her first book was entitled *Friendly Visiting Among the Poor* (1899). Richmond greatly enlarged and enhanced the art of investigation. Her method was to ask literally dozens of questions about an individual and his or her relationships. In a later book Richmond described the three most successful casework policies as the following: "encouragement and stimulation, the fullest possible participation of the client in all plans, and the skillful use of repetition" (Richmond, 1922, p. 256).

It is the second of these that is significant. For the first time, the poor or deviant person being studied was given some part in his or her own treatment. Richmond elaborated on this principle and gave it the name by which it is still known: "self-determination." The next step was obvious, the training of professionals. In 1897 Richmond had already made the first plea for a School of Applied Philanthropy. Social casework and social work became almost synonymous.

The new profession of social work was now ready for Freud. Here was an acceptable scientific theory that explained much of what had puzzled caseworkers when clients did not respond to reason, and here also was an answer to the moralism of earlier social work practice which was then beginning to fall out of favor.

A New Definition of Justice

Mary Richmond, as we have seen, had enunciated a pragmatic principle that she called self-determination. Freud gave scientific sanction to the principle. Finally, it became recognized as a philosophical and eventually a religious belief.

Self-determination as a principle certainly produced a much more humane treatment of the poor. At times it may have led to indulgence, to protecting people from the law or the natural consequences of their actions. At times, in Freudian terms, it liberated the id at the expense of the superego. But it did much to counter the disregard for human dignity that had been taken for granted as part of the fate of anyone who asked for help - submission to the will of the helper and restrictions on his freedom to manage his own life. It was a great corrective to pride arising out of exercising social control.

Self-determination did more. Politically it helped to develop a welfare system that established, for the first time, a legal right to assistance. While social workers were developing their theories of self-determination, the government in the United States was reacting to the Depression with a relief system that seemed to promise some dignity to the poor.

What was really new in the Social Security Act of 1935 were the categories of public assistance - at that time Old Age Assistance, Aid to the Needy Blind, and Aid to Dependent Children. These spelled out for the first time a legal and enforceable right to assistance if certain eligibility conditions were met. The act set aside the goal of earlier welfare reformers who had tried to change human nature, and accepted the fact that government will always be engaged in spending for welfare. What was conceded was that the poor will always be with us.

It is true that the law did not guarantee the adequacy of assistance. The principle of less eligibility could still be practiced. There was also resistance from those who could not accept the idea that the poor had the right to live their lives free from efforts to reform or rehabilitate them. Nevertheless, the moral right had now been given statutory form protected by a system of appeals or fair hearings in which due process was to be observed. Money payments were interpreted to mean unrestricted payments which the recipient could spend as he or she wished, free from social control. With the passage of the Social Security Act, the federal government became, in fact, the protector of the rights of the poor and of the least popular among them—a role not unlike that of the medieval church.

The public, however, found commutative justice hard to accept. Most of them still thought of assistance as a "dole" and were convinced that many of the recipients of public assistance were cheats. Less eligibility was still rife in the system. The grants rarely, if ever, were sufficient for more than minimum health and decency, and many states paid only a fraction of their own estimate of minimum needs. Despite the federal government's insistence that clients should be the principal source of information about their situation, as they are, for instance, in paying income tax, they were subjected to a degrading and often rigorous investigation, which almost assumed that they intended to lie or to cheat.

The Services Solution (rehabilitation)

As a result, by 1956, "services" again became an integral part of these programs. Probably there is no clearer indication of the way basic programs were changed than the revisions made in the Aid to Dependent Children (ADC) program. This was the year in which parents and other caretakers of dependent children were officially recognized as recipients, and the name of the program changed from Aid to Dependent Children to Aid to Families with Dependent Children. The goals of the program were no longer simply to provide a parent with the money to care for her children. They became rehabilitative goals, incumbent on the parent. The "right to assistance" and the unrestricted money grant were still the law, but they had been modified in practice as well as in the announced purpose of the program.

At the beginning of the 1960's, social workers and others persuaded Congress that the answer to the rising costs of welfare was more social services to those in need. The outcome was President Johnson's "War on Poverty." The "War on Poverty" did not abolish poverty. An assessment in 1976 estimated there had been substantial progress in overcoming poverty, measured in absolute terms—that is, reaching a minimum level of well-being. However, there was no progress either in the ability of people to do without government help or in the incidence of relative poverty. In other words, living standards had improved and the welfare system was more generous, but economic inequality remained (Plotnick, 1976). Nevertheless, by 1980, something of a floor had been placed beneath most of the poor—a somewhat shaky floor perhaps, but some assurance that most would not be without adequate food or medical services.

Back to the Poor Law

The actions of the Reagan/Bush administration that came into power in 1980 were not simply an attempt to cut back on welfare programs in order to reduce federal spending. They were an attempt to return America to the principles of controlling pauperism, principles that were current a hundred or two hundred years ago. Clinton campaigned with the promise to "end welfare as we know it." Identifying solutions to dependency had become high politics, with governors, legislators, and policy experts attempting to win public approval for their welfare reform proposals.

The proposals were all very similar. All emphasized that poor women, specifically AFDC recipients, must be coerced to break the habit of dependency on the state. Most solutions relied on market coercion, and a few on a combination of both market and state coercion. Charles Murray (1984) recommended simply abolishing income supports, forcing poor mothers to expose themselves to the curative discipline of the labor market. Lawrence Mead (1985) was less optimistic about the ability of the poor to respond to market sanctions, and called instead for an "authoritative work policy" that would include systematic monitoring by government, along with rewards and sanctions to force the poor to behave in socially-approved ways. Yet, ironically, even the government's own research studies indicated while the range of tested pilot welfare-to-work programs modestly improved people's income, they proved unlikely to move most people out of poverty (Gueron & Pauly, 1991). In fact, for many, they were worse off and without any lasting protection.

In 1997, Congress passed the Personal Responsibility Act, ending over fifty years of federal legal protection for many poor persons. Although early outcomes show a decrease in welfare roles, the effects on poverty rates and on the poor themselves are not as clear or optimistic.

This brief historical review highlighting the motives and attitudes of helpers has shown how easily our best motives, even our cherished Christian values, can very easily be diverted or distorted. As can be seen, we frequently have lost our direction or have been diverted from the goal of properly caring for the poor.

Biblical Principles and Attitudes

What are the biblical principles and attitudes related to poverty? What is our responsibility in caring for the poor? Will we always have the poor with us? What does the Bible really have to say about poverty?

First of all, one of the central, if not *the* central social concern of the Bible is the plight and suffering of the poor. Yet, interestingly enough, the Bible almost never addresses the poor themselves, but rather the nonpoor. The Bible asks the prosperous to set right the condition of the poor.

Amos saw firsthand the terrible oppression of the poor. He saw the rich "trample the head of the poor into the dust of the earth" (2:7), and perceived that the lifestyle of the rich was built on the oppression of the poor (6:1-7).

Many other biblical texts assert how God lifts up the poor and disadvantaged. God aids the poor, but the rich He sends away empty. He actively opposes the rich, not because they are rich, but because they oppress the poor and neglect the needy. Jesus clearly warns against the possession of wealth, and almost every time Jesus offers an opinion about riches, it is negative. Jesus' advice to the rich young ruler (Luke 18:18-30) calls for him to abandon his possessions, and give them to the poor. Either God or wealth is one's master or "employer" (Matthew 6:24). In the parable of the rich man and Lazarus, the rich man was found guilty for neglecting the poor man at his gate (Luke 16:19-31).

Psalm 146 is one among many passages relating God's concern for the hungry and the oppressed. Indeed, care for the poor is central to the nature of God. God not only acts in history to liberate the poor, but He identifies with the weak and destitute.

Luke pictures the Good News as a message of salvation for the poor, sick, sorrowful, weak, lowly and outcast (4:18-19). The parable of the Good Samaritan (Luke 10:25-37) and of the Last Judgment (Matthew 25:31-46) are two of the better known lessons by Jesus on this subject. A living faith is one that demonstrates compassion for those in need: "If a brother or sister is ill-clad and in lack of daily food, and one of you says to them, 'Go in peace, be warmed and filled,' without giving them the things needed for the body, what does it profit?" (James 2:15-16)

The biblical message is clear, poverty exists because we try to serve both God and money, and the love of self is more important than love of neighbor. In short, the cause of economic poverty is found in moral poverty, but not the morality of the poor. In the Bible, moral poverty, described as misplaced hope, distorted love, and perverted faith in money and in oneself, is found with those who are not poor. A true Christian explanation of poverty in affluent America, therefore, is to be found not in the concept of the culture of poverty, but in the concept of the culture of wealth.

Concluding Reflections

The God of the Bible is not a neutral God. The above biblical passages show how pervasive concern for the poor is in the Bible. The Bible depicts God as on the side of the poor, God biased in favor of the poor. This conclusion is hard to contest. Nevertheless, some comments and clarifications are in order.

First of all — although the Bible says many times that God is on the side of the poor and that Jesus identifies himself with the poor, what difference does this make? As long we read these texts merely as if they were saying something beautiful about God, an additional attribute of God, they will make very little if any difference. But all true *theo*-logy, that is speaking about God, is also *anthropo*-logy. These texts are not to be read as if they were speaking only about God. The biblical authors always speak of God as He reveals Himself to us, as He manifests Himself to us, and challenges us. Therefore, every text that says that God is on the side of the poor should also be read as a challenge addressed to us: you who say you believe in the God of the Covenant, who say you are on His side, should be where the Bible says that God is, namely on the side of the poor. To identify, to know, to meet the poor — is to identify, to know, to meet God.

Second, it is clear from the biblical message that poverty has to be opposed and its main causes, injustice and oppression, have to be counteracted. This calls for unrelenting work for justice. The concrete ways and means to attain justice will certainly differ in every given situation. But the biblical texts clearly suggest that this action for justice will include a concrete willingness to share what one has (Luke 3:11; 19:8), and the true measure of this sharing is not the "surplus" of the haves, but the need of the have-nots.

Lastly, in the course of this study of the poor, the central place of the Covenant needs to be made clear. Texts challenging God's people to do justice in the Old Testament are given as conditions of the Covenant. The Old Testament prophets fiercely attacked social injustice in order to recover the lost ideal of the Covenant. The reference point for all biblical texts on social justice is the Covenant community, a people equal among themselves and equal before God, among whom there shall be no poor.

The title of this chapter comes from a verse in Deuteronomy. Deuteronomy comprises the so-called Deuteronomic Code of Law (Deut. 12-26) edited within the framework of two discourses attributed to Moses, represented as both prophet and lawgiver. The central theme of Deuteronomy is the election of Israel as the people of God by means of the Covenant. Deuteronomy's prescriptions concerning the sabbatical year (Deut. 15:1-11) are as follows:

> (1) At the end of every seven years you shall grant a release. (2) And this is the manner of the release: every creditor shall release what he has lent to his neighbor; he shall not exact it of his neighbor, his brother, because the Lord's release has been proclaimed. (3) Of the foreigner you may exact it; but whatever of yours is with your brother your hand shall release. (4) *But there will be no poor among you* ... (7) If there is among you a poor man, one of your brethren, in any of the towns within your land which the Lord your God gives you, you shall not harden your heart or shut your hand against your poor brother, (8) but you shall open your hand to him, and lend him sufficient for his need, whatever it may be .... (10) You shall give to him freely, and your heart shall not be grudging when you give to him; because for this the Lord your God will bless you in all your work and in all that you undertake. (11) *For the poor will never cease out of the land* (you will have the poor always with you); therefore I command you, You shall open wide your hand to your brother, to the needy and the poor, in the land.

At the beginning of this biblical passage stands an old precept (verse 1), which is legally interpreted (verse 2), and then developed like a sermon (verses 3-11). This sermon invites us to meet the poor at all times with an open hand and an open heart. The interest of the *law-giver* is satisfied when he has made an ordinance obligatory. But the *prophet* is concerned with the conscience of the people at whom the law is aimed. In this context, the covenant ideal of a people equal before God and equal among themselves is expressed: "there will be no poor among you" (verse 4). But, considering the way people are running things, the *prophet* sadly concedes that in reality "the poor will never cease out of the land" (verse 11). The presence of the poor, therefore, is not to be considered a fact of life which we should accept as unavoidable. On the contrary, it is to be considered a scandal, contradicting God's vision of the human community, and therefore, must be counteracted by all means.

As Christians in social work we have a similar responsibility to respond to the problems of poverty and wealth in our communities and the world. With poverty rates rising and the gap between the haves and have-nots continuing to widen, will we as Christian social workers respond obediently to God's Word? Will we advocate for the poor and work for God's ideal "that there will be no poor among you." Or will we also distort God's ideal, or simply minimize the goal, finding the task too difficult or unpopular? Being a Christian in social work provides the unique opportunity to respond to this significant Christian challenge.

Notes

I am indebted and wish to acknowledge Alan Keith-Lucas's book *The Poor You Have With You Always*(1989) for much of the outline, themes and many of the illustrations offered in this chapter. Portions of the chapter are descriptions from this book. I refer the reader to his book for a more complete and detailed analysis of this topic.

References

Alexander, Cecil. (1845). All Things Bright and Beautiful. In *Hymns Ancient and Modern*, 1924 edition.

Brown, James. (1855). Confidential Instructions to Visitors of the AICP. In Ralph Pumphrey & Murial Pumphrey (Eds.), *The Heritage of American Social Work*. New York: Columbia University Press.

Gilder, George. (1981). *Wealth and Poverty*. New York: Basic Books.

Gueron, Judith M. & Edward Pauly with Cameron M. Lougy. (1991). *From Welfare to Work*. New York: Manpower Demonstration Research Corporation.

Gurteen, Humphreys S. (1882). A Handbook of Charity Organization. In Ralph Pumphrey & Muriel Pumphrey (Eds.), *The Heritage of American Social Work*. New York: Columbia University Press.

Mead, Lawrence. (1985). *Beyond Entitlement: The Social Obligations of Citizenship*. New York: Free Press.

Murray, Charles. (1984). *Losing Ground*. New York: Basic Books.

Niebuhr, Reinold. (1932). *The Contribution of Religion to Social Work*. New York: Columbia University Press.

Plotnich, Robert D. (1976). Progress Against Poverty? *Social Welfare Forum*, 104-115.

Richmond, Mary E. (1899). *Friendly Visiting Among the Poor*. New York: Russell Sage Foundation.

Richmond, Mary E. (1922). *What is Social Case Work?* New York: Russell Sage Foundation.

Troeltsch, Ernest. (1931). *The Social Teaching of the Christian Churches*. Translated by Olive Wyon, New York.

Uhlhorn, Gerhard. (1883). *Christian Charity in the Ancient Church*. Edinburgh.

Weber, Max. (1930). *The Protestant Ethic and the Spirit of Capitalism*. London.

CHAPTER 11

WHEN SOCIAL WORK AND CHRISTIANITY CONFLICT

Lawrence E. Ressler

His name is Emory and he is a Christian. To be more specific, he is a Mennonite. He may not look like what you expect a Mennonite to look like, but he is. When Emory was young, his family followed more traditional customs. They drove only black cars, for example. His dad wore a plain coat and his mom wore a white bonnet and dark stockings. They had no radios or televisions. His relatives, who have remained committed to traditional Mennonite customs, would not approve of the mustache he now wears, the television, stereo, computers, and gold colored car he has. What is more important to know about Emory, however, is that while he has abandoned many of the traditional customs, he still has the soul of a Mennonite. It is the framework that provides structure and purpose to his living. A story might help illustrate the influence that being Mennonite has on his life.

When Emory was about 13, he earned money by mowing lawns. One day, when he went to mow a lawn for a customer, he found another boy at the same house with a lawnmower. Emory informed the boy he had been hired to do the mowing, to which the boy replied he had been hired to do it. Emory insisted the job was his and before he knew what happened, the other boy drew back and hit Emory squarely on the jaw, knocking him to the ground. Emory got up and did what he thought was proper. He turned his face to one side and said, "Here, do you want to hit this side too." After all, Jesus had said, "Turn the other cheek." To Emory's surprise, the boy hit him a second time. Rather than fight about the lawn, Emory got up and went home. Even as an adolescent, Emory was guided by the Mennonite commitment to nonviolence.

Emory's personal sense of history begins in January 1525 when Conrad Grebel and Felix Mantz chose to be rebaptized as adults in Zurich, Switzerland. They did so based on their reading of the Bible. The choice to be a Christian, they believed, should be a voluntary adult decision rather than a procedure imposed on infants as was the custom of the day. Such an idea ran counter to official church policy and the law that required infant baptism. This issue may not seem significant today, but at that time adult baptism was considered both heresy and treason.

Adult baptism was considered so egregious during the sixteenth and seventh centuries that it could result in capital punishment.

The adult baptisms of Grebel and Mantz marked the beginning of the Anabaptist (rebaptizer) movement which was an extension of the Protestant Reformation begun by Martin Luther in 1517. The word Mennonite was given to followers of Menno Simons, an Anabaptist leader in Holland in the latter part of the sixteenth century. Menno Simons and his followers were deeply committed Christians who desired to use the Bible as a guide to living, particularly the New Testament and the teaching of Jesus. Over the years, a distinctive Mennonite theology and life style developed. This included such things as nonconformist living, service to others, community accountability, and simple living. The visible application of this theology included dressing distinctively, rejecting some technology, a worldwide voluntary service system to help people in need, and living a modest lifestyle. Central to their belief system was a commitment to nonresistant love which was to be put into consistent and practical action. Love, following the teaching of Jesus, was to be extended even to one's enemies.

Anabaptists, including Mennonites, were so empowered by and committed to their faith, that while they would not kill to preserve their beliefs, they were willing to die for them. The commitment to their faith was put to the greatest of tests. Anabaptists were persecuted for several hundred years in Europe because of their beliefs and lifestyle with over 3000 men, women, and children being burned to death, drowned, and beheaded (Bracht, 1837). Take Michael Sattler and his family who were rebaptized in 1525, for example. The Sattlers were arrested, tried, found guilty of heresy and treason, and instructed to recant. Because Michael would not, his tongue was cut out and red hot tongs were applied three times to his body. When he continued to refuse to abandon his beliefs, he was driven to the countryside and had red hot tongs applied five more times to his body. When he still would not renounce his Anabaptist beliefs, he was burned at the stake. His wife and sisters were later drowned because they also would not recant (Baergen, 1981).

In Emory's own direct family, his grandfather seven times removed was sentenced to prison in 1710 for his religious beliefs. The family, along with many other Mennonites, came to America in 1715 primarily in search of religious freedom. James Madison specifically mentions the "Menonists" in the influential apology for religious liberty written in 1785 entitled "Memorial and Remonstrance" (Gaustad, 1993, p. 145). For Emory's ancestors, the First Amendment to the Constitution was a welcome end to several hundred years of religious oppression.

Like his ancestors, Emory has no interest in killing to protect his rights. While Emory cannot state for certain that he would take persecution to the point of death for his beliefs, in his soul he would want to. Religious beliefs are as dear to Emory as they were to his ancestors. Emory may not look like what you would expect a Mennonite to look like, but the teachings of Christ, respect for the Bible, the Mennonite theology, and a lifestyle which emerges from them are as important to him as those who dress and live in a distinctive manner.

Emory is also a social worker. He has a bachelor's degree, a master's degree, and a doctorate in social work. He has worked as a social worker in both religious and secular settings and has attended or worked in social work educational institutions for two decades. Emory has also had leadership roles in both the National Association of Social Workers (NASW) and the North American Association of Christians in Social Work (NACSW).

Emory is equally committed to his faith and the social work profession. He has found the social work profession to a be a particularly meaningful vocation. His motivation for social work is related to his understanding of what it means to be a faithful follower of Christ. I John provides a particularly clear connection between his theology and his interest in social work:

> We know love by this, that he laid down his life for us—and we ought to lay down our lives for one another. How does God's love abide in anyone who has the world's goods and sees a brother or sister in need and yet refuses help? Little children, let us love, not in word or speech, but in truth and action. (I John 3:16-18)

Emory is an example of what can be called a Christian social worker. While Emory is comfortable with the label, others are not. The phrase Christian social worker, for some, is an oxymoron. Rather than see social work and Christianity as allies, Christianity, for them, is viewed as a major barrier to accomplishing social work ideals. The linking of Christianity and social work, for some social workers, is a troublesome connection.

There are, in other words, points of tension between social work and Christianity. The purpose of this chapter is to explore the reasons for the conflict between Christianity and social work. In addition, several suggestions for reducing the tension between the two are offered.

Spirituality and Religion

To fully understand the tension between Christianity and social work, it is important, first of all, to distinguish between spirituality and religion.

Definitions

Spirituality, in the popular social work use of the term, refers to "the basic human drive for meaning, purpose, and moral relatedness among people, with the universe, and with the ground of our being" (Canda, 1989, p. 573). Human beings from this perspective are viewed as more than physical beings determined by their basic drives as Freud suggested, by the economic system as Marx believed, or by the environment as Skinner argued. A spiritual perspective holds that at the core of the human being is a search for meaning, the desire to know, and the yearning to be connected.

Spirituality is distinguished from religion which is defined as "an institutionally patterned system of beliefs, values, and rituals" (Canda, 1989, p. 573). Religion involves the organization of ideas about the relationship of the supernatural world and the natural world. It also includes the organization of activities and people that stem from an understanding of the supernatural and natural worlds. Whereas spirituality is largely philosophical in tone and speaks to human nature issues, religion is more sociological and theological. Spirituality is a personal phenomenon while religion is a social phenomenon.

A Typology

Using contemporary definitions, an analysis of spirituality and religion results in a fourfold typology. The first category could be called **Spiritual and Non- Religious**. This would include people who are actively engaged in a search for or have found meaning and connection in life. They do so, however, outside of a religious framework. They do not attend a church and are not involved in what is considered religious activities. Meaning in life and connectedness come from non-religious sources such as nature, a job, special relationships, or even the mundane aspects of daily living that are approached with a spiritual attitude. The second type could be designated **Religious and Disspirited**[1]. This would be typical of people who go to church, follow religious rituals, and even support the religious organization. Their life, however, has no meaning and they do not feel connected to others. They may be involved in religious activity but it does not provide meaningful structure or purpose for life. The third classification could be referred to as **Disspirited and Non- Religious**. This would involve persons who are not consciously purposeful about life nor connected. They may well feel aimless and isolated from others. They also are not involved in religious activities, do not embrace a religious belief system, and are not part of a religious community. The fourth category could be called **Spiritual And Religious**. This would consist of persons whose meaning in life is related to their religious experience. Emory, described earlier, is in this category. The person of Jesus Christ and the Bible as well as an awareness of the Holy Spirit give form and substance to his life. The Mennonite theology helps organize how he understands the world, history, and the future, and it influences how he lives. Going to church, reading the Bible, praying, singing, worshiping with others, and attending church conferences provide inspiration and motivation. His religion is a source of hope and strength.

Spirituality, Religion, and the Social Work Profession

After decades of neglect, the topic of spirituality has become increasingly popular in social work in recent years. Spirituality, for example, is being addressed more frequently in social work journals. A keyword search in the Social Work Abstracts, for example, found 70 entries related to spirituality in the past 20 years with 86% published in the last 10 years. After being dropped from the Council on Social Work Education's (CSWE) curriculum policy statement in 1970, the term spirituality has been reinserted in the 1996 revision (Marshall, 1991). An organization called the Society for Spirituality and Social Work has been developed complete with a newsletter, chapters across the country, and an annual convention. Although the change is not yet evident, there is also some indication that social work textbooks, which have seriously neglected spirituality (Cnaan, 1997), are beginning to address the topic (e.g. Bullis, 1996). In sum, the concept of spirituality appears to be gaining support in the profession.

The topic of religion, like spirituality, has been largely ignored in social work for the greater part of the twentieth century (Cnaan, 1997; Loewenberg, 1988). There appears to be an interesting paradox with respect to recent attitudes in the social work profession related to religion, however. On the one hand, there is increasing recognition of the importance of religion to clients and colleagues. This is evident most notably in the revised 1996 NASW Code of Ethics where religious diversity has been given increased status. Religion is now included as one of the groups which social workers are implored to be sensitive to along with race, ethnicity, national origin, color, sex, sexual orientation, age, marital status, political belief, and mental or physical disability. Social workers are instructed in the NASW Code of Ethics to "obtain education about and seek to understand the nature of social diversity and oppression" related to religion as well as diverse groups (1.05). Social workers are further instructed to "avoid unwarranted negative criticism of colleagues" related to religion (2.01), to "not practice, condone, facilitate, or collaborate with any form of discrimination" on the basis of religion (4.02), and are required to "act to prevent and eliminate domination of, exploitation of, and discrimination against any person, group, or class" on the basis of religion (6.04). In other words, respect for religious diversity seems to be of equal importance to other types of diversity.

At the same time, there has been significant tension in the profession with respect to religion, especially those who are in the **Spiritual** and **Religious** category. Alan Keith- Lucas highlighted the crux of the matter with this question in 1958, "What happens, then, to the social worker who is not content with religious generalizations and who really believes and acts by what he says in his creed?" (Keith-Lucas A., 1958, p. 236). Keith-Lucas, who wrote prolifically about the integration of Christianity and social work for 40 years, believed that with careful theology and a good understanding of social work the two were compatible. He states, "The task of beginning to make such a synthesis will not, however, be an easy one. It will require an exploration for those willing to undertake it, of what theology really teaches and not what most people take for granted that it teaches, or remember from Sunday School...It must be intellectually rigorous, conducted by people who are amateurs neither in religion nor social work. It will have to do with the 'hard paradoxes' rather than the 'easy correspondences'" (p. 236).

Not everyone has taken Keith-Lucas's position. In spite of clear evidence that social workers do not feel adequately prepared to deal with religious issues which arise in social work practice (Joseph, 1988; Sheridan, 1992), some social workers resist giving increased attention to the topic. Clark (1994), for example, argues, "If we want the social work profession to maintain its political and technological gains, we must not move religion to a position of central importance" (p. 15). Increased attention to religion in social work, Clark argues, will place the profession on a "slippery slope."

One of the most visible and volatile clashes in social work took place recently between the Council on Social Work Education (CSWE) and religiously-affiliated institutions. At the center of the conflict was an accreditation standard developed in 1982 which extended mandatory nondiscrimination to political and sexual orientation. The requirement that sexual orientation be included in the social work program nondiscrimination statement conflicted with a policy in some religiously-affiliated institutions that prohibits sexual intimacy outside of marriage[2]. Interestingly, the CSWE acknowledged in a publicly distributed memorandum that the sexual orientation requirement was added knowing that it violated the religious beliefs of some institutions (CSWE Commission on Accreditation, 1996).

From 1982 to 1995, the conflict was dormant because the policy was not enforced. That changed beginning in 1995 when a number of schools were told by CSWE that they would not be accredited if they did not comply with the standard. A number of religiously-affiliated schools responded by threatening a lawsuit on several accounts. First, the 1982 standard was viewed as a violation of the profession's commitment to religious diversity and being denied accreditation was seen as a violation of the principle of social justice. Second, denying accreditation to religiously-affiliated institutions for policies related to their religious beliefs was interpreted as a violation of the First Amendment guarantee of religious freedom. Third, since eliminating religiously-affiliated institutions from accreditation would result in their students being ineligible for state licenses, anti-trust concerns were raised.

The CSWE Commission on Accreditation (COA) made an attempt to resolve the conflict by proposing an exemption to the nondiscrimination standard similar to the American Bar Association and the American Psychological Association. In part, the proposed revision read, "Religious institutions that qualify for religious exemption under federal laws and regulations may apply for an exemption if they cannot comply with these standards" (CSWE Commission on Accreditation, 1996). Concern was raised by both religiously-affiliated institutions that would benefit from the revised standard and gay and lesbian advocates who favored having sexual orientation in the standard. The common concern, however, came from very different sources. Religious affiliated institutions feared a social stigma if granted an exemption. Gay and lesbian advocates saw the proposal as abandoning historic commitments to the oppressed. As a result of the negative and widespread feedback, the COA withdrew the proposal.

A second effort to resolve the dilemma was attempted in 1996 by removing the 1982 nondiscrimination standard entirely and replacing it with a new standard. The proposed standard called for "specific, continuous efforts to provide a learning context in which understanding and respect for diversity (including age, color, disability, ethnicity, gender, national origin, race, religion, and sexual orientation) are practiced" (CSWE Commission on Accreditation, 1997). The proposal was received favorably by the religiously-affiliated institutions who had expressed dissatisfaction with the 1982 standard. The proposal was resisted by gay and lesbian advocates who wanted a policy that required nondiscrimination based on sexual orientation. The second statement was approved by the CSWE Board of Directors by a narrow margin in June of 1997. While a new policy has been put into place, the debate uncovered a significant level of animosity among some social work educators and practitioners toward religious persons and institutions, especially those whose spirituality stems from a more conservative theology.

Why the Conflict Between Social Work and Christianity?

At one level, there seems to be a natural compatibility between Christianity and social work. Take the six core values and related ethical principles espoused in the newly revised NASW Code of Ethics, for example. Related to the value of **Service** is the following ethical principle, "Social workers primary goal is to help people in need and to address social problems." For Christians, this brings to mind the statement of Jesus, "Whoever wishes to be great among you must be your servant, and whoever wishes to be first among you must be your slave just as the Son of Man came not to be served but to serve, and to give his life a ransom for many" (Matt 20:26-28). The value of service appears to be highly esteemed in both social work and Christianity.

The second of the social work values is **Social Justice** with the ethical principle stated as follows, "Social workers challenge social injustice." Some theologians, such as Donahue (1977) argue that justice is the central theme in the Bible. The admonition of Micah 6:8 seems to fit quite nicely with the NASW principle. "He has told you, O mortal, what is good; and what does the LORD require of you but to do justice, and to love kindness, and to walk humbly with your God."

The third NASW value is **Dignity and Worth of the Person** and the fourth value is **Importance of Human Relationships**. The related ethical principles are that "Social workers respect the inherent dignity and worth of the person" and that "Social workers recognize the central importance of human relationships." Both of these principles appear to have striking Christian parallels. The most dominant symbol in Christianity, the cross, is a powerful reminder to Christians of God's unconditional love. The NASW commitment to social relationships seems compatible with Jesus' admonition to love your neighbor as yourself (Luke 10:27). Indeed, Christians are called to love one's enemies and to do good to those who hate them (Luke 6:27).

The fifth and sixth values are **Integrity** and **Competence** with the related ethical principles being "Social workers behave in a trustworthy manner" and "Social workers practice within their areas of competence and enhance their professional expertise." While the Bible does not speak to these issues directly, they would easily fit the Christian imperative to be holy (Ephesians 1:4) and to be above reproach (I Timothy 5:4).

In other words, at the principle level of the NASW Code of Ethics, there exists what appears to be an easy fit between social work and

Christianity. At this level, social work appears to be a natural profession for Christians who want to help.

Incompatible Christian Issues

While similarities can be demonstrated between Christianity and social work at the value and ethical level, there are many areas of difference, some of which result in significant tension. Some of these differences derive from Christian tradition and thought.

Spiritual Reductionism

One source of tension between social work and Christianity stems from a strain of thought I will call spiritual reductionism. Reductionism, according to Babbie (1995), is an overly strict limitation on the kinds of concepts and variables to be considered as causes in explaining a broad range of human behavior" (p. 93). Spiritual reductionism is rooted in the ancient Greek philosophy of gnosticism that embraced a dualistic view of the world. To oversimplify, the material world was seen as evil while the spiritual world was viewed as good. Gnostics believed they had secret knowledge which would lead people to return to the goodness found in the spiritual world.

In a similar way, contemporary Christian spiritual reductionism has a bifurcated view of existence. The material world, including the human body, is viewed as fallen, doomed, and temporary. The spiritual world, including the human soul, is eternal. Heaven and Hell are places where good and bad reign for eternity. The ultimate destiny of the soul depends on spiritual decisions made prior to death. Since the soul is viewed as eternal and the material world as temporary, saving a person's soul is the only action that really matters.

Spiritual reductionism can have a significant impact on how Christians conduct themselves. For example, shortly after I moved to a new house once, two representatives from a local church knocked on my door. Bluntly they asked, "Are you a born again Christian?" I was shocked by their directness and was speechless. I mumbled something and they went away. The only issue that concerned them was my spiritual welfare. I suspect I said yes and that seemed to be all they were concerned about.

This type of theology can also have a direct impact on social attitudes about social work. Dwight Moody and Billy Sunday, famous turn of the century evangelists for example, spoke out actively against social work arguing that it detracted from the more important work of saving souls (Loewenberg, 1988). Moberg (1977), in *The Great Reversal: Evan-*

gelism and Social Concern, examines the split between "fundamentalists" and "social gospelers" that took place between 1910 and 1930. He
describes in considerable detail the rejection of social welfare concerns
by fundamentalists who embraced a gnostic-like theology.

Christian spiritual reductionism can impact the practice of social
work as well. Food, clothing, or shelter, for example, may be used as a
means to an end. Material needs may be addressed only as a way to get
to the spiritual aspect of clients which is viewed as the more important
aspect. Christian spiritual reductionism can also result in a myopic assessment of problems. Placing a higher value on the spiritual dimension
than other aspects may result in the belief that if spiritual problems are
resolved, other problems will dissipate. It can also reduce intervention
strategies to those which address spiritual issues. Furthermore, Christian spiritual reductionism can result in a dependence on religious language when working with clients. Not only may the social worker rely
heavily on religious language when assessing problems, they may establish client use of religious language as a measure of success. Finally,
working in contexts which prohibit the use of religious language for
legal or other reasons, may lead to employment frustration for spiritual
reductionistic social workers because of their inability to deal with what
they consider to be the most important area of life.

Unbalanced Social Work Practice

A second tension between social work and Christianity stems from
an understanding of evangelism that has the potential to clash with the
profession's commitment to client self-determination. I received a letter
once from a Christian social worker who shared this dilemma:

> It is the dying person who seems content without "religion"
> that truly frustrates me. I fear for his/her death based on my
> own spiritual beliefs that death without Jesus Christ equals
> Hell. Yet, I continue to practice my commitment to not force
> discussion about his/her spiritual apathy in honor of my pro-
> fessional value: self-determination. So I ask the following ques-
> tion: How can I profess to be a Christian and practice ethical
> social work? (personal correspondence, 1996)

The more a person's theology emphasizes evangelism and Hell,
the more difficult it may be to remain committed to the social work
value of self-determination. If one believes "death without Jesus Christ
equals Hell," the most caring act one could engage in would be to lead
the person into a saving knowledge of Christ and into eternal life. The

more intense the conviction, the more extreme the measures may be to "save" people. Indeed, in its most extreme form, forcing someone to confess their sins is interpreted as a loving act even if causing pain is necessary. Sadly, some Christians have used beating, torture, drowning, and burning people to death in an effort to save their souls.

Religious Tyranny

A third source of tension between social work and Christianity results from a phenomenon I will call religious tyranny. Religious tyranny, like other types of tyranny, imposes one way of doing things on others. It ignores diverse perspectives and may even be threatened by them. Whether the social policies are unintentionally insensitive to diverse groups or intentionally controlling, the result is the same; a second class of citizenship results.

One form of religious tyranny stems from a belief that the United States is or should be a Christian nation. Elsen (1954) illustrates this conviction:

> Let us be honest. Our kind of democracy depends on religion. It depends on the Christian religion. Its ideas are Christian ideas. Its ideals are Christian ideals. Its goals are Christian goals. Allow Christian faith and practice to languish, and democracy as we know it begins to disintegrate. (p. 175)

Numerous American colonies in the eighteenth century in fact had laws that were deferential to Christianity including Connecticut, Delaware, Georgia, Maryland, Massachusetts, New Hampshire, New Jersey, North Carolina, Pennsylvania, South Carolina, and Vermont. The South Carolina constitution, for example, stated, "The Christian Protestant religion shall be deemed, and is hereby constituted and declared to be, the established religion of this State" (Gaustad, 1993, p. 171). Numerous colonies limited public offices to persons who would affirm Christianity. Pennsylvania, for example, required the following: "Each member [of the legislature], before he takes his seat, shall make and subscribe to the following declaration, viz: 'I do believe in one God, the creator and governor of the universe, the rewarder to the good and punisher of the wicked. And I do acknowledge the Scriptures of the Old and New Testament to be given by Divine inspiration'" (Gaustad, 1993, p. 170).

State sponsored religion was declared illegal for all of the entire nation in 1868 when the Fourteenth Amendment to the Constitution was adopted[3]. The Fourteenth Amendment required that states honor the Constitutional bill of rights including freedom of religion in the

First Amendment which states, "Congress shall make no law respecting an establishment of religion, or prohibiting the free exercise thereof" (Gaustad, 1993, p. 44).

Neither the First Amendment nor the Fourteenth Amendment, however, have eliminated the belief for some that Christianity should be the preferred religion and that laws and legislators need to be consistent with it. The most visible advocate in recent years is Pat Robertson, the president of the Christian Broadcast Network, who ran for president in 1992. He states in a recent book, "There is absolutely no way that government can operate successfully unless led by godly men and women operating under the laws of the God of Jacob" (Robertson, 1991, p. 227).

This issue is for some Christian social workers one of the most troubling dilemmas. The NASW Code of Ethics calls on social workers to be dually committed to clients and to the general welfare of society (e.g. NASW Code of Ethics, 1.01, 6.01). Consequently, if one believes that Christianity is the one true religion and that biblically supported lifestyles are necessary to achieve a healthy society, there is a sense of obligation to advocate for Christian ways of doing things. At the same time, the Code of Ethics calls for respect for diversity. These two standards result in a perplexing ethical dilemma for some.

It needs to be pointed out that this is not just a Christian dilemma. All social workers have a vision of what constitutes the general welfare of society. Each social worker must wrestle with the tension between the patterns which are consistent with this vision and ideas or practices that are at odds with it. This tension was illustrated most clearly to me at a seminar focused on religious fundamentalist families that I attended. A social worker convinced of the rightness of egalitarian family structure indicated she would never be able to work with a family that had a hierarchical structure. Her vision of what constitutes a healthy family system was at odds with a model that others embrace. Her dilemma was fundamentally the same as that faced by many Christians.

Oppressive Aspects of Social Work

There is, however, another side to the social work and Christianity tension that is less frequently acknowledged in the profession. The tension between social work and Christianity can also stem from an aspect or body of social work thought that is religiously oppressive and lacks commitment to religious diversity. Ironically, some social workers, in their attempt to pursue social justice for certain groups, condone prejudice and discrimination against certain religious groups with whom they disagree.

Social Work Secularism

Secularism is a way of thinking that denies or ignores the spiritual dimension of life and discredits the value and contribution of religion. While there is widespread agreement that social work has a religious foundation (Niebuhr, 1932; Marty, 1980; Goldstein, 1987; Loewenberg, 1988; Midgley, 1989; Keith-Lucas, 1989), it is also clear that social work was significantly influenced by the progressive mindset of the late nineteenth century which promoted a positivist worldview and devalued spirituality and religion. Empirical evidence and logic, the twin pillars of science, were embraced in the social sciences as superior ways of knowing.

Karl Marx, Emile Durkheim, and Sigmund Freud, key social scientists upon which social work theory relied during much of the twentieth century, all viewed religion with suspicion and doubt. Religion for Marx was oppressive, for Durkheim was a social construction, and for Freud a neurotic impulse. With respect to social work, friendly visiting was replaced with scientific charity, while religiously motivated compassion and caring gave way to social diagnosis.

Evidence for the secular influence in social work is provided by Cnaan and Wineburg (1997). In reviewing papers given at the CSWE Annual Program Meeting, they found that only 30 out of 1500 (2%) papers given at the CSWE Annual Program Meeting from 1990 - 1994 dealt with religion and service delivery, with only 2 papers addressing "contemporary concerns of religiously based social services" (p. 7). Their study found that, with few exceptions, the 20 most popular texts "made no mention of any congregational or sectarian aspect of social work with the exception of the obligatory Charity Organization Societies" (p. 8). Furthermore, their study found that only 10 of 50 social welfare syllabi reviewed mentioned religiously-affiliated social service provision.

Positive sentiments from social work pioneers about spirituality and religion have been largely expunged from historical accounts of social work. Seldom acknowledged, for example, is Jane Addam's view of the critical role of Christianity in the settlement house movement. Referring to Christian humanitarianism, she states, "Certain it is that spiritual force is found in the Settlement Movement, and it is also true that this force must be evolked and must be called into play before the success of any Settlement is assured" (Addams 1910: p.124, as quoted in Garland, 1994, p.81).

Likewise, little has been said about the positive attitude the renowned Mary Richmond had about the role of the church. She states:

After all has been said in objection to past and present methods of church charity, we must realize that, if the poor are to be effectively helped by charity, the inspiration must come from the church. The church has always been and will continue to be the chief source of charitable energy; and I believe that, to an increasing degree, the church will be the leader in charitable experiment and in the extension of the scope of charitable endeavor...The church has always been the pioneer in such work. (Richmond, 1899, p. 174-175)

Cnaan and Wineburg (1997) conclude that a "bias of omission" related to religiously-based social service provision exists in social work.

A second aspect of social work secularism is related to the broader church/state legal issue. While there has been no Supreme Court decision that has directly addressed the relationship of religion and social work, the profession has been influenced by the secular philosophy advanced by the Supreme Court in other arenas, the most significant of which have taken place in education. The dominant church/state philosophy endorsed by the Supreme Court in the twentieth century was first articulated by Justice Black in 1947 when he wrote, "The First Amendment has erected a wall between church and state. That wall must be high and impregnable" (Eastland, 1993, p. 67). This philosophy has resulted in Supreme Court decisions that have consistently ruled against religion in the public arena. Carter (1993), in a recent bestseller about politics and religion, concludes that the law has trivialized religion and needs to move towards a more accommodating stance.

Since the growth of the social work profession has been closely correlated with the growth of the welfare state, the "high and impregnable wall" philosophy suggested by Justice Black has had a significant impact on how religion was dealt with by social workers. Namely, religion in publically funded agencies has been treated as a phenomenon outside the purview of social work. In order to observe the "high wall" separation of church and state, religious issues, if acknowledged at all, were seen as best dealt with by religious representatives. While no study has been completed to document the impact of the "high wall" philosophy on social work, there is a wealth of anecdotal evidence from social workers in public agencies who report being strictly forbidden to address religious or spiritual issues, to use religious language, or to pray with clients even if it was in the client's best interest and desired by clients. While dealing with religious issues is surely a complicated professional matter, the principle strategy followed by the profession was to refuse to deal with them.

The secularization of social work practice has gone beyond social workers working in publicly funded agencies, however. Religious-free social work practice has been presented as the only responsible professional position. There have been individuals and organizations over the years who have explored and supported an accommodating philosophy of religion but with little public acknowledgment and presented only in obscure literature. Most notable among those addressing the relationship of Christianity and social work is the North American Association of Christians in Social Work (NACSW) which has been in existence since 1950 and has published the journal *Social Work and Christianity* since 1974. As for individual contributions, Alan Keith-Lucas was by far the most productive writer on the integration of faith and social work (Ressler, 1992). In general, however, little attention has been given to the relationship of religion and social work even in private agencies not constrained by the First Amendment.

Religi-phobia and Religious Discrimination

Religious prejudice and discrimination are reported with surprising frequency by religiously active social workers. While no study has been completed to evaluate the full extent of the problem, one small study (Ressler, 1997) found that 12 of 18 persons (67%) who placed themselves in the **Spiritual** and **Religious** category had experienced prejudice or discrimination within the profession. For example, the respondents reported the following:

> They act like you are a fanatic if your religion permeates your life...In a board meeting, I heard someone talking about "those born-again' folks in a derogatory manner. There have been times that born-again [persons] are accused of extreme behaviors and portrayed as lunatics, when in fact, the person may have had difficulty without born-again affiliation...My religious values, especially my personal interpretation of scripture concerning homosexuality, resulted in my being told by a supervisor that I shouldn't be a therapist because I couldn't be objective enough to work with gay and lesbian clients...A vivid memory occurred as an undergraduate when a professor jumped on me in the classroom for including Scripture in a paper. A peer was ridiculed in the classroom for her faith by another instructor...Mostly subtle beliefs that Christian values are somehow different than those of others and should never be expressed.

Religious discrimination has made inroads into some social work institutions which has resulted in screening out of students with certain religious belief systems. The social work faculty at St. Cloud State University, for instance, in 1992 developed a position paper entitled, "The S.C.S.U Social Work Department's Position on Attitudes Towards Gay and Lesbian People" (St. Cloud State University Department of Social Work, 1992). Referring to themselves as gatekeepers for the profession, the position statement attempted to outline what was expected of students related to gay and lesbian people. The initial paper stated, "The only legitimate position of the social work profession is to abhor the oppression that is perpetuated in gay and lesbian people and to act personally and professionally to end the degradation in its many forms...Many of our students come from religious backgrounds that do not accept homosexuality...It is not okay in this case to "love the sinner and hate the sin"...Students who have predetermined negative attitudes towards gay and lesbian people, and who are not open to exploring these values will not find this program very comfortable and should probably look elsewhere for a major" (p. 2).

The social work program also required that student applicants participate in an admission interview that "made a point of examining students' attitudes towards homosexuality" (Hibbard, 1994, p. 1). With the support of the Christian Legal Society, the American Jewish Congress, American Jewish Committee, the Center for Individual Rights, the Intercollegiate Studies Institute, and the Minnesota Civil Liberties Union, the statement and interview was challenged by some students. As a result, the statement was revised and reference to a student's religion was dropped. The interview has been replaced with an "admissions meeting in which students 'formally introduce' themselves to the department" (p. 1).

Social Work Tyranny

Hidden in the question about religious values being in conflict with social work values is an issue which the social work profession needs to address. Some social workers advocate a form of professional tyranny with the notion that there is one correct social work worldview and one set of values in social work that all must agree with. Social workers, they believe, who do not accept this worldview and agree with the popular application of social work values should be censured or even banished from the profession.

This argument was made by the University of Buffalo with respect to the CSWE non-discrimination statement on sexual orientation described earlier. The faculty at the University of Buffalo signed a petition that stated, "We, the faculty at the University of Buffalo, are disappointed and outraged at CSWE's proposal to exempt social work programs at religious institutions from nondiscrimination on the basis of sexual and political orientation...If these programs want to receive CSWE accreditation, they must be held to nondiscrimination policies" (State University of New York at Buffalo, School of Social Work, 1996).

Jones (Parr, 1996) in her argument against allowing religious institutions to be exempt from the sexual orientation non-discrimination standard suggested that programs that did not comply should, among other things, be "explicitly identified by CSWE in its listing of accredited programs" and "should be monitored with particular diligence and asked to demonstrate their efforts in these areas at an additional time midpoint between accreditation site visits" (p. 310). Her recommendation that there be public identification of those who are different and that there be close monitoring of their behavior are reminiscent of tactics advocated by oppressive dictators.

The tone in the NASW lesbian and gay issues policy has a similar exclusivist and intolerant tone. The policy statement reads, "NASW affirms its commitment to work toward full social and legal acceptance and recognition of lesbian and gay people. To this end, NASW shall support legislation, regulations, policies, judicial review, political action changes in social work policy statements, the NASW Code of Ethics, and any other means necessary to establish and protect the equal rights of all people without regard to sexual orientation" (p. 163). There is no recognition of diversity among groups and no room for variation. The position is dictatorial.

Where to From Here

The current tension between social work and Christianity, in other words, has both a Christian aspect and a social work aspect. Reducing the tension involves adjustments from both the Christian community and the social work community.

Christian Adjustments

First, Christians need to embrace a wholistic Christian understanding of creation that acknowledges the spiritual dimension of life but with a balanced view of the world, including the psychological, social, biological, economic, political, and environmental aspects. Christians who have a wholistic theology will likely find much in common with the person in environment framework which undergirds social work.

Second, it is important for Christian social workers to develop a theology of evangelism that does not abandon self-determination. Most Christian theologies view self-determination as a basic human right and one that God has afforded to each of us. If, as most Christians believe, God provided humans with the ability and responsibility to choose, including the freedom to make bad decisions, surely Christian social workers need to allow clients to make their own choices. Self-determination is a sound Christian principle even for evangelicals, as well as a central social work value.

The self-determination dilemma may also involve a mistaken assumption about what self-determination in social work means. Self-determination does not mean that a social worker does not confront and cause discomfort when working with clients. Self-determination means, that first, you do what you do with the awareness and consent of the client, and second, that you respect the right of clients to make their own decisions.

Third, Christian social workers will need to develop a confident understanding of their own role and the contribution of Christianity in society while remaining committed to diversity, even if laws and individual behavior do not fully support a Christian sense of morality. This begins with a Christian humility that holds we "see through a glass darkly" and that "all have sinned and fallen short of the glory of God." It further acknowledges that God permits humans to live in ways that violate His intended plans. Finally, the temptation to impose Christian values can be reduced by interpreting the Christian role as one of salt and light rather than conquerors.

Having said this, Christians need to be afforded the right of others to participate in public conversation about what constitutes the general welfare and to be involved in the political process.

Social Work Adjustments

There are adjustments the social work profession can make as well to reduce the tension. This involves, first of all, adopting positions on social issues which are inclusive rather than exclusive. Interestingly, on the abortion and euthanasia issues, the social work profession has made a conscious effort to respect and accommodate diverse values. For example, on the abortion issue the 1996 NASW position statement relates that, "In acknowledging and affirming social work's commitment to respecting diverse value systems in a pluralistic society, it is recognized that the issue of abortion is controversial because it reflects the different value systems of different groups. If the social worker chooses not to participate in abortion counseling, it is his or her responsibility to provide appropriate referral services to ensure that this option is available to clients" (NASW, 1994, p. 3). For the individual, diversity is acknowledged and honored. With respect to social policy, the position is moderate. "In states where abortion services are not available as one option, those members of NASW who so desire may work toward legalization, planning, funding, and implementation of such services" (p. 3).

With respect to the euthanasia position, the NASW policy states, "In acknowledging and affirming social work's commitment to respecting diverse value systems in a pluralistic society, end of life issues are recognized as controversial because they reflect the varied value systems of different groups. Social workers should be free to participate or not participate in assisted-suicide or other discussion concerning end of life decisions depending on their own beliefs, attitudes, and value systems" (p. 59). Social worker diversity is respected individually. With respect to social policy, the position is conservative. "It is inappropriate for social workers to deliver, supply, or personally participate in commission of an act of assisted suicide when acting in a professional role" (p. 60).

Furthermore, if the profession is going to respect religious beliefs, then it will have to allow for diversity among institutions. This is the position that the Commission on Higher Education has taken. In a recent publication they state, "The Commission respects and honors the diversity of institutions it accredits and recognizes institutional limits created by law, government, or religious tenets. It does not find the diversity of its member institutions incompatible with the principles of equity and diversity within those institutions" (Commission on Higher Education, April 1996, p. 1).

Toward a Common Agenda

The fact that there are differences between Christianity and social work should not be a surprise to either Christians or social workers. For Christians, the very nature of the created world assumes differences between people and groups by extension. The belief in sin and redemption, the Kingdom of God and the Kingdom of this world presumes differences between the Christian and non-Christian. Likewise, the social work profession supports the notion of differences through its concept of diversity. Differences are to be expected.

Furthermore, neither Christians nor social workers should be surprised that some differences result in tension. Jesus warned His disciplines many times of the likelihood of conflict (e.g. John 15:18-19).

Likewise, the NASW Code of Ethics acknowledges the reality of tension between social workers with different points of view. The Purpose of the NASW Code of Ethics includes this statement, "Reasonable differences of opinion can and do exist among social workers with respect to the ways in which values, ethical principles, and ethical standards should be rank ordered when they conflict."

The reality of tension does not need to lead to destructive interaction, however. Christians are called to live at peace with everyone as much as is possible (Romans 12:18) and to pray for leaders so that "we may live peaceful and quiet lives in all godliness and holiness" (I Timothy 2:1-2). The social work profession, for its part, has a section in the NASW Code of Ethics that requires responsible handling of conflict between colleagues (2.03, 2.04).

Tensions exist in part because the differences reflect differing values. Tensions also reflect the fact that not all things are of equal worth and policies and actions make a difference in the lives of people in society. Tensions exist over differences because things matter. The goal, therefore, is not to eliminate all differences since this is impossible. The goal is not even to eliminate all tension since this, too, is not possible. The goal is to reduce the tension as much as possible and to avoid oppressive behavior while making room for as much freedom as possible.

Reducing tension requires differing parties respect each other and engage in dialogue about the differences we see and the tensions we feel. It is particularly critical to listen to those who see injustice and feel oppressed. Listening, it needs to be pointed out, does not mean one agrees nor does it necessarily resolve the tensions. It does, however, provide information which may lead to wiser, healthier, and more empathic decisions.

Christians must insist on their right to live according to their faith but they must extend the same right to others. The goal is to find solutions which make room for as many as possible. This can only happen when people with differences learn to work together to find solutions. Resolving conflict in a way that brings people together is a great challenge of life. How can we be one and yet many? How can we find unity in our diversity? These are not simple questions and there are no simple answers. It seems that social workers and Christians ought to be among those best able to model constructive conflict management. Trying will surely get us closer to living in peace than not trying.

Notes

[1] Since philosophically, all people are viewed as spiritual much like they are sociological and psychological, the term disspirited is used rather than non-spiritual. The fact that a person has no meaning in life or feels unconnected does not mean they are non-spiritual. It rather indicates a negative spirituality.

[2] It should be noted that the concern of faith-based programs tends not to be sexual orientation but sexual behavior. The policies include heterosexual behavior outside of marriage as well as homosexual and bi-sexuality.

[3] There is a debate among Constitutional scholars as to whether the First Amendment prohibits favoring religion in general or one particular state favored religion. The majority on the Supreme Courts since 1947 have favored the religion in general point of view. There has been a minority point of view that argues the intent of the First Amendment was to prohibit one state authorized religion.

References

Babbie, E. (1995). *The practice of social research.* Belmont, CA: Wadsworth.

Baergen, R. (1981). *The Mennonite story.* Newton, KS: Faith and Life Press.

Bracht, T. (1837). *Martyrs' Mirror.* Lancaster, PA: D. Miller.

Bullis, R. K. (1996). *Spirituality in social work practice.* Washington, D. C.; London: Taylor & Frances.

Canda, E. (1989). Response: Religion and social work: It's not that simple. *Social Casework, 70,* 572-574.

Carter, S. (1993). *The culture of disbelief: How American law and politics trivialize religious devotion.* NY: Basic Books.

Clark, J. (1994). Should social work address religious issues? No! *Journal of Social Work Education, 30*(1), 13-15.

Cnaan, R. &., Wineburg. (1997, March 7). Social work and the role of the religious community. Council on Social Work Education. Chicago.

Commission on Higher Education. (April 1996). *Statement concerning the application of equity and diversity principles in the accreditation process.* 3624 Market Street, Philadelphia, PA 19104: Middle States Association of Colleges and Schools.

CSWE Commission on Accreditation, J. N., Chair. (1996, January 22). [Proposed Changes in Accreditation Standards] (Memorandum to Deans and Directors). 1600 Duke Street, Alexandria, VA 22314.

CSWE Commission on Accreditation, J. N., Chair. (1997, February 20). [Proposed Revision to Standard 3.0] (Memorandum to Deans and Directors of Schools of Social Work). 1600 Duke Street, Alexandria, VA 22314.

Donahue, J. (1977). Biblical perspectives on justice. In John Haughty (Ed.), *The faith that does justice,* 68-112.

Eastland, T. (1993). *Religious liberty in the supreme court: The cases that define the debate over church and state.* Washington, DC: Ethics and Public Policy Center.

Elsen, E. (1954). *America's spiritual recovery.* Westwood, NJ: Fleming H. Revell.

Garland, D. (1994). *Church agencies: Caring for children and families in crisis.* Washington, D.C.: Child Welfare League of America.

Gaustad, E. (1993). *Neither king nor prelate: Religion and the new world 1776-1826.* Grand Rapids, MI: Eerdmans.

Goldstein, H. (1987). The neglected moral link in social work practice. *Social Work, 32*(3), 181-186.

Hibbard, J. A., Jungman. (1994). St. Cloud Drops "Attitude" Screening. *The Minnesota Scholar.*

Joseph, M. (1988). Religion and social work practice. *Social Casework, 69*(7), 443-452.

Keith-Lucas, A. (1989). Southern comfort. *Social Services Insight, 4*(8), 1-5.

Keith-Lucas, A. (1958). Readers comments. *Social Casework,* 236-238.

Loewenberg, F. M. (1988). *Religion and social work practice in contemporary American society.* New York: Columbia University Press.

Marshall, J. (1991). The spiritual dimension in social work education. *Spirituality and social work communicator, 2*(1), 12-15.

Marty, M. E. (1980). Social service: Godly and godless. *Social Service Review, 54*(4).

Midgley, J., Sanzenbach. (1989). Social work, religion and the global challenge of fundamentalism. *International Social Work, 32*(4), 273-287.

Moberg, D. (1977). *The great reversal: Evangelism and social concern.* NY: Holman.

NASW. (1994). *NASW Speaks: NASW Policy Statements.* Silver Spring, MD: Author.

Niebuhr, R. 1. (1932). *The contribution of religion to social work.* New York: Pub. for the New York School of Social Work by Columbia University Press.

Parr, R. &., Jones. (1996). Should CSWE allow social work programs in religious institutions an exemption from the accreditation nondiscrimination standard related to sexual orientation. *Journal on Social Work Education, 32*(3), 297-313.

Ressler, L. (1992). Theologically enriched social work: Alan Keith-Lucas's approach to social work and religion. *Spirituality and Social Work Journal, 3*(2), 14-20.

Ressler, L. (1997). Spirituality and religion [A survey of 90 MSW students]. Roberts Wesleyan College.

Richmond, M. (1899). *Friendly visiting among the poor.* Montclair, NJ: Patterson Smith.

Robertson, P. (1991). *The new world order.* Dallas: Word.

Sheridan, M., Bullis. (1992). Practitioners' personal and professional attitudes and behaviors toward religion and spirituality: Issues for education and practice. *Journal of Social Work Education, 28*(2), 190-203.

St. Cloud State University Department of Social Work. (1992, April 29). [The S.C.S.U. Social Work Department's Position on Attitudes Towards Gay and Lesbian People]. St. Cloud, MN.

State University of New York at Buffalo School of Social Work. (1996, February 17, 1996). Petition to the CSWE Board of Directors distributed publically at the Council on Social Work Education Annual Program Meeting. Washington D.C.

CHAPTER 12

INCORPORATING RELIGIOUS ISSUES IN THE ASSESSMENT PROCESS WITH INDIVIDUALS AND FAMILIES

Mary P. Van Hook

Understanding how people interpret events in their lives and the world around them is essential in social work practice with individuals, families, and community groups. The implicit and explicit beliefs of the family and the wider group help shape these interpretations. Religious beliefs and practices influence these interpretations for many individuals, families, and community groups. As a result, understanding how religion shapes people's experiences can be important in social work practice. Including religious issues in the assessment process can also guide the social worker in developing appropriate interventions. The role of religion can be especially salient when people are wrestling with crises and critical junctures in their lives (for example, Loewenberg, 1988; Joseph, 1988; Carlson & Cervera, 1991; Austin & Lennings, 1993; Mailick, Holder & Waltaher, 1994). These events are frequently occasions that prompt people to seek social work help. Such occasions can also be times in which important value choices and issues of meaning are involved. Ignoring religious issues can risk overlooking potential resources and strains in the lives of some client systems. This chapter uses a variety of theoretical approaches to demonstrate how incorporating religious issues in the assessment process can help social workers better understand client systems and develop more effective interventions.

Religion in this chapter refers to "the institutionally patterned system of beliefs, values, and rituals" (Canda, p. 573, 1988). It has both a belief and an organizational participation dimension. A religious person is one who "belongs to a faith group, accepts the beliefs, values, and doctrines of that group, and participates in the required activities and rituals of the chosen group" (Loewenberg, p. 33, 1988). Since people are influenced by family and cultural traditions, the impact of religion can emerge through acceptance of or struggling with aspects of the religious element in these traditions. Religion is a multi-faceted phenomena including beliefs, interpersonal relationships at the family and community level, rituals, and social organizations. As a result, it is helpful to draw upon a variety of theoretical perspectives in analyzing the impact of religion on the lives of people. While this chapter discusses a variety of theoretical approaches to understand religious issues, some aspects will emerge as more important than others in working with a specific client system. It would not be realistic or even necessary for social workers to incorporate all these dimensions in their ongoing assessment of a specific client system or situation. The chapter suggests possible ways to elicit this information as part of the ongoing assessment process, and the nature of information that might be relevant to specific theoretical frameworks or situations. In view of space limitations, this chapter will emphasize individuals and families and will discuss communities and organizations only as they shape them. The case illustrations used demonstrate how incorporating religion from at least one of a variety of theoretical perspectives can be useful in the assessment process and can guide in the development of effective interventions.

Although the emphasis in this chapter is on the assessment of the client system, there is growing recognition that the nature of the relationship between the social worker and the client system is influenced by the characteristics of both the client system and the worker. This interaction process suggests that a religious self-assessment by the social worker can also be important in the assessment and intervention process. Social workers bring to the helping relationship beliefs and practices that influence how they perceive problem situations and possible solutions.

Religious Beliefs

Since it is impossible to do justice to the vast diversity of the world's religions, the following discussion will be limited to the major monotheistic religions of Christianity, Islam, and Judaism. These groups share a core belief in a divine being with an existence separate from human beings with the possibility of a personal relationship between human beings and the divine. As a result, they must answer questions involving how the divine relates to human beings and the world as a whole, and how human beings in turn should relate to the divine and each other. Clients might not be immediately aware of the nature of these underlying beliefs, but this awareness may emerge in the course of exploration regarding the meaning attached to behaviors and more readily recognized beliefs (Miller, 1988). While social workers do not necessarily need complete information about the religious beliefs of their clients, asking clients if they have any religious beliefs that might relate to the presenting problems can both provide useful information and let the client know that these beliefs have a legitimate place in social work efforts with them. The following represent some major themes that might be present in these religious traditions.

"His eye is on the sparrow": This phrase from the Gospel song reflects the belief that God is intimately involved in everything that happens in life. Beliefs about the involvement of God range from this intimate involvement to only remote involvement in major events. Questions of good and evil, free will versus determinism or fatalism, and the intentions of God are raised by these beliefs. These beliefs become especially salient, perhaps comforting or troubling, as people must deal with tragedy in their lives (Kushner, 1981; Smedes 1982). Why did God allow my child to die or my husband to leave me? Why did God allow me to get AIDS? How can I trust a God who would allow this terrible thing to happen to me? Can I gain comfort from believing that nothing happens by chance, that there is a purpose in everything? Is God punishing me for something I did? Is God here for me as I walk through this valley of despair?

Exploring with clients their beliefs in this area can reveal sources of comfort as well as alienation from God and from organized religion. People might be reluctant to voice their anger, doubts, and sense of alienation to other people out of fear that family members and their support system within the church and the community will condemn them for these thoughts and emotions. The experience of raising these issues with someone who can listen without judgment and understands the pain can be an important first step in the healing process. It can also provide an occasion to explore with clients the possibility that there might be other people in their lives who could also understand and accept their views.

God as love/as judgment: Religious traditions vary in terms of whether they view God as relating to people primarily on the basis of judgment against sinful people and a sinful world, or on the basis of love and grace. For members of traditions focused on judgment, feelings of self-worth can be viewed as suspect at best. On the other hand, feeling loved as a "child of God" can be a great source of comfort and self-worth to people. God's love can also be viewed as a gift of grace or something to be earned through specific works and sacrifices. When God's love is linked to works and sacrifice, people may worry that they have not done enough. Yet accepting love as a gift of grace can be difficult for many people even when official religious beliefs affirm this position (Smedes, 1982; Tournier, 1962; Phillips, 1963). Exploring what is the basis of legitimate self-worth within the client's religious tradition can be particularly helpful in working with clients experiencing low self-worth. This exploration can be useful not only with people who are currently religious, but also with those who as adults rejected the reli-

gion of their childhood and their family, because they may still be struggling with deeply entrenched views in this area.

Human nature as good/evil: Human nature can be considered to be
primarily sinful, neutral, or good. Although viewing human beings as
evil has been considered antithetical to the social work belief that people
are capable of good and positive changes (Sanzenbach, 1989;
Loewenberg, 1988), this can sometimes be a false dichotomy. Even religious traditions that view human nature as essentially sinful can allow
for positive change through divine redemption and grace (Smedes, 1982).
Understanding and respecting the client's sense of dependence on God
for this change can be important.

God of dialogue/God of answers: The divine can be viewed as welcoming dialogue with human beings or requiring their unquestioning
acceptance. Tevye in "The Fiddler on the Roof" asks God why he could
not have made him a rich man instead of a poor man. Tevye is comfortable with being in an ongoing and sometimes complaining dialogue
with God. For some people, questioning God for letting a child die or a
factory close would be very difficult. Feelings of anger toward God for
these events would create guilt or perhaps fear of retribution. While it
may be useful to indicate to such people that sometimes even devoutly
religious people feel angry with God, the social worker must also understand their reluctance to acknowledge these feelings personally because of their fear that doing so might come at a very high price.

Basis/Context for Religious Beliefs

In addition to specific beliefs, religious groups also vary in terms of
the legitimate basis for their religious beliefs. For some groups, the legitimate basis for religious beliefs can be limited to a literal interpretation of
the sacred text, while for others it can include tradition. These later groups
adopt a less literal view of interpretation and/or are willing to include the
insights of science, history, and culture. Understanding this perspective
enables the social worker to identify the types of information that clients
and their reference groups would consider valid. A strongly fundamentalist
Christian, for example, would not be swayed by social science or cultural
information in terms of the scriptural passages regarding sex roles that con-
tradicted their interpretation of the Bible.

Organizational context of beliefs: Although membership in a specific religious denomination plays a less important role in defining be-

liefs of individuals than it did previously, understanding the belief system of specific groups can give some insight into potential sources of pain or support on particular issues. This is particularly true if the group holds highly specific views on an issue (Loewenberg, 1988). As an example, Mark returned home to his parents in the terminal stages of AIDS. His parents belonged to a conservative church that viewed homosexuality as a grievous sin and AIDS as God's punishment for those who have sinned. Understanding the strain experienced by his parents who were caught between their love for their son and the tenets of their church and religious support system can be important in responding to the pain experienced by Mark and his family.

Families living in rural areas can experience a compounding of stigma (McGinn, 1996). Mrs. James, a Roman Catholic woman, sought counseling for depression following the birth of a baby born blind. For years she had been dreading God's punishment for her earlier divorce and marriage outside the church. When her baby was born, she was convinced that this was God's punishment on her. Fortunately a referral to understanding Roman Catholic sisters and a priest helped her recognize that the church did not teach that God would punish her baby in this way.

In working with grieving families facing a death in the family, understanding how their religious group views life after death can identify potential sources of support or additional grief. Families who are Baptist or Jehovah's Witness, for example, are likely to derive very different types of comfort from their religious beliefs in dealing with the death of a child from Sudden Infant Death Syndrome.

Social Support: The social support systems of individuals and family members can be an important resource as they seek to cope with a variety of stressful life events. As a result, understanding potential sources of support and possible barriers to using these sources can be extremely important in the process of helping people cope. Social support in this context includes both emotional and material support. Religion can play an important role in the social support system of clients. Religion can influence this support basis through the nature of the resources available—a caring church congregation or specific programs offered by religious groups. The nature of these supportive networks can also be influenced by the ethnic traditions of the individuals involved. As indicated in a subsequent discussion in this chapter regarding racial/ethnic groups, African Americans have a strong tradition of interdependence in which the church plays a central role (Hines & Boyd-Franklin, 1982).

In addition to understanding basic group traditions regarding the role of the church community, it can also be important to identify how the nature of the problem might effect potential sources of help within the church. Religious groups vary in terms of their attitudes toward specific life difficulties and the type of help that is viewed as appropriate. Typically problems relating to a death or illness in the family are likely to evoke sympathy and support. Yet if the illness is due to AIDS acquired through a homosexual relationship, attitudes of judgment regarding the illness may diminish either actual support or people's willingness to seek help due to fear of judgment (McGinn, 1996). Attitudes toward divorce, alcoholism, and mental health problems can influence either actual available support or the client's perceptions about seeking such help. A recent study of economically distressed farm families revealed a mixed picture regarding available support from the church. The attitudes of church members and the economically hurting family members toward this extremely complex problem made it difficult for some people to seek or receive the help they needed (Van Hook, 1990). Use of an eco-map that identifies potential sources of support and strains can be useful in eliciting information from clients about the role of the church in this regard.

Personality Theories

Several important personality theories can help social workers understand the interplay between religion and the experiences of clients. An understanding of this interplay can help the social worker develop effective helping approaches. This section discusses how aspects of cognitive-behavioral and psychodynamic/ego psychology can be used in this regard.

Cognitive behavioral: According to contemporary cognitive-behavioral theory, our beliefs influence our behavior, our emotions, and our thoughts. Religious beliefs can influence the core beliefs that are especially influential in this process. Helping based on this theory uses a collaborative partnership between the client and the social worker to identify the nature of these beliefs and to test out their accuracy. The process begins with a series of questions asked of and with the client. These questions are designed to identify how the client views the world. These might include questions such as, "What do you think would happen if you told your parents that you want to switch to social work as a major?" The client and worker also engage in a process of testing these beliefs by a series of further questions or activities. The client, for example, might tell her or his parents about the switch to a social work major and the reasons for doing so to test out what really will be the parents' reaction.

Miller (1988) describes the use of this approach with a male seminary student with a strong sense of duty who was suffering from depression. His initial attempt was to help the man through progressive relaxation of the muscles of this body and scheduling of pleasant activities. This approach was unsuccessful because it did not fit with the client's sense of purpose in life. Miller then used a common approach in cognitive treatment. A person is asked to keep a record of when a certain problem arises, the situations in which the problem occurs, and the person's reaction to these events. The student was asked to record the situations in which he felt depressed, his self-statements in these situations, and his resulting emotions. Several crucial themes emerged. Three potentially healing religious themes surfaced in this process: "Even servants have to be restored" (in response to his relentless driving of himself), "Grace" (a message he wished to communicate to others but did not fit with his own driving perfectionism), and "Focus on others" (which was impeded by his worry about himself). The social worker used this understanding to develop a more effective helping strategy with John. John began to experiment with replacing his driven perfectionism with alternative self-statements that were consistent with important elements of his core religious belief system. "1. — Even Jesus took time to rest and recharge, 2. — If I want to serve, I also need to take care of myself, 3. — God, through Jesus Christ, accepts me as I am, 4. — Don't worry about how people are evaluating me. Focus on their needs instead. And 5. — I have good news to share." Within this context John was able to use the techniques of relaxation and scheduling of pleasant events because these efforts were compatible with efforts to change the way he was thinking — a process called "cognitive-restructuring" (Miller, 1988).

Cognitive-behavioral strategies like these can also help clients identify other issues that might be camouflaged by religious thoughts and interpretations of events. Sue's parents, for example, contacted their pastor because their daughter Sue felt that she was demon possessed. The pastor assured the family that God would not let this happen to one of His children and suggested they contact a mental health program. Sue, age 13, was able to identify the thoughts, emotions, and bodily sensations that she associated with being demon possessed. The social worker asked her to keep a log identifying the situations in which she had the sensations that made her feel that she was demon possessed. The following week she returned for counseling pleased that she had discovered the nature of the problem. She experienced it when she was lonely and afraid the other children in her new community would not want to be her friends. She and her family had recently moved to the community and she was experiencing the anxiety of trying to make friends in her new school and community. Her insight clearly established the direction for counseling and gave her a very different view of herself and her problem.

Psychodynamic/ego psychology: One important aspect of psycho-dynamic/ego psychology is the theory of object relations. According to object relations theory, people gradually identify a sense of self separate from the world around them. A child, for example, quite early on becomes clear that there is a "me" that is separate from others. In the course of this process, children internalize a series of mental images (objects) of the people who are important to them. These internalizations are subjective and reflect how the child has experienced these other people. These subjective interpretations in turn influence how children view themselves as well as experience the world around them and subsequent relationships with other people. A child who has experienced parents and other caretakers as loving and meeting his needs is likely to view himself as lovable and to trust that other people will also be loving and trustworthy. On the other hand, a child who has experienced abuse is likely to distrust that other people will love her or meet her needs appropriately.

From an object relations perspective, the concept of God is not an illusion. Instead it represents an important reality. Part of being human is our capacity to create nonvisible realities (Rizzuto, 1979). The concept of God develops very early in a child's psychological development in the context of the child's developing a sense of separation from nurturing parents (Fuller, 1988). Although God is often called the "Heavenly Father," a child's concept of God represents more than just an internalization of the father. It involves a combination or gestalt of many powerful factors: the characteristics of the mother and the father, the dynamics of the twofold need to merge with a higher power and yet at the same time to experience oneself as autonomous, and the general social, historical, and religious background of the family (Fuller, 1988). As a result, children develop an image of God that reflects their own experiences with significant individuals and their own developmental needs. Belief in a powerful God can serve as an important transition object as children develop a growing sense of separation from their parents (Fuller, 1988). The internalization of an all powerful and all knowing God with the power to judge based on parental relationships can be a source of considerable distress if it is based on rejecting parental experiences and a source of comfort when based on trusting or caring relationships with these individuals.

Because these internalized views (objects) of other people color a person's relationships with others and their view of themselves, understanding the client's early and basic view regarding God and the impact of this perspective on their lives can be important. Questions about one's experiences with parents as well as about how one views God can provide important clues in this area. Joyce illustrates how early family relationships combined with the belief system of the group profoundly shaped her view of God, herself, and others. She was a member of a strongly religious group that stressed God's judgment and the sinfulness of human beings. Yet most members of this group manage to live relatively satisfying lives. In contrast, she lived a life preoccupied with fear of the rejection of others and of God. She was convinced that she was completely unlovable and totally undeserving of any happiness. Exploration of her life revealed that her image of God was shaped in part by a realistically very frightening relationship with her father. Her father, who has been in a nursing home for several years, had suffered severely during World War II and later immigrated to the United States. After his move to the United States and while the children were growing up, he frequently had paranoid delusions in which Joyce and another sibling were Nazi soldiers. He would then try to attack them and her mother would have to hide them from their father. As a result of these events and their rural setting, the family was generally isolated from other families so there were few other adults to serve as benign and protective role models that might create a balance in her life. By the time she entered school she was so traumatized that she withdrew from others and experienced herself as the object of ridicule. For Joyce, her early experience of terror and rejection by her father and her mother's inability to protect her from the emotional trauma created a strong introject of a powerful and rejecting God. At an intellectual and beliefs systems level her perspective was further reinforced by the doctrines of her religious group, but her early life experiences set the stage for her sense of fear. She needed a helping relationship that demonstrated that she was a person deserving of concern, and to help her with her difficulty in trusting others.

Family Issues

The family plays a primary role in the formation of religious beliefs. These beliefs are further shaped by relationships within the family and family events. Family rituals in turn reinforce these religious beliefs and practices. As a result of the key role of the family, understanding the interaction between family and religious issues can be especially fruitful (Dudley & Dudley, 1986; Friedman, 1985; Cornwall, 1987; Joseph, 1988; Loewenberg, 1988; Raider, 1992). This section examines families in terms of life-cycle issues, rituals, and family patterns and rules.

Families can be understood in terms of the development of the family over time — the life-cycle of the family. This process in turn is influenced by the developmental process of individual family members. As children enter adolescence, it becomes important for them to establish their own sense of identity. While the family is important in this sense of identity, adolescents frequently need to distance themselves from their parents in various ways. Some adolescents do so by distancing themselves from their parent's religious beliefs, practices, and rituals. This process can be the source of considerable tension within the family.

Families also face important transitions in the life-cycle of the family. Transitions that involve the breaking of old bonds and identities and the establishment of new ones are frequently marked by rituals, including religious ones (Friedman, 1985). Baptism in the Christian tradition and circumcision (*bris*) in the Jewish tradition represent the entry of a child into the religious community, and the assumption by parents of the responsibilities of raising the child in the religious traditions. Confirmations, Bar Mitzvahs, and other religious rites symbolize growth and approaching adulthood and the personal adoption of an identity within religious groups. Weddings mark the establishment of new commitments and boundaries with the accompanying need to create a new family structure. Religious rituals surrounding death help family members relinquish the lost family members and bind remaining family members together. The inability to carry out these rituals, on the other hand, can be the source of great distress (Harari & Wolowelsky, 1995; Friedman, 1985). Asking family members about the nature of pertinent rituals and how family members experienced these rituals can open the door to important information in this area.

Examining how individuals maintain and experience religious and other family rituals can provide clues to the nature of relationships within the family system, but also the extent to which family members are tied to their religious traditions. Harari and Wolowelsky (1995) describe how exploring changes in family observance of religious rituals following a death in the family can be an entrée into possible changes in family roles generally. This can be the opportunity to identify, for example, who are the individuals that others turn to in difficult times, and shifts in power within the family due to illness or the response to a death.

It is always important to explore what these family religious rituals mean to family members. Clients can be asked what these rituals mean to them, how they experienced them, and how they felt participating (or not participating) in them. These rituals convey messages of belonging or alienation. They can be sources of healing or further occasions to evoke the memory of an aching void or the pain of disrupted relationships. Exploring which family members are included or excluded from important family rituals also provides valuable information about family coalitions, cohesion or disengagement in the family, reasons for cutoffs in families, and family communication patterns.

Because family religious rituals frequently are invested with great meaning, failure to carry out previously treasured rituals or the institution of new rituals can be a source of considerable tension within an extended family. For immigrants, especially the elderly, difficulties in carrying out the religious rituals that were important in their home country can be a source of distress. Tensions can also be present if younger family members become acculturated and subsequently devalue these rituals. The Li family who came to the United States as refugees following the Vietnam war illustrate these tensions. They were later joined by her parents and extended family. When Mrs. Li became pregnant the extended family wanted her to carry out a religious ceremonial ritual that members of their traditional group viewed as an essential protection for a baby during pregnancy. While this ritual continued to be vitally important to Mrs. Li's parents and other relatives, Mr. and Mrs. Li had changed their religious beliefs and refused to carry it out because they felt it was not necessary, and doing so would violate their new religious beliefs. The extended family became frantic, fearing that the baby would be born deformed and were very angry with the Li's for their actions. Although the baby was born without any birth defects, this event contributed to lasting tensions within the family system.

Social workers also need to be alert to ways that religious rituals can be used to control other family members. Religious rituals are one of the ways family members use to enforce family patterns and rules on other members. One way this can be done is by excluding family members from important family rituals, for example, a Bar Mitzvah or Christening, if family members are viewed as straying from family beliefs or practices.

The K family illustrates how the religious ritual of prayer can be used in a coercive manner. Mrs. K and her husband had agreed to an amicable divorce but her parents were furious with her because of this action. Mrs. K was eager to explain to her parents the reasons for her action and to find some way to maintain a relationship with her parents. As a result, a meeting was arranged between Mrs. K, her parents, the minister (who was supportive of Mrs. K's decision) and the social worker. Mrs. K's parents continued to be adamant in terms of their disapproval of her actions with her mother indicating she would rather have Mrs. K dead than divorced. With no resolution of the issue, her mother indicated at the end of the meeting that she wanted to have a closing prayer and launched upon one designed to make Mrs. K feel guilty of letting both her parents and God down. Fortunately the pastor was sensitive to this issue and offered a second prayer that spoke of forgiveness and reconciliation.

Families not only generate a sense of identity but also loyalty to the family group and members. Contextual family therapy points out the power of these family legacies or loyalty and obligations from one generation to the next (Broszormenyi-Nagy, 1986). As a result, individuals feel obligated to believe or act in a certain way in response to these family legacies. Family loyalty issues can emerge in powerful and sometimes painful ways in family groups. These issues frequently come to the fore as people begin to establish their own way of understanding the world ("worldviews" — including religious beliefs) appropriate to their own family and personal existence. In his book *Blood of the Lamb*, novelist Peter DeVries (1960) tells a poignant story of a man whose beloved daughter dies of cancer. As an adult he had rejected the religious beliefs of his childhood and family and raised his daughter as an atheist. After her death he again becomes attracted to a religious faith. Now he cannot accept this faith out of a sense of loyalty and obligation to his dead child. He cannot accept a faith that he denied her. Clients who have rejected the religious beliefs of their family members may struggle with a sense of betrayal to their family tradition.

Individuals change and establish their own identities in the history of families. This process can also create the risk of alienation from the family. Religious issues have been the source of intense emotional cutoffs in families whereby family members either totally or partially eliminate contact with another family member. If the client is aware of previous cutoffs in the family history due to religious intermarriage or departures from the family's religious beliefs and practices, they too may fear abandonment by family members.

Genograms are an effective way to identify religious themes within families (Raider, 1992). A genogram is a visual map of the family as it exists through several generations. It can reveal intergenerational expectations within families. A genogram, for example, that reveals a long line of family members who served the church in various ways can suggest unfulfilled expectations and issues of betrayal on the part of a person who has left the family church and religion. In contrast, as one minister's wife said after doing a genogram, "I realize I had to either become a minister or marry one." For her, the genogram confirmed a pattern that was consonant with her current life choices. The impact, however, would be quite different for an individual who had left the church or was struggling with the religious tradition of the family. Genograms also reveal cutoffs within families due to religious reasons. Use of a genogram can not only help identify and objectify family patterns but also be an occasion to examine how similar or different a client's current situation is from past events in the family.

Ethnicity

Studies of ethnicity reveal the important role of religious beliefs, practices, and organizations in the lives of many groups. These beliefs shape expectations regarding relationships among family members, ways that events are experienced, and the nature of acceptable resources. The growing body of literature regarding ethnicity reveals how important religion is in shaping the lives of members of these groups. The following represent several religious themes which are present in the ethnic traditions of client systems. In this context, it is important to remember that such themes run the risk of becoming stereotypes, and social workers always need to explore the perspectives and experiences of specific individuals and families (Caple, Salcio, & Cecco, 1996; Yellow Bird, Fong, Galindo, Nowicki & Freeman, 1995; McGolderick & Giordano, 1996).

Confucian ideas and beliefs about filial piety and sense of respect for elderly persons have strongly influenced Chinese, Japanese, and Koreans (Browne & Broderick, 1996). As a result, it is especially important to demonstrate respect for family members of authority and not to expect family members to provide information that would be demeaning to other family members in the assessment process. To do so would be to ask family members to bring shame to the family (Shon, 1982).

Ethnicity can influence views regarding the nature of illness and health and appropriate healers. Beliefs in the connection with the spiritual world, the nature of both "natural" and "supernatural" illnesses suggest the important role that folk healers (*curandero*) can play, especially for elderly Mexican-Americans (Applewhite, 1996). Folk healing traditions combining Spanish Catholic practices with African and other belief systems can be present in some Cuban families (Bernal, 1982). Traditional healers can also be important for Native Americans (Attneave, 1982). In addition, Al-Krenawi and Graham (1996) describe the importance of traditional healing rituals and healers for the Bedouin people.

Religious beliefs and organizations have long played essential roles for African Americans. The church has served as a source of dignity and self-esteem, as a mutual aid society, and as a focal point for activism for social change. Church leaders have played central roles within African American communities. As a result, eliciting information about religion and the church may identify important emotional, spiritual, and material resources for African American individuals and families. In terms of community practice, assessing the presence and roles of the church within the African American community can help discover essential resources for mobilizing people and other community resources (Hines & Boyd-Franklin, 1982).

The Roman Catholic church and beliefs have traditionally played an important role in the life of Irish individuals and families. Irish Catholicism has historically emphasized the need for personal morality while viewing human nature as intrinsically evil. Sin and guilt have been strong elements. Prior to Vatican II the church held a strongly authoritarian stance with people in terms of morality, and the role of the priest is still very influential (McGolderick, 1982).

Jewish families vary widely in terms of their adherence to Jewish rituals and beliefs. "Familism" which makes the family and the procreation and raising of children central, remains important to the Jewish traditions of all groups. It is useful to elicit from Jewish clients how they view their family obligations and how their current actions fit with the expectations of their family and cultural group. Discovering how Jewish clients observe religious rituals can also be an important clue to how closely they identify themselves with the Orthodox, Conservative, and Reform groups, and the salience of these traditions for the life of the family (Herz & Rosen, 1982; Friedman, 1985).

Defensive Use of Religion

Religion can protect people from anxiety in ways that help people cope more effectively or can contribute to problems in functioning. According to ego psychology, people protect themselves from being overwhelmed by anxiety or guilt by defense mechanisms. These defense mechanisms can be thoughts, feelings, and actions. As Brenner points out (1981), virtually any aspect of life can be used as a defensive mechanism to ward off anxiety. An individual with terminal cancer might not be able to believe the words of the doctor about the seriousness of the illness. This sometimes also takes the form of people avoiding dealing with painful personal issues by putting them in religious terms or context (York, 1989). For example, a parent who cannot deal with his own rage and is physically abusive to a child, might rationalize this behavior by saying that a parent must exercise proper discipline because "sparing the rod would spoil the child."

Religious involvement in symptoms and problems can sometimes be readily identified in clients as problematic, for example, the individual who is obviously psychotic and out of touch with reality and who talks about being a special messenger of God. Typically the situation is less obvious. There are times in which religion is used defensively to avoid acknowledging other personal problems. In evaluating the role of religion in this regard, it is important to view the religious beliefs and practices of the client in the context of the total life and functioning of the client. The individual who finds it hard to believe that she has a terminal illness might initially be less anxious because her religious beliefs help to cushion the shock. The denial of the seriousness of the illness becomes problematic, however, if she continues to refuse treatment for the illness, spends large amounts of money or goes through a series of doctors in order to find someone who says that the problem is not life-threatening, or refuses to seek treatment because "God will protect me."

In assessing the role of religion, social workers and others in the helping professions must also be aware of how their own views about religion are affecting their evaluation of deviance and pathology. They need to be aware of the danger that they will use their own beliefs as the basis for viewing the religious beliefs and practices of a client as pathological (Bindler, 1985). There is always the danger of the process called "countertransference," whereby the social worker reacts to clients based on the social worker's own life experiences and personal issues, rather than the reality of the client's situation. Because religious issues can evoke strong feelings, social workers need to be alert to the danger of this process when dealing with religious clients or religious issues generally. A social worker, for example, who is reacting negatively to the religious practices of his own parents risks being overly judgmental of a client whose religious beliefs and practice mirror those of the parents. Defensive uses of religion can sometimes be identified because these religious concerns are more intense or effect more of life than is typical of others who belong to a similiar religious group. Peter's situation demonstrates how religious views can protect against other life concerns. He was preoccupied by his religious obligation to forgive an abusive father. He felt that his religion obligated him to forgive him but he had difficulty doing so. The issue became especially acute when his father became ill and needed his help. While his religious belief system included the theme of forgiveness, he seemed to be placing unduly harsh expectations on himself. Further exploration revealed that his religion protected him against having to acknowledge his ambivalence toward his father. He yearned for a sense of closeness while he feared being hurt again. This understanding permitted the social worker and Peter to work together to learn ways that he could cope with his father during the illness, and in the process to come to terms with the reality of his relationship with his father.

Or consider the situation of Joan, who could virtually talk of little else than her fear that she had committed the "unpardonable sin" and was, therefore, dammed by God. While this belief was a part of her religious group's belief system, most members rarely think about it or can easily dismiss it because they have been taught that people who have committed it do not worry about doing so. As a result, her religious preoccupation met the criteria of being an undue preoccupation accompanied by rigidity, ongoing unhappiness, and lack of productivity. As the helping process unfolded, it became apparent that her obsession represented a desperate way of eliciting interest from others, including the social worker. Even when Joan had realistic issues in her life that would naturally elicit interest from others, she would fall back on her obsession of the unpardonable sin. Her story included a sister who had been severely mentally ill for years and a brother who had recently been arrested for attempted murder. As a child, she had felt ignored by her parents because her father was preoccupied with religion and her mother with her sister's illness. The social worker's understanding of the role of this religious obsession in the total economy of her life and demonstration of interest in other aspects of Joan's life helped her to diminish substantially her obsession. The social worker helped Joan experience that it was possible to relate to others on the basis of healthy aspects of her person.

Spero (1985) suggests several characteristics of religious beliefs and practices that might suggest the presence of a disordered psychological need or conflict.

1. The individual's total religious affiliation, or the current intensity and sense of religious meaning and conviction, is of relatively recent and rapid onset. It has also involved the person in severing of one or more significant family, social, or professional ties and roles.

2. The individual's past history includes numerous religious "crises" or episodes of changing religious affiliation or levels of belief.

3. The individual's religious behaviors and beliefs indicate that the person remains or has returned to a way of relating to God and others that is more immature than is appropriate for one's age. This can be evidenced by several themes.

   a. There is a predominance of immature themes of relationships that do not fit with developmentally appropriate relationships with other people. This might be evidenced by an adult who does not believe that she must prepare herself for a professional service role because she believes "God will provide the way."

   b. There is lack of integration between the individual's mode of religious expression and adaptive ego functioning—the individual may be careful in the use of money in most of the areas of their life, but gives without questioning the value of a program, if it is described in religious terms.

   c. The individual is unable to successfully accomplish appropriate psychosocial tasks— a young man who neglects his own young children because he spends so much of his time helping the youth program in the church.

4. The religious individual is preoccupied either with a directly acknowledged or intellectually masked fear of back-sliding. The individual then becomes very rigid, and extremely concerned with a rigid interpretation of belief and behavioral codes to deal with such fears. Sometimes this takes the form of strict interpretations of religious laws even when others in the group typically follow more lenient interpretations of the laws.

5. Continued unhappiness and unproductivity following religious conversion or awakening. The individual has turned to religion to conquer a drinking problem that persists despite growing religious zeal designed to conquer the drinking.

6. Excessive idealization of a religious movement or leader, and the use of such idealization to resolve problems of autonomy, identity, impulse control, and so forth. The Jonestown, Waco (Texas) and recent Heaven's Gate tragedies represents extreme cases of this pathological use of religion. People gave up their individuality, their possessions, and their own and their children's lives because they had idealized their religious leaders.

Because religious groups vary widely in terms of beliefs and practices, an assessment of the defensive use of religion might require further study about the groups involved or perhaps conversations with relevant religious leaders. As with cultural groups, lack of this understanding can lead to either one of two errors: attributing personal pathology to the religious group or evaluating members of a group that is different from one's own experience as disturbed.

Conclusion

As suggested by previous discussions, assessment includes an analysis of the fit between the client and possible types of interventions. Religion can influence the nature of interventions that are viewed as acceptable by clients. As with other cultural issues, it may be necessary to interpret interventions from the perspective of the religious views of clients. The example of the seminary student who could not use relaxation and pleasure scheduling until after cognitive interventions made these acceptable, illustrates the need to place interventions in an appropriate context. Understanding religious beliefs and practices can also identify potential sources of healing within the religious tradition. Prayer, for example, might be an important source of comfort for many Christians. It may also be important as a source of support, to reconnect people with important religious rituals within their religious traditions.

Religion is a multi-faceted phenomena that can influence the lives of people in many complex ways. Incorporating religious issues in the social work assessment process helps identify ways in which religion can be either a resource or a strain for clients, provides meaning for present and past life events, and points to the types of interventions that might be helpful in managing their problems. Many theories from social work and psychology further this understanding. The specific nature of the appropriate theoretical perspective will depend on the nature of the problem situation. The importance of social work practitioners being aware of their own religious beliefs and those of other ethnic and cultural groups in order to make appropriate assessment and intervention decisions is becoming a prerequisite for competent professional practice.

References

Al-Krenawi, A. & Graham, J. (1996). Social work and traditional healing rituals among the Bedouin of the Negev, Israel. *International Social Work*, 38, 365-377.

Applewhite, S. (1996). *Curanderissmo*: Demystifying the health beliefs and practices of elderly Mexicans Americans. In P. Ewalt, E. Freeman, S. Kirk, & D. Poole (Eds.), *Multicultural issues and social work*. Washington, DC: NASW Press.

Attneave, C. (1982). American Indians and Alaska Native families: Emigrants in their own homeland. In M. McGolderick, J. Pearce, & J. Giordana (Eds.), *Ethnicity and Family Therapy*. New York: Guilford Press.

Austin, D. & Lennings, C. (1993). Grief and religious belief: Does belief moderate depression. *Death Studies,*17(6), 487-496.

Bernal, G. (1982). Cuban families. In McGolderick, J. Pearce, & J. Giordana (Eds.), *Ethnicity and family therapy*. New York: Guilford Press.

Bindler, (1985). Clinical manifestations of religious conflict in psychotherapy. In M. Spero (Ed.), *Psychotherapy of the Religious Client*. Springfield: C.Thomas.

Boszormenyi-Nagy, (1986). Transgenerational solidarity: The expanding context of therapy and prevention. *American Journal of Family Therapy*, 14(3), 195-212.

Brenner, C. (1981). Defense mechanism. *Psychoanalytic Quarterly*, Oct. 557-569.

Browne, C. & Broderick, A. (1996). Asian and Pacific Island Elders: Issues for social work practice and education. In P. Ewalt, E. Freeman, S. Kirk & D. Pool (Eds.), *Multicultural issues and social work*. Washington, DC: NASW Press.

Canda, E. (1988). Spirituality, religious diversity, and social work practice. *Social Casework*, 69, April, 238-247.

Caple, S. Salcio, R. & Cecco, J. (1996). Engaging effectively with culturally diverse families and children. In P. Ewalt, E. Freeman, S. Kirk, & D. Poole (Eds.), *Multicultural issues and social work*. Washington, DC: NASW Press.

Carlson, B. & Cervera, D. (1991). Incarceration, coping, and support. *Social Work*, 36(4), 279-85.

Cornwall, M. (1987). The social basis of religion: A study of factors influencing religious belief and commitment. *Review of Religious Research*, 9(1), 4-56.

DeVries, P. (1960). *The Blood of the Lamb*. Boston: Little, Brown.

Dudley, R & Dudley, M. (1986). Transmission of religious values from parents to adolescents. *Review of Religious Research*, 28(1), 3-15.

Friedman, E. (1982). The myth of Shiska. In M. McGolderick, J. Pearce, & J. Giordano (Eds), *Ethnicity and family therapy*. New York: Guilford Press.

Friedman, E. (1985). *From generation to generation: Family process in church and synagogue*. New York: Guilford Press.

Fuller, R. (1988). *Religion and the life cycle*. New York: Haworth Press.

Harari, V. & Wolowelsky, J. (1995). Family therapy after a death in the traditional Jewish family. *Journal of Family Therapy*, 17, 243-251.

Herz, F. & Rosen, E. (1982). Jewish Families. In McGolderick, J. Pearce, & J. Giordana (Eds.), *Ethnicity and family therapy*. New York: Guilford Press.

Hines, P. & Boyd-Franklin, N. (1982). Black families. In McGolderick, J. Pearce, & J. Giordana (Eds.), *Ethnicity and family therapy*. New York: Guilford Press.

Joseph, M.V. (1987). The religious and spiritual aspects of clinical practice: A neglected dimension of social work. *Social Thought*, 13(1), 12-23.

Joseph, M.V. (1988). Religion and social work practice. *Social Casework*, 70(Sept), 447-457.

Kunshner, H. (1981). *When bad things happen to good people*. New York: Avon.

Loewenberg, F. (1988). *Religion and social work practice in contemporary American society*. New York: Columbia University Press.

Mailick, M. Holden, G. & Walther, V. (1994). Coping with childhood asthma: A caretaker view. *Health and Social Work*, 19(2), 103-111.

McGinn, F. (1996). The plight of rural parents caring for adult children with HIV. *Families and Society*, (May), 269-278.

McGolderick, M. (1982). Irish families. In M. McGolderick, J. Pearce, & J. Giordana (Eds.), *Ethnicity and family therapy*. New York: Guilford Press.

McGolderick, M & Giordano, J. (1996). *Ethnicity and family therapy*. New York: Guilford Press.

Miller, W. (1988). Including clients' spiritual perspectives in cognitive behavior therapy. In Wm. Miller & J. Martin (Eds.), *Behavior therapy and religion: Integrating spiritual and behavioral approaches to change*. Thousand Oaks: Sage.

Phillips, J. (1963). *Your God is too small*. New York: MacMillan.

Raider, M. (1992). Assessing the role of religion in family functioning. In L. Burton (Ed.), *Religion and the family: When God helps*. New York: The Haworth Pastoral Press.

Rizutto, A. (1979). *The birth of the living god*. Chicago: University of Chicago Press.

Smedes, L. (1982). *How can everything be all right when everything is all wrong*. New York: Harper and Row.

Spero, M. (1985). Diagnostic guideline for psychotherapy with the religious client. In M. Spero (Ed), *Psychotherapy of the religious client*. Springfield: Charles C. Thomas.

Tournier, P. (1962). *Guilt and Grace*. New York: Harper and Row.

Van Hook, M. (1990). Family response to the farm crisis: A study in coping. *Social Work,* 35(5), 425-431.

Yellow Bird, M., Fong, R., Galindo, R., Nowicki, J. & Freeman, E. (1996). The multicultural mosaic. In P. Ewalt, E. Freeman, S. Kirk, & D. Poole (Eds.), *Multicultural issues in social work*. Washington, DC: NASW Press.

York, G. (1989). Strategies for managing the religious-based denial of rural clients. *Human Services in the Rural Environment,* 13(2), 16-22.

CHAPTER 13

DOING THE RIGHT THING:
A CHRISTIAN PERSPECTIVE ON ETHICAL
DECISION-MAKING FOR CHRISTIANS IN
SOCIAL WORK PRACTICE

David A. Sherwood

You are on the staff of a Christian Counseling Center and in the course of a week you encounter the following clients:

1. A minister who became sexually involved with a teen-age girl at a previous church several years ago. His current church is not aware of this. He says he has "dealt with his problem."
2. A Christian woman whose husband is physically abusive and who has threatened worse to her and their young child if she tells anyone or leaves him. She comes to your office with cuts and bruises, afraid to go home and afraid not to go home. She doesn't know what she should do or can do.
3. A single mother who is severely depressed and who is not taking adequate care of her two young children, both under the age of four. She denies that her personal problems are affecting her ability to take care of her children.

The list could easily go on. Helping professionals, Christian or otherwise, are daily confronted with issues that are immensely complex and which call forth judgments and actions that confound any attempts to neatly separate "clinical knowledge and skill," our preferred professional roles and boundaries, and, fundamentally, our world-view, faith, moral judgment, and character. Much as we would like to keep it simple, real life is messy and all of a piece. All kinds of things interconnect and interact. How would you respond to clients like the ones I just mentioned?

Christian social workers need to know who they are and what resources they have to do the right thing as children of God—personally, socially, and professionally. What are our resources and limits in choosing and acting ethically as Christians who are placed in helping relationships with others? I will try to review briefly a Christian perspective on:

• When we have a moral problem.
• Conditions under which we choose and act.

- Faith and the hermeneutical spiral (understanding God's will).
- How the Bible teaches us regarding values and ethics.
- A decision-making model which integrates the deontological (ought) dimensions with the teleological (purpose and consequences) dimensions of a problem.
- The fundamental role of character formed through discipleship and the guidance of the Holy Spirit.

We cannot devise or forcibly wrench out of the scriptures a set of rules which will simply tell us what to do if we will only be willing to obey. It appears that God has something else in mind for us as He grows us up into the image of Christ. Ultimately, "doing the right thing" results from our making judgments which grow out of our character as we are "changed into his likeness from one degree of glory to another; for this comes from the Lord who is the Spirit" (II Cor. 3:18).

When Do We Have a Moral Problem?

When do we have a moral "problem?" I would argue that value issues are so pervasive in life that there is virtually no question we face that does not have moral dimensions at some level. Even the choice regarding what brand of coffee to use (or whether to use coffee at all) is not a completely value-neutral question. However, for practical purposes I think it is helpful to realize that moral "problems" tend to be characterized by the following conditions:

1. **More than one value is at stake and they are in some degree of conflict.**
   This is more common than we would like to think. It need not be a conflict between good and bad. It is more usually differing goods or differing bads. A maxim that I drill into my students is "You can't maximize all values simultaneously." Which is to say life continually confronts us with choices and to choose one thing *always* means to give up or have less of something else. And that something else may be a very good thing, so serious choices are usually very costly ones. A familiar, lighthearted version of this is the adage "You can't have your cake and eat it too." This is one of life's truisms which is very easy to forget or tempting to ignore, but which is at the heart of all value and moral problems. No conflict, no problem.
2. **There is uncertainty about what values are, in fact, involved or what they mean.**
   For example, what are all the relevant values involved in a decision regarding abortion? And what, exactly, is meant by choice,

right to life, a person? Where do these values come from? What is their basis? How do they put us under obligation?

3. **There is uncertainty about what the actual facts are.**

What is the true situation? What are the relevant facts? Are they known? Can they be known? How well can they be known under the circumstances?

4. **There is uncertainty about the actual consequences of alternative possible choices and courses of action.**

Often we say that choices and actions should be guided by results. While it is true that their morality is at least in part influenced by their intended and actual consequences, Christians believe that God has built certain "oughts" like justice and love into the creation and that results always have to be measured by some standard or "good" which is beyond the naked results themselves. It is also crucial to remember that consequences can never be fully known at the time of decision and action. The best we can ever do at the time is to *predict*. We are obligated to make the best predictions we can, but we must be humbled by the limitations of our ability to anticipate actual results. However, unintended consequences turn out to be every bit as real and often more important than intended ones, especially if we haven't done our homework.

Under What Conditions Do We Have to Choose and Act?

Given this understanding of a moral "problem," it seems to me that real-life value choices and moral decisions are always made under these conditions:

1. **We have a problem.**

An actual value conflict is present or at least perceived. For example, we want to tell the truth and respect our dying parent's personal rights and dignity by telling him the prognosis but we don't want to upset him, perhaps hasten his death, or create possible complications for ourselves and the hospital staff.

2. **We always have significant limitations in our facts, knowledge, understanding, and ability to predict the consequences of our actions.**

What causes teen-age, unmarried pregnancy? What policies would lead to a decrease in teen-age pregnancy? What other unintended consequences might the policies have? Correct information and knowledge are very hard (often impossible) to come by. As Christians we know that human beings are both finite (limited) and fallen (liable to distortion from selfishness and other forms of sin). The more we can do to overcome or reduce these limitations the better off we'll be. But the beginning of wisdom is to recognize our weakness and dependence.

3. **Ready or not, we have to decide and do** *something*, **at least for the time being, even if the decision is to ignore the problem.**

   Life won't permit us to stay on the fence until we thoroughly understand all the value issues, have all the relevant data, conduct a perfectly complete analysis, and develop a completely Christ-like character. So, we have to learn how to make the best choices we can under the circumstances.

4. **Whatever decision we make and action we take will be fundamentally influenced by our assumptions, world-view, faith**'*whatever* **that is.**

   "Facts," even when attainable, don't sustain moral judgments by themselves. They must be interpreted in the light of at least one faith-based value judgment. Where do my notions of good and bad, healthy and sick, functional and dysfunctional come from? Never from the "facts" alone.

5. **We would like to have definitive, non-ambiguous, prescriptive direction so that we can be completely certain of the rightness of our choice, but we never can.**

   Not from Scripture, not from the law, not from our mother. We want to *know* without a doubt that we are right. This has always been part of the allure of legalism, unquestioning submission to authorities of various stripes, and simplistic reduction of complex situations. The only way (to seem) to be saved by the law is to chop it down to our own puny size.

6. **We may not have legalistic, prescriptive formulas, but we *do* have guidance and help.**

   Doing the right thing is not just a subjective, relativistic venture. God knows the kind of help we really need to grow up in Christ and God has provided it. We need to be open to the kind of guidance God actually gives instead of demanding the kind of guidance we think would be best. What God has actually given is Himself in Jesus Christ, the story of love, justice, grace, and redemption given witness in Scripture, the Holy Spirit, and the community of the church, historically, universally, and locally.

7. **Ultimately, doing the right thing is a matter of identity and character.**

   In the last analysis, our morality (or lack of it) depends much more on *who* we are (or are becoming) than what we know or the procedures we use. We must become persons who have taken on the mind and character of Christ as new creations. And it turns out that this is precisely what the Bible says God is up to'growing us up into the image of Christ, from one degree of glory to another. The "problem" of making and living out these moral decisions turns out to be part of the plot, part of God's strategy, suited to our nature as we were created. Instead of fight ing and resenting the hardness of moral choice and action, maybe we should *embrace* it as part of God's dynamic for our growth.

Faith and the Hermeneutical Spiral

Walking By Faith Is Not Optional

Christian or not, consciously or not, intentionally or not, we all inevitably approach understanding the world and ourselves on the basis of assumptions or presuppositions about the nature of things. Walking by faith is not optional. All human beings do it. We do have some choice (and responsibility) for what we continue to put our faith in, however. That's where choice comes in.

Is love real or a rationalization? Does might make right? Do persons possess inherent dignity and value? Are persons capable of meaningful choice and responsibility? Are human beings so innately good that guilt and sin are meaningless or destructive terms? Is human life ultimately meaningless and absurd? Is the physical universe (and ourselves) a product of mindless chance? Is there a God (or are *we* God)? These are a few of the really important questions in life and there is no place to stand to try to answer them that does not include some sort of faith.

Interpreting the Facts

Like it or not, the world, life, and scripture are not simply experienced or known directly. Things are *always* interpreted on the basis of assumptions and beliefs we have about the nature of the world which are part of our faith position. Knowingly or not, we are continually engaged in hermeneutics, interpretation on the basis of principles.

My interpretation of the meaning of scripture, for example, is strongly affected by whether or not I believe the Bible is a strictly human product or divinely inspired. It is further affected by whether or not I assume the Bible was intended to and can, in fact, function as a legal codebook providing specific prescriptive answers to all questions. My beliefs about these things are never simply derived from the data of the scripture only, but they should never be independent of that data either. In fact, a good hermeneutical principle for understanding scripture is that our interpretations *must* do justice to the actual data of scripture.

The same is true regarding our understanding or interpretation of the "facts" of our experience. The same event will be seen and interpreted differently by persons who bring different assumptions and expectations to it. On the day of Pentecost, the Bible records that the disciples "were filled with the Holy Spirit and began to speak in other tongues as the Spirit enabled them" (Acts 2:4). Some in the crowd didn't know anything about the Holy Spirit, but were amazed by the fact that they heard their own native languages. "Are not all of these men who are speaking Galileans? Then how is it that each of us hears them in his native tongue" (Acts 2:7-8). Some, however, heard the speech as drunken nonsense and said, "They have had too much wine" (Acts 2:13). Different interpretive, hermeneutical frameworks were in place, guiding the understanding of the "facts."

As a child, I occasionally experienced corporal punishment in the form of spankings from my mother (on one memorable occasion administered with a willow switch). The fact that I was spanked is data. But what did those spankings "mean" to me? Did I experience abuse? Was I experiencing loving limits in a way that I could understand? The experience had to be interpreted within the framework of the rest of my experiences and beliefs (however formed) about myself, my mother, and the rest of the world. And those "facts" continue to be interpreted or re-interpreted today in my memory. In this case, I never doubted her love for me or (at least often) her justice.

The Hermeneutical Spiral

We come by our personal faith position in a variety of ways'adopted without question from our families, friends, and culture; deliberately and critically chosen; refined through experience; fallen into by chance or default'or, more likely, it comes through some combination of all of these and more. However it happens, it is not a static, finished thing. Our interpretation and understanding of life proceeds in a kind of reciprocal hermeneutical spiral. Our faith position helps order and integrate (or filter and distort) the complex overload of reality which we confront. But at the same time reality has the capacity to challenge and at least partially modify or correct our assumptions and perceptions.

Once the great 18th century English dictionary-maker, writer, conversationalist, and sometime philosopher Samuel Johnson was asked by his biographer Boswell how he refuted Bishop Berkeley's philosophical theory of idealism (which asserted that the physical world has no real existence). Johnson replied, "I refute it *thus.*" He thereupon vigorously kicked a large rock, causing himself considerable pain but gaining more than enough evidence (for himself, at least) to cast doubt on the sufficiency of idealist theory as a total explanation of reality.

This is a hermeneutical spiral. You come to interpret the world around you through the framework of your faith, wherever you got it, however good or bad it is, and however embryonic it may be. It strongly affects what you perceive (or even look for). But the world is not a totally passive or subjective thing. So you run the risk of coming away from the encounter with your faith somewhat altered, perhaps even corrected a bit, perhaps more distorted. Then you use that altered faith in your next encounter. Unfortunately, there is no guarantee that the alterations are corrections. But, *if* the Bible is true, and *if* we have eyes that want to see and ears that want to hear, we can have confidence that we are bumping along in the right general direction, guided by the Holy Spirit.

How Does the Bible Teach Us?

The Heresy of Legalism

For Christians, the desire for unambiguous direction has most often led to the theological error of legalism, and then, on the rebound, to relativism. Legalism takes many forms but essentially uses the legitimate zeal for faithfulness to justify an attempt to extract from the Bible or the traditions of the elders a system of rules to cover all contingencies and then to make our relationship to God depend on our understanding and living up to those rules.

It is theological error because it forces the Bible to be something that it is not—an exhaustive theological and moral codebook yielding prescriptive answers to all questions. It distorts the real nature and meaning of God's self-revelation in the incarnation of Jesus Christ, the Holy Spirit, the Scriptures, and even nature. Taken to its extreme, it effectively denies the gospel of justification by faith in Jesus Christ and substitutes a form of works righteousness. It can take the good news of redeeming, reconciling love and distort it into a source of separation, rejection, and condemnation.

The paradigm case in the New Testament involved some of the Pharisees. Jesus had some very strong words for them. When the Pharisees condemned the disciples for breaking the Sabbath by gathering grain to eat, Jesus cited the example of David feeding his men with the temple bread, also a violation of the law, and told them, in effect, that they were missing the point of the law' "The sabbath was made for man, not man for the sabbath" (Mk. 2:23-28). In the parable of the Pharisee and the tax collector Jesus warned about those who "trusted in themselves that they were righteous and despised others" (Lk. 18:9-14). He talked of those who strain out gnats and swallow camels, careful to tithe down to every herb in their gardens but neglecting the "weightier matters of the law, justice and mercy and faith" (Mt. 23:23-24). When a group of Pharisees condemned the disciples because they didn't wash their hands according to the Pharisees' understanding of the requirements of purifica tion, saying "Why do your disciples transgress the tradition of the elders?" Jesus answered "And why do you transgress the commandment of God for the sake of your tradition? . . . For the sake of your tradition you have made void the word of God. Hear and understand: not what goes into the mouth defiles a man, but what comes out of the mouth" (Mt. 15:1-11).

The Heresy of Subjective Relativism

If the Bible isn't a comprehensive lawbook out of which we can infallibly derive concrete, pre scriptive directions for every dilemma, what good is it? Aren't we then left to be blown about by ev ery wind of doctrine, led about by the spirit (or spirits) of the age we live in, guided only by our subjective, selfish desires? This is a good example of a false dichotomy, as though these were the only two alternatives. Either the Bible is a codebook or we land in total relativism. Yet this is the conclusion often drawn, which quite erroneously restricts the terms of the discussion. Once we cut loose from the deceptively certain rules of legalism it is very easy to become the disillusioned cynic—"I was tricked once, but I'm not going to be made a fool again." If the Bible can't give me all the an swers directly then its all just a matter of human opinion. So the false dilemma is stated.

The Orthodoxy of Incarnation—What if God Had a Different Idea?

Such conclusions assume that, to be of any practical use, God's revelation of His will can only be of a certain kind, an assumption we are more likely to take *to* the Bible than to learn *from* it. It as sumes that divine guidance must be exhaustively propositional, that what we need to be good Christians and to guide our moral lives is either specific rules for every occasion or at least principles from which specific rules can rationally be derived. What if such an assumption is wrong? What if it is not in keeping with the nature of God, the nature of human beings, the nature of the Bible, the nature of the Christian life?

What if the nature of Christian values and ethics cannot be adequately embodied or communicated in a book of rules, however complex and detailed? What if it can only be embodied in a life which is fully conformed to the will of God and communicated through the story of that life and its results?

What if God had to become a man, live a life of love and justice, be put to death innocently on the behalf of others, and raise triumphant over death to establish the kingdom of God? What if the Bible were book about that? A true story of how to become a real person?

The point I am trying to make is that if we go to the Bible for guidance on its *own* terms, not de ciding in advance the nature that guidance has to take, what we find is neither legalism nor relativism but precisely the kind of guidance that suits the kind of reality God actually made, the kind of crea tures we actually are, the kind of God with whom we have to do.

We learn that ethical practice has more to do with our identity, our growth in character and virtue than it does with airtight rules and that the Bible is just the kind of book to help us do this. It may not be as tidy as we would like. It may not be as easy as we would like to always tell the good guys from the bad guys. We may not always be able to act with the certain knowledge that we are doing just the right (or wrong) thing. But we will have the opportunity to get closer and closer to the truth of God, to grow up into the image of Christ. Growth is not always comfortable. But the Bible tells us *who* we are, *whose* we are, and *where* we're going.

God is Bigger Than Our Categories but the Bible is a Faithful Witness

The reality of God and biblical truth shatters our categories. At least, none of them, taken alone, can do the God of the Bible justice. Taken together, our categories have the potential to balance and correct each other. Human language can only carry so much divine freight in any particular car.

We are *all* susceptible to distorted use of Scripture. We need the recognition that we (*all* of us) always take preconditions to our Bible study which may seriously distort its message to us. In fact, we often have several *conflicting* desires and preconditions at work simultaneously. For example, we have the hunger for the security of clear-cut prescrip-tive answers ("Just tell me if divorce is always wrong or if I have a scrip-tural right to remarry") *and* a desire to be autonomous, to suit ourselves rather than submit to anyone or anything ("I don't want to hurt anyone, but my needs have to be met").

So, how do I think the Bible teaches us about morality? How does it guide us in making moral judgments in our professional lives? Strug-gling to rise above my own preconditions and to take the Bible on its own terms, to see how the Bible teaches and what the Bible teaches, I think I am beginning to learn a few things.

God's Project: Growing Us up into the Image of Christ

It seems to me that God is trying to reveal His nature and help us to develop His character. And it seems that the only way He could do that is in *personal* terms, creating persons with the dignity of choice, developing a relationship with a nation of them, becoming one of us Himself, revealing His love, grace, and forgiveness through a self-sacrificial act of redemption, and embarking on a process of growing persons up into His own image. The process requires us to be more than robots, even obedient ones. It requires us to make principled judgments based on virtuous character, to exercise wisdom based on the character of Christ. Neither legalism nor relativism produce this.

According to the Bible, growing us up to have the mind and character of Christ is an intrinsic part of God's redemptive project. We are not simply forgiven our sins that grace may abound but we are being rehabilitated, sanctified—being made saints, if you will. The theme is clear, as the following passages illustrate.

In Romans 6:1-2, 4 Paul says that, far from continuing in sin that grace may abound, we die to sin in Christ, are buried with him in baptism, and are raised that we too may live a new life. Romans 12:2 says that we do not conform to the pattern of this world but are to be transformed by the renewing of our minds which makes us able to test and approve what God's will is. II Corinthians 3:17-18 says that where the Spirit of the Lord is, there is freedom and that we are being transformed into His likeness with ever-increasing glory. Ephesians 4:7, 12-13 says that each one of us has been given grace from Christ to prepare us for service so that the body of Christ might be built up until we all reach unity in the faith and knowledge of the Son of God and become mature, attaining to the whole measure of the fullness of Christ. I John 3:1-3 marvels at the greatness of the love of the Father that we should be called children of God and goes on to affirm that, although what we shall be has not yet been made known, we do know that when Christ appears we shall be like him. In Philippians 2, Paul says that, being united with Christ, Christians should have the same servant attitude as Christ, looking out for the interests of others as well as ourselves. Then he makes this remarkable conjunction—"Continue to work out your own salvation with fear and trembling, for it is God who works in you to will and to act according to his good purpose."

And in I Corinthians 2 Paul says that we speak a message of wisdom among the mature, God's wisdom from the beginning, not the wisdom of this age, revealed to us by His Spirit. He explains that we have received the Spirit who is from God that we might understand what God has freely given us. He concludes, "Those who are unspiritual do not receive the gifts of God's Spirit for they are foolish ness to them, and they are unable to understand them because they are spiritually discerned . . . But we have the mind of Christ."

A Key: Judgments Based on Wisdom Growing Out of the Character of Christ

It would seem that the key to integrating Christian values into professional practice (as in all of life) is making complex judgments based on wisdom growing out of the mind and character of God, incarnated in Jesus Christ.

In our personal and professional lives we face many complex situations and decisions, large and small. Real-life moral dilemmas confront us with having to make choices between (prioritize) values that are equally real (though not necessarily equally important—remember Jesus' comments on keep ing the Sabbath versus helping a human being). Whatever we do, we cannot fully or equally maximize each value in the situation. (If the father embraces the prodigal son and gives him a party, there will be some who will see him as rewarding irresponsibility.) Whatever we do, we have to make our choices on the basis of limited understanding of both the issues involved and the consequences of our actions. Moreover, our decision is complicated by our fallen nature and selfish desires.

In situations like this, the answer is not legalism (religious or scientific) or relativism. The *mind* of Christ helps us to figure out *what* to do and the *character* of Christ helps us to have the capacity (i.e. character or virtue) to actually *do* it. It seems to me that in the very process of struggling through these difficult situations we are dealing with a principle of growth that God has deliberately built into the nature of things. The people of God are continually required to make decisions based on principles embodied in our very identity'the character of who we are, whose we are, and where we are going.

These virtues are not just abstract ones but rather they are incarnated in the history and *character* of Jesus Christ. Love and justice are the fundamental principles but we learn what they mean because Jesus embodies them. (Yes, keep the Sabbath but don't let that keep you from helping someone.)

How should a Christian social worker respond when a client says she wants an abortion? How should parents respond when an unmarried daughter tells them she is pregnant? How should a church respond to a stranger's request for financial aid? Should I be for or against our Middle Eastern pol icy? Should my wife Carol and I invite her mother to come and live with us? How much money can I spend on myself? It appears I have some complex judgments to make in order to live a life of love and justice.

So, one of God's primary dynamics of growth seems to be to place us in complex situations in which decisions based on judgment are required. These decisions require our knowledge of the character of Christ to make and they require that we be disciplined disciples at least beginning to take on the character of Christ ourselves to carry them out. It seems to me there is a deliberate plot here, daring and risky, but the only one that works, which fits the world as God made it.

Can the Preacher Have a Boat?

Permit me a personal example to illustrate the point. I remember a lively debate in the cafeteria as an undergraduate in a Christian College over whether or not a preacher (i.e. completely dedicated Christian) could have a boat. The issue, of course, was stewardship, our relationship and responsibility toward material wealth, our neighbors, and ourselves.

Being mostly lower middle class, we all easily agreed that a yacht was definitely an immoral use of money and that a row boat or canoe was probably o.k. But could it have a motor? How big? Could it possibly be an inboard motor? How many people could it carry? It was enough to cross a rabbi's eyes. Since we believed the Bible to contain a prescriptive answer to every question, we tried hard to formulate a scriptural answer. But we found no direct commands, approved apostolic examples, or necessary inferences that would nail it down.

What we found was much more challenging—things like:

> The earth is the Lord's and the fullness thereof (Psa. 24:1)
> Give as you have been prospered (I Cor. 16:2)
> What do you have that you did not receive (II Cor. 4:7)
> Remember the fatherless and widows (Jas. 1:27)
> Don't lay up treasures on earth (Mt. 6:19-20)
> Follow Jesus in looking out for the interests of others, not just your own (Phil. 2:1-5).

Plenty of guidelines for exercising love and justice, lots of examples of Christ and the disciples in action—in other words, no selfish relativism. But no iron-clad formulas for what to spend or where—in other words, no legalism.

Instead, every time I turn around I am faced again with new financial choices, fresh opportunities to decide all over again what stewardship means—plenty of chances to grossly rationalize, distort, and abuse the gospel, to be sure. But also plenty of opportunities to get it right this time, or at least better. To grow up into the image of Christ.

Gaining the Mind and Character of Christ

So, only persons of character or virtue can make the kind of judg-ments and take the actions required of us. To do the right thing we need to be the right kinds of persons, embodying the mind and character of Christ.

The most direct route to moral practice is through realizing our identity as Christ-Ones. In Galatians 2:20 Paul said "I have been cruci-fied with Christ and I no longer live, but Christ lives in me. The life I live in the body, I live by faith in the Son of God, who loved me and gave himself for me" and in Galatians 5:13-14 he said "You were called to freedom, brothers and sisters; only do not use your freedom as an op-portunity for self-indulgence, but through love become slaves to one another. For the whole law is summed up in a single commandment, 'You shall love your neighbor as yourself.'"

The mind and character of Christ is formed in us by the Holy Spirit as we submit to God's gen eral revelation in creation (Romans 1-2), written revelation in Scripture (II Tim. 3:15-17), and, ultimately, incarnated revela-tion in Jesus Christ (John 1:1-18; Col. 1:15-20). We can only give appropri-ate meaning to the principles of love and justice by knowing the God of the Bible, the Jesus of incarnation, and the Holy Spirit of understanding and power. This happens best (perhaps only) in the give and take of two living communities—Christian families and the church, the body of Christ.

What we have when this happens is not an encyclopedic list of rules that gives us unambiguous answers to every practical or moral issue we may ever encounter. Neither are we left in an uncharted swamp of selfish relativity. And, it should be noted well, we are not given a substitute for the clear thinking and investigation necessary to provide the data. The Bible and Christ Himself are no substitute for reading, writing, and arithmetic (or practice wisdom, theory, and empirical research)'getting the best infor-mation we can and thinking honestly and clearly about it.

Instead, what we have then is the enhanced capacity to make and carry out complex judgment that is more in harmony with God's love and justice than we could make otherwise. We are still limited. We still know in part and "see but a poor reflection as in a mirror" (I Cor. 13:12).

We may be disappointed that the Bible or Christ Himself don't give us the kind of advice, shortcuts, or easy black-and-white answers we would like, but what they give us is much better—the truth. Do you want to live a good life? Do you want to integrate your Christian values and your profes-sional helping practice? Do you want to do what is right? The only way, ultimately, is to know God through being a disciple of Christ. This doesn't mean that only Christians can have good moral character—God's common grace is accessible to all. But it really is *true* that Jesus is the way, the truth, and the life (John 14:6). God is the one who gives *content* to the idea of "good." The mind of Christ is really quite remarkable, filling up and stretching to the limit our humanity with God.

Lord, help us to know
   who we are,
   whose we are, and
   where we are going.

An Ethical Decision-Making Model

Given this understanding of the human situation, how God is working with us to grow us up into the image of Christ and the proper role that the Bible plays in giving us guidance, I would like to briefly introduce an ethical decision-making model for Christian helping professionals. It is a simple "problem-solving" model which assumes and is no substitute for developing the mind and character of Christ. It is simple only in concept, not in application. And it is what we need to do in all of our lives, not just in our work with clients.

Deontological and Consequentialist/Utilitarian Parameters

Ethical judgments and actions can generally be thought of as being based on two kinds of criteria or parameters—deontological and consequentialist/utilitarian. These are philosophical terms for describing two types of measuring sticks of whether or not something is good or bad in a moral sense and either ought or ought not to be done.

Deontological Parameters—The "Oughts"

Deontological parameters or criteria refer to moral obligation or duty. What are the moral imperatives or rules that relate to the situation? What are the "oughts?" For the Christian, it can be summed up by asking "What is the will of God in this situation?" Understanding the deontological parameters of an ethical dilemma we face is extremely important. But it is not as simple as it may first appear. Some think that ethics can be determined by deontological parameters only or that deontological parameters operate without consideration to consequences in any way. For example, the commandment "Thou shalt not lie" is taken to be an absolute, exceptionless rule which is to be obeyed in all circumstances and at all times, regardless of the consequences. By this principle, when Corrie Ten Boom was asked by the Nazis if she knew of any Jews, she should have led them to her family's hiding place.

Trying to answer all moral questions by attempting to invoke a particular deontological principle in isolation, even if it is biblical, may wind up leading us into actions which are contrary to God's will. That is the legalistic fallacy which we discussed before. Normally we have an ethical dilemma because we are in a situation in which more than one deontological principle applies and they are in conflict to some degree. Do we keep the sabbath or do we heal? The Ten Commandments or the Sermon on the Mount, for example, contain deontological principles that are vitally important to helping us understand the mind of Christ and doing the will of God. But they cannot be handled mechanistically or legalistically or we will become Pharisees indeed. Does "turning the other cheek" require us to never resist evil in any way?

Most Christians properly understand that God's will is fully embodied only in God's character of love and justice, which was incarnated in the person of Jesus Christ. Love and justice are the only "exceptionless absolutes" in a deontological sense. The moral rules and principles of scripture provide important guidelines to help us to understand what love and justice act like in various circumstances, but they cannot stand alone as absolutes nor can they be forced into a legal system which eliminates the need for us to make judgments.

Consequentialist/Utilitarian Parameters—The "Results"

For God and for us, moral reality is always embodied. Part of what this means, then, is that the deontological "oughts" can never be completely separated from the consequentialist/utilitarian parameters. The consequentialist/utilitarian parameters refer to the results. Christian ethical decisions and actions always have to try to take into account their consequences. What happens as a result of this action or that, and what end is served?

Many people (quite erroneously) believe that moral judgments or actions can be judged exclusively on the basis of their results. Did it have a "good" or desired result? Then it was a good act. If we value the end we implicitly accept the means to that end, no matter what they might be (say, terrorism to oppose unjust tyranny). This is just as much a fallacy as the single-minded deontological judgment. Pure utilitarianism is impossible since there must be some deontological basis for deciding what is a "good" result, and this can never be derived from the raw facts of a situation. And "goods" and "evils" must be prioritized and balanced against one another in means as well as the ends.

It is a fact that some adults engage in sexual activity with children. But so what? What is the moral and practical meaning of that fact? Is it something we should encourage or prevent? Without some standard of "good" or "health" it is impossible to give a coherent answer.

Another major limitation of consequentialist/utilitarian criteria in making moral judgments is that at best they can never be more than guesses or *predictions* based on what we *think* the results might be, never on the actual consequences themselves. If I encourage my client to separate from her abusive husband, I may think that he will not hurt her or the children, but I cannot be sure.

So, ethical and practical *judgments* are always required. They aren't simple. And they always involve identifying, prioritizing, and acting on *both* deontological and consequentialist/utilitarian parameters of a situation.

The Model: Judgment Formed By Character and Guided By Principle

1. **Identify and explore the problem:**
   What issues/values (usually plural) are at stake?
   What are the desired ends?
   What are the alternative possible means?
   What are the other possible unintended consequences?
2. **Identify the deontological parameters:**
   What moral imperatives are there?
   What is the will of God, the mind of Christ?
   What are the principles at stake, especially in regard to love and justice?
   Are there any rules or rule-governed exceptions, biblical injunctions, commands, or codes of ethics which apply?
3. **Identify the consequentialist/utilitarian parameters:**
   What (as nearly as can be determined or predicted) are the likely intended and unintended consequences?
   What are the costs and benefits? How are they distributed (who benefits, who pays)?
   What must be given up in each particular possible course of action? What values will be slighted or maximized?
4. **Integrate and rank the deontological and consequentialist/utilitarian parameters:**
   What best approximates (maximizes) the exceptionless absolutes of love and justice?
5. **Make a judgment guided by character and act:**
   After gathering and analyzing the biblical, professional and other data, pray for wisdom and the guidance of the Holy Spirit.

Make a judgment and act growing out of your character as informed by the character of Christ.

Refusing choice and action *is* choice and action, so you must do the best you can at the time, even if, in retrospect it turns out you were "sinning bravely."

6. **Evaluate:**

Grow through your experience. Rejoice or repent, go on or change.

Character Formed through Discipleship and the Guidance of the Holy Spirit

Ultimately, ethical Christian practice depends on one thing—developing the mind and character of Christ. It depends on our growing up into the image of Christ. This begins in the new birth as we become new creations in Christ. We are filled with the Holy Spirit and called to a life of discipleship in which we bring every thought and action in captivity to Christ (II Cor. 10:5). We present our bodies "as a living sacrifice," not conformed to this world, but "transformed by the renewal of your mind" (Rom. 12:1-2). We hunger and thirst after righteousness. We seek to know God's will through scripture, the guidance of the Holy Spirit, and the community of the church. We identify with Jesus and the saints of God down through the ages. We daily choose to follow Christ as best we know and can. We repent and confess to our Lord when we fall. We thankfully receive his grace. We choose and act again.

Certainly piety is not a substitute for the discipline of professional training, careful research, and thoughtful analysis. Rather, the use of all of these is simply a complimentary part of our stewardship and discipleship. The most solid possible assurance that we will do the right thing in our personal lives and in our professional practice is our discipleship, growing to have more and more of the character of Jesus Christ, as we make judgments more in harmony with God's character and Spirit.

We become a "letter from Christ . . . Written not with ink but with the Spirit of the living God, not on tablets of stone but on tablets of human hearts, . . . ministers of a new covenant, not in a written code but in the Spirit; for the written code kills, but the Spirit gives life . . . .Now the Lord is the Spirit, and where the Spirit of the Lord is, there is freedom. And we all, with unveiled face, beholding the glory of the Lord, are being changed into his likeness from one degree of glory to another; for this comes from the Lord who is the Spirit" (II Cor. 3:3, 6, 17-18).

Notes

This chapter was previously published in *Social Work and Christianity*, 20(2), 1993.

References

Adams, Robert M. (1987). *The virtue of faith*. New York: Oxford University Press.

Hauerwas, Stanley. (1981). *A community of character: Toward a constructive Christian social ethic*. Notre Dame: University of Notre Dame Press.

Hauerwas, Stanley and Willimon, William H. (1989). *Resident aliens: Life in the Christian colony*. Nashville: Abingdon Press.

Holmes, Arthur. (1984). *Ethics: Approaching moral decisions*. Downers Grove, IL: InterVarsity Press.

Keith-Lucas, Alan. (1994). *Giving and taking help*. Botsford, CT: North American Association of Christians in Social Work.

Keith-Lucas, Alan. (1985). *So you want to be a social worker: A primer for the Christian student*. Botsford, CT: North American Association of Christians in Social Work.

Lewis, C. S. (1947). *The abolition of man*. New York: Macmillan.

Lewis, C. S. (1943). *Mere Christianity*. New York: Macmillan.

MacIntyre, Alasdair. (1984). *After virtue: A study in moral theory*. 2nd Ed. University of Notre Dame Press.

Mott, Stephen C. (1982). *Biblical ethics and social change*. New York: Oxford University Press.

O'Donovan, Oliver. (1986). *Resurrection and the moral order: An outline for evangelical ethics*. Grand Rapids: Eerdmans.

Osborne, Grant R. (1991). *The hermeneutical spiral: A comprehensive introduction to biblical inter pretation*. Downers Grove, IL: InterVarsity Press.

Pinnock, Clark. (1984). *The scripture principle*. New York: Harper and Row.

Sire, James W. (1980). *Scripture twisting*. Downers Grove, IL: InterVarsity Press.

Sherwood, David A. (Spring-Fall 1981). Add to your faith virtue: The integration of Christian values and social work practice. *Social Work and Christianity*, 8, 41-54.

Sherwood, David A. (Spring 1989). How should we use the bible in ethical decision-making? Guidance without legalism or relativism. *Social Work and Christianity*, 16, 29-42

Sherwood, David A. (Fall 1986). Notes toward applying Christian ethics to practice: Growing up into the image of Christ. *Social Work and Christianity*, 13, 82-93.

Smedes, Lewis. (1983). *Mere morality*. Grand Rapids: Eerdmans.

Swartley, Willard M. (1983). *Slavery, sabbath, war, and women: Case issues in biblical interpre tation*. Scottsdale, PA: Herald Press.

Verhay, Allen. (1984). *The great reversal: Ethics and the new testament*. Grand Rapids: Eerdmans.

CHAPTER 14

HOSPICE: AN OPPORTUNITY FOR TRULY WHOLISTIC SOCIAL WORK

John E. Babler

The field of social work provides many diverse opportunities for practice and most students wonder what type of practice setting will fit them best. For Christians, the contemplation of practice settings may include consideration of variables such as their own spiritual gifts, their theology of helping, the openness of various social work settings to Christians sharing their faith, and God's call on their life. This chapter will present information about hospice, a social work practice setting that should be of particular interest to Christians in social work.

The Seminary where I teach exists to provide theological training to men and women called to vocational ministry. The department in which I teach focuses on preparing students for ministries of helping. The importance of both demonstrating *and* declaring faith in Jesus while helping is modeled and taught. God calls me personally to overtly express my Christianity when helping others and to teach them that His Word is sufficient to solve problems in living. God continually reminds me what a great resource He has provided in the Bible. Of all the books we have available to us it alone is living and active (Hebrews 4:12) and inspired by God and useful for teaching, reproof, correction and training in righteousness (2 Timothy 3:16-17).

Several years experience in hospice social work and completion of a dissertation on spiritual care in hospice causes me to be excited about hospice as a practice setting for Christians in social work. It is a practice setting that can be a good fit for Christians in social work.

Hospice: History and Overview

Throughout history, writings of philosophers, theologians, and poets have detailed and explored a universal human fascination with and fear of death (Munley, 1983). Missinne (1990) contends that Ameri-

---

Scripture taken from the New American Standard Bible, c. 1977, by The Lockman Foundation.

can attitudes concerning death are negative. In facing death, people are exposed to their weaknesses and encounter feelings such as hostility, denial, and embarrassment. Possessions and physical beauty no longer are important. Death is democratic, the one thing we all have in common is that we all will die. Many of us "fear death far less than...a long and painful dying that leaves us incapacitated, helpless, totally dependent on the good will of strangers—bereft of dignity, comfort, and human warmth" (Bulkin & Lukashok, 1988).

According to Munley (1983), the rapidly advancing medical technology in our society coupled with urbanization and the lack of contact with dying people makes dealing with death even more complex. Dying in America is often a clinical experience filled with machines, tubes, unknown people, strange surroundings, and limited family contact. In contrast, the end of life for a hospice patient is filled with familiar surroundings, close (sometimes constant) support of family and friends, and wholistic care by committed professionals.

Hospice care can be a positive alternative to a "technological" death. Hospices were common in the Middle Ages where they served a variety of purposes. The typical medieval hospice was a combination guest house and infirmary where all who entered were given food, shelter, and care until they died or set out again on their journeys, refreshed and renewed (Munley, 1983). Ley and Corless (1988) emphasize the fact that these medieval hospices had strong Christian roots. They were dedicated to the Scriptural injunctions of Matthew 25 to feed the hungry, give drink to the thirsty, welcome the stranger, clothe the naked, and visit the prisoner as well as to the early church practice of burying the dead. The medieval view that death is a transformation and the belief that what happens to the mind and the spirit are as important as what happens to the body provided the foundation for the modern hospice movement (Stoddard, 1991).

Dame Cicely Saunders was the driving force behind the beginning of the modern hospice movement. Saunders was first trained as a nurse and then her interest in terminally ill patients led her to be trained as a medical social worker, and finally as a physician. As a physician at a hospice operated by the Irish Sisters of Charity, she began to integrate the wholistic care concepts of hospices of the past with modern pain control techniques. She opened St. Christopher's Hospice in London in 1968. St. Christopher's has become a model of modern hospice care and is an international education and research center that attracts hospice professionals and those interested in hospice from around the world (Munley, 1983).

St. Christopher's was "founded on the ancient Christian concept of hospice dating back to the fourth century A.D.—a place to care for pilgrims and travelers, the poor, the sick, and the dying" (Ley & Corless,

1988). Strong religious affiliation was one of the major characteristics of the development of the hospice movement in England, but in the United States a more pluralistic and secular tradition exists and the religious aspect may not appear to be so significant (O'Connor, 1986).

The hospice movement in the United States has Elizabeth Kubler-Ross as its "lightning rod." Her commitment to meeting the needs of the dying and their loved ones as demonstrated by her life and teaching and her book *On Death and Dying,* helped many in the medical community to see the need hospice could fill. Hospice Incorporated in New Haven, Connecticut and Hospice of Marin in Marin County, California were among the first hospice programs in the United States. Hospice of Marin was begun by committed professionals who volunteered their time to care for terminally ill cancer patients in their homes (Stoddard, 1991; Munley 1983).

Less than twenty years since its humble beginnings in this country, hospice has grown and changed significantly. No longer dependent upon volunteers, hospices employ many to meet the needs of the terminally ill and their families. Hospice services are covered by Medicare, Medicaid, and many private health insurance plans. The National Hospice Organization currently represents over 1600 hospice organizations. In the midst of change and growth, many of the emphases of the past continue on today. Among these are the inter-disciplinary team approach to providing care and a continuing emphasis on the necessity of treating the whole person. The National Hospice Organization sums up this emphasis as a standard for hospices, stating that a specially trained team of hospice professionals and volunteers work together to meet physiological, psychological, social, spiritual, and economic needs of patients and families facing terminal illnesses (National Hospice Organization, 1994).

Hospice does nothing to hasten or slow the process of death. A common sentiment is that hospice does not deal with death, but rather with making the end of one's life as positive as possible. An appropriate understanding of hospice stresses a "good death" or "the good in dying" (Jennings, 1997). Due to a belief that people should not suffer needlessly, palliation or pain control is a major priority of hospice. Sometimes, very large doses of pain relievers such as morphine are required to keep the patient comfortable.

Since hospice has a very high success rate at keeping patients comfortable, it serves as a positive alternative to the argument that assisted suicide is necessary to keep people from dying painful deaths. Hospice takes very seriously the other needs of patients and their families, as well. These needs are widely varied and may relate to emotional support, financial struggles, out of home placement, spiritual issues, personal hygiene of the patient, counseling, crisis intervention, and grief.

The interdisciplinary team of hospice professionals and volunteers work together to meet the wholistic needs of the hospice patient and the patient's family, friends, and co-workers. Requirements for hospice admission include a diagnosis of a terminal illness with less than six months to live and a desire to *not* seek further curative treatment. After admission to a hospice program, assessments are made of the patient and family by the various team members and the team designs and implements a care plan for the family.

The inclusion of social work services as a part of hospice care is required and social workers are a vital part of the hospice team (National Hospice Organization, 1994). The comprehensive skills that a social worker has obtained through education and experience find many applications in hospice care. The team approach allows social workers a voice in a wide variety of issues, and ongoing relationships with other professionals, hospice patients, and their families and friends provide abundant opportunities for intervention.

Hospice: Meeting Psychosocial Needs Through Social Work

The National Hospice Organization (1994) provides the following guidelines for the availability and scope of social work services:

1. Social work services should be offered to every patient/family/significant other.
2. A thorough social work/psychosocial assessment should be done by a social worker at the time of admission or as soon as possible thereafter. The social worker should be involved in the initial and ongoing care planning.
3. Social work services should be reflective of traditional social work roles and include, but not be limited to: psychosocial assessment, counseling, consultation, education, resource and referral services, advocacy, and discharge planning.
4. The scope of services should be clearly defined in the policies and procedures of the organization or social work department.
5. Ongoing social work services should be provided based on the social work assessment and plan of care. Additionally, services may be initiated upon referral at any time by any member of the interdisciplinary team, the patient or family. (p.1)

While the above guidelines provide a foundation for hospice social work, published articles that address social work in hospice are rare (MacDonald, 1991). Those that have been written focus primarily on the roles and functions of hospice social workers (Quig, 1989; Rusnack,

Schaefer, & Moxley, 1988). There continues to be a need for research that clarifies the importance and efficacy of social work in hospice (Richardson, 1997).

Social workers are a necessary component of hospice care. Strengths brought to the hospice team include a focus on the patient as not only a part of a family, but as part of a community and society. Social workers have many varied opportunities to practice social work roles in hospice, but there is a need to formalize the interventions and skills as well as outcomes sought and achieved. The advocacy role of the social worker in hospice is vital in the current environment of health care reform. The demands of reform give social workers in hospice the opportunity to clarify their importance to the health care industry as well as the profession (Richardson, 1997). The practice of social work in hospice is emotionally intense and very demanding. It requires well developed skills and an ability to be flexible based on the needs and demands of others.

Social work in hospice is accomplished at several different levels. First and foremost is the work that is accomplished with the patients, families and loved ones. This work requires excellent assessment skills as well as wisdom to know which problems require intervention and which issues are normal for people facing their own mortality. Sometimes the social worker is called on to assist the family in group problem-solving. Knowledge of group dynamics as well as an ability to work with groups is necessary. Social workers also practice advocacy for patients and families with other hospice team members during team meetings and in other settings. Since hospice social work requires the social worker to make their own schedule and do home visits, self-discipline is a must.

Hospice social workers are frequently called on to present grief workshops and work with bereaved family members. This requires public speaking skills and compassion as well as an understanding of grief. Networking and crisis intervention round out the responsibilities of hospice social workers.

Gambrill (1997) emphasizes the importance of nonverbal behaviors such as facial expression, gaze, posture and position, proximity, gestures, touch, and physical appearance. These nonverbal communications are even more important and less defined in hospice work. People who are receiving hospice services all have different needs, but all are in "chronic crisis" and many are ultra-sensitive to nonverbal as well as verbal communication.

Hospice provides a setting where a social worker will have the opportunity to use almost all the skills learned in the classroom and field education. It also provides the opportunity to use skills in spiritual care that, unfortunately, are not typically a part of social work.

Hospice: An Opportunity for Truly Wholistic Social Work

As has been mentioned, the hospice movement in the United States does not have the same strong emphasis on religious affiliation as hospices in England. Despite the differences, the religious and spiritual components of hospice in the United States are vital to caring for the dying. By accepting patients with no hope of recovery and offering them hope of spiritual restoration, hospice has called forth the spiritual force in society by challenging the mortality of humans (O'Connor, 1986). Even for patients who have not been active in a church or synagogue, religious concerns often become important as death nears and they may welcome the opportunity to discuss religious matters with a chaplain, pastoral counselor, friends, family, or staff members (Rhymes, 1993).

While there is agreement that spiritual needs of hospice patients and families are important and need to be addressed and that hospice programs need to provide spiritual care, the spiritual care component of hospice care is the most undefined area of service (Meogrossi, 1991). Missinne asserts that providing spiritual care is as important as meeting biophysical and psychosocial needs (Missinne, 1990).

Ed Holland of Methodist Hospital in Minneapolis describes one way hospices attempt to meet the spiritual needs of patients and families. Chaplains in his program are the designated spiritual care providers. In this approach, the chaplains are the team members who provide spiritual care (Holland, Hay, & Rice, 1991). This approach is similar to the medical model utilized at most hospitals of referring all spiritual needs to the chaplain and is the preferred approach of many medical personnel.

In this medical model of spiritual care, if a patient or family member expresses any sort of spiritual concern it is referred to the chaplain. If a team member observes anything he or she believes needs spiritual intervention it is referred to the chaplain. The chaplain acts as a liaison between the patient/family and the mental health professionals on the team. The chaplain is responsible for spiritual/emotional support, pastoral counseling, acting as liaison to community clergy, acting as support group facilitator, providing grief instruction and counseling, coordinating bereavement services, and facilitating religious rituals and worship.

In addition to the familiarity that medical professionals have with it, the acceptance of the referral approach to spiritual care by some hospices may be motivated by a focused definition of spiritual caregiving. A narrow definition of spiritual care "includes specifically priestly acts, administration of sacraments, prayers, Scripture reading, and talking about explicitly religious or theological concerns: theodicy, sin, forgiveness, salvation, and eternal life" (Irion, 1988). Acceptance may also be motivated by the lack of definition of the chaplain role as pointed out by True Ryndes, "You experience role-blurring a great deal with some of the team members, especially social work..." (Schwarz, Schmoll, Ryndes, & Hay, 1991).

Christian social workers who find themselves working in a hospice that utilizes this referral approach to spiritual care will struggle with role-blurring with the chaplain. The overlap of the responsibilities mentioned above with social work are obvious. The social worker who is committed to helping the whole person will also be responsible for providing spiritual/emotional support. Social workers are trained and equipped in advocacy and often serve as liaisons to various individuals and institutions in the community. Social workers have advanced skills in group work and many have had course work that covers issues of grief. While this role-blurring may be frustrating, Christian social workers are equipped to deal with it on two different levels.

Social workers receive education and experience in dealing with role difficulties in practice. Conflict can occur around issues of age, race, ethnicity, culture, and authority. The skills utilized by a young, single social worker to deal with concerns expressed by a mother of four seeking help parenting can be transferred to a situation where a chaplain doubts the ability of a social worker to intervene in a particular situation. Other skills and emphases inherent in social work such as the importance of honest communication are also beneficial in dealing with role confusion. Although social work skills and training can be helpful in dealing with role-blurring, the Christian social worker is equipped to deal with the issue even more effectively. Christians have Jesus' example of servant-leadership (as when He washed the disciples feet in John 13:1-15) as a foundation upon which to build relationships. This servant-leadership avoids the power struggles or "turf wars" that are so common in role-blurring between professionals and additionally is a witness to the world that we are Christ's disciples (John 13:34-35).

Milton Hay of San Diego Hospice describes another way hospices attempt to provide spiritual care to patients and families. This approach emphasizes using all team members to provide spiritual care and sees pastoral care as a religious specialization. He explains that at San Diego Hospice, spiritual care is the *broader* application of the work of the chaplains in the Department of Pastoral Care. Assessments are completed by a team consisting of a nurse and a social worker. The intake social worker completes the initial spiritual assessment. This is a part of the overall psycho-social assessment and includes questions about religious beliefs and involvement as well as questions about feelings and emotions related to the impending death of the patient. When a spiritual "problem" is identified, the ongoing social worker is responsible for resolving it. One of the options the social worker has available is referral to a chaplain. The patient's and family's spiritual needs are continually re-assessed and addressed, but not all see a chaplain. Spiritual assessment and intervention by non-chaplain team members is always appropriate and referrals to chaplains can be made by any team member. These referrals are coordinated by the social worker who works closely with the chaplains regarding spiritual issues (Holland, Hay, & Rice, 1991).

This inter-disciplinary team approach fits well with general hospice philosophy. Hospice is not anti-specialization, but it encourages specialists to adopt a team approach that values role flexibility, "...in a hospice, a social worker may carry a tray, a maintenance worker may comfort a patient, and a physician may promise a prayer" (Munley, 1983).

It almost goes without saying that hospice workers and volunteers should respect spiritual and religious views different than their own. "Hospice provides spiritual care services that are consistent with patient/family beliefs and desire for service..." (National Hospice Organization, 1993). The provision of spiritual care in hospice needs to take into account the patient's and family's right to self-determination. No matter what conclusion the hospice program comes to regarding who will provide spiritual care utilizing which approach, if the patient and family conclude their spiritual needs are not being met, the spiritual care component is not successful.

Truly wholistic social work includes meeting the spiritual needs of clients. Hospice as a field provides opportunities for Christians in social work to be exposed to and meet spiritual needs. The greatest need every individual has is for a personal relationship with Jesus Christ. For those who already have a relationship with Jesus, the greatest need is to grow to become more like Him through discipleship. Social workers pride themselves on helping the whole person. However, most social workers focus only on meeting the physical and emotional needs of their clients. To help the whole person, the Christian social worker must be committed to the practice of evangelism and discipleship. Truly wholistic social work both demonstrates and declares the Good News of Jesus. Hospice can at times provide opportunities for the Christian social worker to overtly engage in evangelism and discipleship.

I have frequently heard that if you give a man a fish you feed him for a day, but if you teach him to fish you feed him for a life time. It wasn't until a recent mission trip to the Philippines that I heard the complete version of this illustration. If you give a man a fish you feed him for a day, if you teach him to fish you feed him for a lifetime, but if you introduce him to the Creator of the fish he will be fed for eternity. Hospice is one practice setting that can at times provide opportunities for Christians in social work to meet needs at all three levels.

The Bible calls us to witnessing and ministry. In Mark 1:17 Jesus commands us to follow Him and promises to make us fishers of men. Jesus tells us to go and make disciples and promises to be with us (Matthew 28:19-20). Acts 1:8 shows that witnessing is not just voluntary or mandatory, but is inevitable. If Christ is in our hearts, He will be in our talk (Atkinson & Roesel, 1995). Ministry unto the least is presented to people of every nation as ministry unto Jesus (Mt. 25:31-46).

People that the social worker will encounter in hospice are in crisis. Either a loved one or they themselves are dying. When people are in crisis and facing the issue of death, they frequently have questions and are open to spiritual issues. I remember caring for a young single woman (I'll call her Ellen) whose 3 month old baby (I'll call her Jennifer) was dying. Over the months we got to know each other I not only demonstrated Christ's love for her, but I verbally presented the Good News of Jesus.

Ellen was a nineteen year old single mother who did not finish high school, she lived with her parents in a rural setting away from her friends, her parents did not approve of the baby's father, and she was making life and death decisions for Jennifer. She had many physical, spiritual, and emotional needs. In my role as hospice social worker I had the opportunity to walk with Ellen through this crisis and meet some of her many needs. I accomplished many traditional social work tasks. I advocated for her and for Jennifer with doctors, children's hospital staff, The Ronald McDonald House, and governmental agencies. I counseled her regarding difficult decisions she had to make. I counseled with the entire family and attempted to facilitate and improve communication. I sat with her and her family during the last few hours of Jennifer's life. I attended the funeral and encouraged Ellen as she continued her life after the death of her dear daughter.

But my "intervention" with Ellen was so much more than just traditional social work—focusing on meeting physical and emotional needs while ignoring the spiritual. Through an emphasis on true evangelism, which includes both demonstration and declaration of the Gospel, Ellen's ultimate need was met. Throughout our relationship we talked about God and heaven and faith until one visit I shared with her the plan of salvation. God convicted her of her sin, she responded in humble repentance and asked Jesus to be her Lord and Savior. She was truly changed by God and began to exhibit the spiritual fruit that only God can develop (Gal. 5:22-23).

At Southwestern Seminary we call the combination of demonstration and declaration of the Gospel with the meeting of physical and emotional needs Ministry-Based Evangelism. The focus of Ministry-Based Evangelism is to develop a relationship through which needs are met in the name of Jesus and true evangelism takes place. As my experience with Ellen demonstrates, hospice can provide a unique opportunity for the Christian social worker to do truly wholistic social work.

Many of the people I encountered in hospice were committed Christians. As I attempted to meet their needs I was able to disciple and challenge them from God's Word. People in crisis have many questions and God has provided everything we need for life and Godliness (2 Peter 1:3). The idea of discipling someone who is more mature is a challenge that can best be met by making sure our counsel is from God's Word (Heb 4:12, 2 Ti. 3:16-17).

Many Christian professionals who have studied the behavioral sciences have become accustomed to looking first to science for answers and often ignore the greatest resource available—The Bible. Providing not only the foundation for our service, The Bible is the living truth (Heb 4:12) that God uses to change lives. I have found it very important to share actual Scripture verses rather than just Biblical insight. Some of the verses I have found helpful to share with hospice clients are listed below.

For Evangelism:

John 14.6 Jesus said to him, I am the way, and the truth, and the life; no one comes to the Father, but through Me.

Rom. 3:23 For all have sinned and fall short of the glory of God.

Rom. 6:23 For the wages of sin is death, but the free gift of God is eternal life in Christ Jesus our Lord.

Rom. 10:9-10 That if you confess with your mouth Jesus as Lord, and believe in your heart that God raised Him from the dead, you shall be saved; for with the heart man believes, resulting in righteousness, and with the mouth he confesses, resulting in salvation.

To Show That God Understands Grief and is Compassionate:

Is.53:3-4 He was despised and forsaken of men, a man of sorrows, and acquainted with grief; and like one from whom men hide their face, He was despised, and we did not esteem Him. Surely our griefs He Himself bore, and our sorrows He carried; yet we ourselves esteemed Him stricken, smitten of God, and afflicted.

2 Chr.30:9 For if you return to the Lord, your brothers and your sons will find compassion before those who led them captive, and will return to this land. For the Lord your God is gracious and compassionate, and will not turn His face away from you if you return to Him.

Ps.22:24 For He has not despised nor abhorred the affliction of the afflicted; neither has He hidden His face from him; but when he cried to Him for help, He heard.

Ps.25:6 Remember, O Lord, Thy compassion and Thy loving kindnesses, for they have been from of old.

Ps.31:7 I will rejoice and be glad in Thy loving kindness, because Thou hast seen my affliction; Thou hast known the troubles of my soul.

Ps.40:11 Thou, O Lord, wilt not withhold Thy compassion from me; Thy loving kindness and Thy truth will continually preserve me.

Ps.51:1 Be gracious to me, O God, according to Thy loving kindness; according to the greatness of Thy compassion blot out my transgressions.

Ps.103:8 The Lord is compassionate and gracious, slow to anger and abounding in loving kindness.

Ps.103:13 Just as a father has compassion on his children, so the Lord has compassion on those who fear Him.

Ps.111:4 He has made His wonders to be remembered; the Lord is gracious and compassionate.

Ps.116:5 Gracious is the Lord, and righteous; yes, our God is compassionate.

Pr.28:13 He who conceals his transgressions will not prosper, but he who confesses and forsakes them will find compassion.

Lu.15:20 And he got up and came to his father. But while he was still a long way off, his father saw him, and felt compassion for him, and ran and embraced him, and kissed him.

Jn.11:35 Jesus wept.

Heb.4:15 For we do not have a high priest who cannot sympathize with our weaknesses, but One who has been tempted in all things as we are, yet without sin.

The above verses are just a small sample of all that the Bible says to those in hospice. I encourage you to look them up and read them in context to better understand their application for hospice social work. It is my prayer that whatever social work setting you find yourself in, you will search the Scriptures and allow them to provide the foundation and the vehicle for helping people.

Conclusion

The world would have us believe that death is something to fear and that those facing the death of themselves or a loved one will receive little comfort or hope. For many years hospice has provided comfort for dying patients and their families. Christian social workers in hospice have an opportunity to provide both comfort and hope. The Bible provides many verses that tell us about our hope and encourage us to share it (Rom. 15:4; 1 Pet. 3:15; Col. 1:5; Tit. 2:13; He. 6:18-19; 1 Pet. 1:3). We can share the message that "God is able to do exceeding abundantly beyond all that we ask or think, according to the power that works within us (Eph. 3:20)." Finally, in the midst of our own grief in helping people facing death, as members of God's family we can rest on and share the family secret: "And WE KNOW that God causes all things to work together for good to those who love God, to those who are called according to His purpose (Rom. 8:28)."

References

Atkinson, Donald A. & Charles L. Roesel. (1995). *Meeting Needs Sharing Christ*. Lifeway Press: Nashville, TN.

Bulkin, Wilma & Herbert Lukashok. (1988). Rx for Dying: The Case for Hospice. *New England Journal of Medicine*, February 11, 378-80.

Gambrill, Eileen. (1997). *Social Work Practice*. Oxford University Press: NY.

Holland, Milton Hay & S. Rice. (1991). Don't Put a Round Plug in a Square Hole! Developing an Effective Spiritual Care Model for Your Hospice. Tape recording of presentation made at National Hospice Organization's First National Conference on Spiritual Care in Hospice, Kansas City, MO.

Irion, Paul E. (1988). *Hospice and Ministry*. Nashville: Abingdon Press.

Jennings, Bruce. (1997). Individual Rights and the Human Good in Hospice. *The Hospice Journal*, 12(2), 1-8.

Ley, Dorothy & Inge Corless. (1988). Spirituality and Hospice Care. *Death Studies*, 12,101-05.

MacDonald, Douglas. (1991). Hospice Social Work: A Search for Identity. *Health and Social Work*, 16 November, 274-80.

Meogrossi, Romuald J. (1991). A Comparison of Patient Satisfaction of Persons Treated in Church-related and Nonchurch-related Hospices. D.P.C. dissertation, Loyola College in Maryland.

Missinne, Leo. (1990). Death & Spiritual Concerns of Older Adults. *Generations, 14* Fall, 45- 49.

Munley, Anne. (1983). *The Hospice Alternative*. New York: Basic Books.

National Hospice Organization. (1994). *Standards of a Hospice Program of Care.* Arlington, VA: National Hospice Organization.

O'Connor, Patrice. (1986). Spiritual Elements of Hospice Care. *Hospice Journal,* 2 Summer, 108-19.

Quig, Lois. (1989). The Role of the Hospice Social Worker. *The American Journal of Hospice Care,* 6 (July/August),22-23.

Rhymes, Jill. (1993). Hospice Care in the Nursing Home. *Nursing Home Medicine,* 1 (November), 16.

Richardson, Joan. (1997). Embracing The New, Guarding The Past. *The Hospice Professional,* Spring, 13-14.

Rusnack, Betty, Sarajane McNulty Schaefer, & David Moxley. (1988). "Safe Passage": Social Work Roles and Functions in Hospice Care. *Social Work in Healthcare, 13,* 3-19.

Schwarz, Jack, Betty Schmoll, True Ryndes, & Milton Hay. (1991). The State of the Art of Spiritual Caring in the 1990's Science of Hospice. Tape recording of presentation at National Hospice Organization's First National Conference on Spiritual Care in Hospice, Kansas City, MO.

Stoddard, Sandoll. (1991). *The Hospice Movement.* New York: Vantage Books.

CHAPTER 15

SPIRITUALLY SENSITIVE ASSESSMENT TOOLS FOR SOCIAL WORK PRACTICE

Timothy A. Boyd

In the social work endeavor, assessment has been a mainstay of the social workers' effective helping of clients. Without proper and thorough assessment, it is difficult to know how to structure and implement intervention strategies that fit the individual client. Effective assessment individualizes the intervention plan, and allows it to be tailored to the specific needs of the client—effective interventions flow out of effective assessments.

The hallmark of social work assessment, and the thing that differentiates it from assessments done by other disciplines, is its emphasis on a holistic picture of the client. Social work assessment focuses on the person-in-situation, and insists on the exploration of the interactions between the person and the various systems that affect that person. The assessment, therefore, is transactional in nature. It is a fluid, dynamic, and ongoing process, rather than a static product. The results of this kind of assessment leads the worker to a complex, multi-faceted understanding of the client, rather than to a diagnostic category based upon symptoms and their configuration. While social workers can and do use diagnostic systems such as the DSM-IV (Diagnostic and Statistical Manual of the American Psychiatric Association), they often feel torn between the need to work within the prevailing classification systems of modern therapy, and the need to describe the client in more holistic terms. Many social workers find difficulty with an emphasis on the medical model-based systems that tend to classify people according to symptoms rather than describing them in a way that includes strengths, resources, coping skills and the environmental forces that impinge upon their lives. As Goldenberg (1983) states, assessment needs to "obtain a picture of a person's strengths, assets, and adaptive functions as well as weaknesses, deficits, and dysfunctions; to look beyond the individual alone in order to see and understand his or her behavior and experience within a broader context" (p. 82-83).

In order to have a truly multi-dimensional assessment and a complete picture of the clients' functioning, it is necessary to gather data and understandings of the total person, both internal and external. This requires multiple sources of information. Rauch (1993) says, "assessment can be defined as the process of gathering, analyzing, and synthesizing salient data into a multi-dimensional formulation that provides the basis for action decisions" (p. XIV). It includes both the factors that maintain a problem as well as the resources that can be mobilized for change. Jordan and Franklin (1995) list five factors that encompass a multi-dimensional assessment:

- The nature of the clients' problems
- The functioning of clients and significant others (strengths, limitations, personality assets and deficiencies)
- The motivation of clients to work on their problems
- The relevant environmental factors that contribute to the problem
- The resources that are available or are needed to ameliorate the client's difficulties (p. 3)

Since professional social work values and works with many dimensions of a client's life, it would seem logical that social work assessments would be inclusive of all the following; the biological, psychological, social-cultural, *and* religious/spiritual dimensions. In fact, Jordan and Franklin (1995) make the assumption that well-qualified practitioners are knowledgeable about numerous assessment methods. It is curious, however, that most social work assessment texts and writings seem to ignore or give cursory examination to the religious/spiritual dimension, while affording a thorough examination of the other dimensions. An exploration of the various assessment tools, tests, and surveys used in the field reveals a paucity of resources that social work practitioners can utilize in their attempts to do holistic assessments. On the positive side, there does seem to be a growing awareness in the field of the importance of the religious/spiritual dimension, and an attempt to integrate this perspective into social work education and practice. Perhaps this will result in the development of a variety of assessment tools that can be used to explore this dimension.

Evidence of the growing awareness of the importance of the religious/spiritual dimension in assessment can be seen in the change that was enacted in the fourth edition of the Diagnostic and Statistical Manual (DSM-IV) (1994). The fourth edition, in a change from the third, included a V-Code (which describes additional conditions, other than clinical disorders, that may be the focus of clinical attention) for Religious and Spiritual Problems (p. 685). The Manual states that this category can be used when the focus of clinical attention is a religious or spiritual problem, and gives examples such as loss or questioning of faith, problems associated with conversion to a new faith, or the questioning of spiritual values (p. 685). The P-I-E System (Person In Environment System, 1994), which is one of the newest classification systems, has been developed by social workers and has the endorsement of the NASW (National Association of Social Workers). P-I-E has a category under "Voluntary System Problems" for problems related to religious groups. These problems could involve lack of a religious group or choice, lack of community acceptance of religious values, or other religious group problems (1994, p. 32). The P-I-E Manual also lists religious discrimination and religious member role problems as possible sources of client distress. Both the DSM-IV and the P-I-E System, however, only focus on the problematic aspects of a person's religious/spiritual life, and do not address the beneficial effects.

Religion is of prime importance in the lives of a majority of Americans. Gallup surveys indicate that 2/3 of the population of the U.S. consider religion to be important or very important in their lives (Religion in America, 1985). A Gallup poll (Gallup & Castelle, 1989) revealed that 94% of the U.S. population believes in God and report their relationship with God has influenced their beliefs. 40% of Americans attend religious services one time per week and 60% have a religious membership of some sort (Bellah et al, 1985, p. 219). Bullis (1994) cites a 1988 study done by Greif and Porembski that illustrates one example of how religion plays a key role in the coping response of a population in crisis. Bullis said that the researchers "looked at the coping mechanisms of individuals, families, and friends faced with the crisis of AIDS" and found that "a renewed or continued faith in God, both for themselves and the person with AIDS, was a factor, if not the most important factor for 9 out of 11 respondents" (p. 12). Derezotes (1995) succinctly summed up the importance of this issue when he said that "the social worker has a responsibility to assess each client's unique spiritual development and religiosity, and to provide interventions that reflect both developmental levels and religious doctrines and rituals" (p. 11).

Is there a difference between the religiosity of social workers and the population in general? A study by Bergin and Jensen (1990) found that 44% of their sample of clinical social workers were regular religious service attendees, 83% said that they tried hard to live by their religious beliefs, and 46% said their whole approach to life was based upon their religion (contrasted to 72% of the general public). Bergin's conclusion, in another article (1991), was that therapists are generally more religious than would be expected, although less so than the general public. In light of this finding, Bergin (1991) puzzled over his findings that only 29% of therapists rated religious content in the process of psychotherapy as important in guiding and evaluating treatment with

many or all clients. Bergin conjectured about a "religiosity gap" between clients and therapists, and suggested that this gap may explain
why people in distress often prefer counsel from clergy rather than counsel by mental health professionals (citing a 1981 study by Veroff, Kulka,
& Donovan).

A survey done by Elhiany, McLaughlin, Brown, and Bertucci (Unpublished paper) used a sample of 30 social work educators, 30 practitioners, and 90 social work students. They found that 96% of the educators,
93% of the practitioners, and 92% of the students felt that client religious
and spiritual beliefs are important in treatment, but only 8% of the educators, 13% of the practitioners, and 15% of the students said that they discuss a client's in-depth religious and spiritual beliefs during an initial assessment. Also reported was that 37% of the educators, 43% of the practitioners, and 30% of the students felt that these beliefs should be discussed
only when the client presents the issue to the worker. Another survey which
presents an apparently different conclusion, was carried out by Bullis (1992)
with a sample of 116 clinical social workers in Virginia. On a 5-point scale
(1=Not at all to 5=Always) respondents had a mean of 3.57 on the factor of
"Frequency of Use of Religion or Spiritual Factors in Assessment." Respondents also had a mean of 3.77 on a 5-point scale (1=Not at All Important to
5=Extremely Important) on the factor of "Importance of Religious and Spiritual Factors in Assessment."

It appears that, although a majority of social workers are religiously
or spiritually involved themselves, many may be reluctant for a variety
of reasons to pursue an in-depth exploration of spiritual and religious
issues in their client's lives. Bergin (1992) wondered if this reflects "that
such matters have not been incorporated into clinical training as have
other modern issues such as gender, ethnicity, and race" (p. 396). Another factor might be located in a concern on the part of social workers
that a more focused exploration of religious/spiritual issues might lead
to an imposition of personal values on the client, which would be a
violation of the ethical principle of self-determination. Perhaps there is
some avoidance of these issues related to the ongoing debate over the
functional versus dysfunctional aspects of religion. A number of theo-
rists, most notably Sigmund Freud and Albert Ellis, have written about
the immaturity inherent in an individuals' need for involvement in religion. As many practitioners have been influenced by these ideas in their
professional training and development, an ambivalence may have been
created in many professionals who now fear being too positive toward
religious involvement. In addition, personal observations of the negative effects of dysfunctional belief systems on clients may also reinforce
this reluctance.

Importance and Relevancy of Religious/Spiritual Assessment

For the purposes of this chapter, a distinction will be made between religion/religiosity and spirituality. In religion, people usually have some kind of identification or affiliation with an institutional structure. Such an affiliation involves religious roles, practices, doctrines, and identities. Spirituality is a broader, less well-defined term that refers to a person's attempt to find meaning in their life, to move toward higher states of consciousness, or to transcend themselves. It may or may not find expression in some form of institutional membership, beliefs or practices. Spirituality is a universal — every person has a spiritual self. Dombeck and Karl (1987) state that "every person can be understood to have a spiritual life, although some persons do not subscribe to any established religion" (p. 184). All persons have worldviews, belief systems, and value systems that orient their life decisions.

In addition to assessing information regarding a person's religious affiliations and the actual content of their spirituality, it is important to assess the process whereby their spiritual identity was developed, and how that identity is translated into principles for living. These more complex dimensions may require somewhat more sophistication in the assessment process, but are key to a holistic understanding of the person's capacities for change and growth. Victor Frankl (1968) went as far as to say that "the proper diagnosis can be made only by someone who could see the spiritual side of man" (p. ix).

The social worker who is sensitive and informed about a persons' religious/spiritual life is better equipped to engage and develop rapport with a client, as well as to develop intervention strategies that will be successful. Netting (1982) states that ethical decision-making in both micro and macro practice often includes an understanding of religious values. If a social worker is reluctant to explore religious/spiritual issues that are important to a client, it leaves the unspoken message that these issues are to be avoided, and subsequently, clients may be hesitant to offer information about such concerns. To ask about a person's religious beliefs, values, and affiliations is to affirm their importance. It is important to note that clients are affected by what we ask or do not ask, and by the manner in which we ask and by our responses to their verbalizations.

In a review of the empirical literature from 1974 to 1987 on religious counseling, Worthington (1986) suggests that highly religious clients have two fears about participating in psychotherapy with non-religious therapists; first, that their values will be challenged, and second, that they will be misunderstood and misdiagnosed. This fear may have some basis in reality. A study done by Gartner, Harmatz, Larson, and Gartner (1990) found evidence that religiously and politically extreme patients were assigned psychiatric diagnoses more frequently than patients whose religious and political views were unknown. In an article by Canda (1988), in which he describes the results of interviews with 18 social workers who had demonstrated knowledge concerning spirituality and social work, he reports comments relating to the importance of religious/spiritual self-awareness on the part of practitioners. A comment given by one of the interviewees was that a "social worker has to be in touch with [her] own feelings...about spiritual [and] religious beliefs [and] be aware of [her] own unresolved issues about institutional religion," and that a "social worker must be comfortable with his/her beliefs in order to learn appropriate skills for exploring these issues without the distortions of countertransference" (p. 244). Canda, in the article, reminds social workers that clients sometimes have spiritually significant experiences that sound unfamiliar and bizarre, but that it is important to not confuse insights achieved during peak experiences or altered states of consciousness with psychopathology (p. 246).

Another advantage of a thorough religious/spiritual assessment of clients at intake is in the awareness gained which can facilitate an optimal matching of client to worker. Research has demonstrated that clients prefer a counseling approach consistent with their worldview (Lyddon & Adamson, 1982). Denton (1990), in an article on the religiously fundamentalist family, said that religion for these families tends to permeate every aspect of family life (including interpersonal relationships, roles, family boundaries, relationship to community, and help-seeking behaviors). Denton expressed the belief that unique assessment skills are needed in working with these families, because they are so different from other families. He further described the ethical dilemma that is encountered when the therapist believes that the families' beliefs are pathological, or perceives the families' problems to be caused by their religion (p. 10).

A possible benefit for clients in being asked to participate in a religious/spiritual assessment can be found in the effect of the procedure itself. The worker's initiative to explore spiritual issues may act as a catalyst for clients to recognize and grapple with the questions of worth and meaning that underlie their life experiences. Sensitive and well-timed inquiries can serve to help clients enter a process of self-reflection, look beyond their circumstances to the broader context, and evaluate the principles and values they use to give direction to their lives. The worker's interest in these issues may help deepen the client's interest in their own spiritual journey. Being asked a timely question can promote a substantive dialogue between worker and client about religious issues that are at the heart of the client's dilemma.

Lastly, the exploration of a client's religious affiliations can help both worker and client discover linkages to religious social support systems that may be advantageous in the identification of resources to aid the helping process. Religious leaders, clergy, and spiritual healers can be utilized as consultants to the worker, and can serve as reinforcement and support for the changes that a client is attempting to make. Abbot, Berry, and Meredith (1990) list five ways that religion can be an asset to family functioning:

- By enhancing the family's social support network
- By sponsoring supportive family activities and recreation
- By promoting supportive family teachings and values
- By providing family social and welfare services
- By encouraging families to seek divine assistance with personal and family problems (p. 443)

Dimensions of Religious/Spiritual Assessment

Just as there are several dimensions to a holistic assessment of clients, there are also several dimensions within a holistic assessment of religious/spiritual life. Attempts to explore these dimensions allows the worker to develop a more robust or texture-filled assessment. The assessment of the religious/spiritual life of clients ranges from the more basic collection of factual information to a more sophisticated assessment of factors such as level of religious development and spiritual maturity. It may be useful to assess a client's categorical religious affiliations (what kind of religious institutions or denominations the client is involved with), but it is also vital to know the degree to which he/she is involved in that group, the degree of commitment she/he has to the group, and the amount of support received from the group. Doing a holistic assessment does not mean that the worker has the goal of exploring every conceivable religious/spiritual question, but rather, crafts the assessment in light of its' overall purpose or usefulness. The worker always maintains an integrative focus with the client's presenting and ongoing problems. The assessment must be well integrated with the intervention goals, and should be prescriptive of treatment. This is part of the art of assessment — knowing what to explore and when to explore it.

Because assessment is an ongoing process, the worker does not need to pressure the client or themselves into finding out all there is to know. An effective assessment unfolds over time, depending on a number of factors. Because religious/spiritual issues are usually very personal and clients experience a sense of vulnerability about them, workers must approach their exploration with utmost sensitivity and discretion. This is especially true for those clients who have had negative or harmful experiences in their past religious/spiritual life. An astute worker possesses the skills to effectively assess persons from a wide range of religious systems and personal backgrounds, which often requires study into the cultural context of those systems.

The social work setting (where the assessment is being carried out) is also important to the manner in which an assessment is conducted. First, and most obvious, are the particular parameters for practice that have been established by the agency or organization. It is important that the worker be in concert with the practice guidelines of their agency.

There are some social work settings where religious/spiritual factors are especially cogent, by virtue of the variety of religious issues that regularly surface. Two examples can be found in work with elderly clients and hospice clients. Issues related to the afterlife, doing life reviews (an examination of life events and relationships carried out as a means of coming to terms with their life), and emotional responses to the process of aging and/or dying are regularly encountered with these populations, especially as they confront their own impending death. Religious/spiritual issues come to the forefront for many people at these times. Watson, Howard, Hood, and Morris (1985) demonstrated that intrinsic religiosity (religion as a master motive in one's life) is significantly associated with age.

Another setting which has traditionally involved the spiritual dimension in the process of help is the field of chemical dependency. The 12-Step program, with it's focus on the relationship between the chemically dependent person and their "higher power," naturally requires the assessment of religious/spiritual issues. In addition to this setting, there are certain other population groups in which religious affiliations seem to be of particular centrality to the socio-cultural matrix of the client. For example, many immigrant clients find a strong source of personal stabilization in their identifications with their religious groups as they negotiate the process of transitioning and acculturation.

Social workers assess client religious/spiritual issues also with regard to both the functional and dysfunctional effects on the individual. This involves some judgment on the part of the worker related to what may have a positive effect on client functioning, as well as what may have a negative impact. This aspect of assessment gauges a clients's "health" from a spiritual perspective. The judgments are slippery, and the worker must attend to their own countertransferences and biases in order to remain objective. The classification process can become subjective, for example, when a client's group affiliation is called a "cult," a term which is often experienced by clients as a pejorative or inaccurate description. The label "fundamentalist," as another example, carries the same kind of subjective coloring. While some clients may welcome such a descriptor, others might feel misunderstood. It is important in the assessment process, therefore, to explore the client's own meanings and evaluations. What kind of designations, labels, and descriptions do they give (ascertaining their own descriptive words and metaphors)? Workers serve their clients well by being sensitive to their use of language. Some clients may be comfortable with assessment questions that are contextualized in "religious language" while other clients are more comfortable with less religiously oriented language. Canda's (1988) interviews with social workers led him to the conclusion that spiritually sensitive practitioners attuned themselves to the specific beliefs and needs of the clients without imposing their own beliefs, and were able to maintain an appreciation for the diverse spiritual beliefs of their clients, yet maintained a strong commitment to their own beliefs (p. 245).

A number of studies have established a clear correlation between religiosity and a person's general sense of well-being. Koenig, Kvale, and Ferrel (1988) found a significant positive correlation between intrinsic religiosity, organizational religious activity, ability to cope, and morale. Koenig, George, and Siegler (1988) discovered a positive relationship between religious behaviors and well-being, and Willits and Crider (1988) also identified a relationship between religiosity and overall well-being and satisfying relationships. In exploring the beneficial aspects of a religious/spiritual orientation, the worker may want to know such things as how the client's religious /spiritual connections:

- Foster pro-social attitudes and behaviors (help the client maintain fulfilling relationships with others)
- Help to maintain positive support networks with their environment
- Foster growth, health, and life-style improvements
- Give comfort and solace in time of crisis
- Give help in problem solving and ethical decision-making
- Provide stability at times of stress and loss
- Provide goods and resources, social services, and social opportunities

The worker will also need to explore how people use their beliefs in the process of coping. Religious/spiritual defense mechanisms can serve a purpose in the clients' attempts to negotiate their life events, even if they may not be the most functional ways to do so. Although past negative religious/spiritual experiences may cause a client to be indifferent, or even hostile toward their background, the client is still effected by what has been experienced and internalized. An assessment of negative religious/spiritual experiences can be vital in the selection and utilization of interventions. Client willingness and readiness to incorporate and act upon certain interventions depends upon what meaning those experiences have to them.

A thorough assessment of religious/spiritual issues will not only identify the beliefs and practices of an individual, but will also explore how those beliefs and practices are operationalized in the client's life. A consideration in this regard is the degree that a client has a committed or consensual faith; ie. what degree of commitment does she/he have to the beliefs and doctrines of their religious affiliation or group. This understanding may help explain how a person can identify with a particular religious group, but not necessarily be invested in meeting the behavioral expectations of the group. It is important to remember that there is within religious groups a significant amount of diversity among adherents, such that one cannot assume that people from a particular faith group are homogeneous in their commitments to their beliefs and practices.

A prime issue for consideration in the assessment of families is the way that religion permeates family life. Denton (1990) outlines five major questions for consideration in family assessment:

- Is religion used for extrinsic (social) or intrinsic (spiritual) purposes?
- Do family members vary in their investment in the religious community and belief structure?
- Is the family enmeshed in the church community?
- To what degree is the problem given a religious interpretation, which will dictate the   extent to which the worker will have to make use of religious beliefs in order to change the family system?
- To what degree is religion used as a control mechanism? (p. 10-11)

The family assessment will need to examine, therefore, the way family structure, roles, and boundaries are effected by the family's religious system, with these considerations having major implications for intervention planning.

Religious/spiritual assessment usually incorporates three time dimensions — past, present, and future. The historical perspective (past) explores such things as the events, experiences, and individuals that have shaped a person's life. The present dimension explores how a person is currently manifesting their spiritual self — their current beliefs and affiliations. The future dimension focuses on the person's hopes and desires for spiritual growth, their spiritual "vision," their anticipation about the afterlife, and issues such as "How will I raise my children in regard to their spiritual life?"

Lastly, the social worker may need to take a developmental perspective when doing the assessment, focusing on understanding the level or stage of the client's moral and spiritual development. The developmental dynamics of spiritual well-being can be difficult to measure, however. Canda (1988) called for criteria that would establish a client's level of moral and spiritual development, but also cautioned that the development of these criteria requires much work. He states that "perhaps a client's spiritual development can be evaluated according to their life satisfaction, degree of caring and love in relationship with others, capacity for sophisticated moral reflection, and willingness to come to terms with morality and other challenges to their sense of meaning and purpose," but cautions that "these criteria should not be used to reduce the client's spirituality to externally observable behavior" (p. 246). It is generally safe to conjecture that a client's level of spiritual development will be a key factor in their responses to the challenges of life. How clients respond to problems, life choices, value conflicts, and suffering, for example, is intimately related to the internalized principles of worth and meaning that they have developed.

Techniques

The techniques used in the assessment of religious/spiritual issues vary little from those used in assessment in general. In fact, some of the most widely used social work tools can be usefully translated into more specific applications in religious/spiritual assessment. Perhaps the simplest is the time line, which allows the client and worker to see the process of development in the client's spiritual life. A time line can be drawn upon which the key religious/spiritual experiences can be depicted (membership in groups, key mentors/spiritual guides/leaders, baptism/conversion/communion/Bar-Mitzvah/rites of passage, etc.). Bullis (1996) suggests that the time line can be "supplemented with photographs or a collage of pictures and drawings" (p. 35).

The genogram can also be adapted for use in a religious/spiritual assessment utilizing the same procedures used for a family system or genetic genogram. Bullis (1996) says that spiritual genograms are a kind of family tree which charts — those persons, places, ideas and experiences that have formed one's spiritual identity or lack thereof (p. 34).

Another tool, the eco-map, can be adapted for use. The eco-map is generally used to identify how a person relates to the variety of systems that impact his/her life, and the "rate, direction, and mutuality of resource exchanges" (Mattaini, 1993, p. 22). One could include the religious/spiritual systems as part of this larger systemic review, or could devote one specific eco-map to a more detailed depiction of the religious/spiritual subsystems and relationships.

Additional assessment techniques could be implemented using drawings, collages, and sculptures. One could ask an adult to draw a picture depicting their current spiritual identity, or a child to draw a picture of what God is like. The family sculpture technique could be modified to depict a family's spiritual life at present, or to show the type of spiritual life a family identifies as a desired goal (with each family member having a chance to do their own sculpture). In addition to these tools, there are other surveys, questionnaires, and tests that can be utilized, although a survey done by this author found the selection to be quite limited. Some of these available tools cover a wider range of religious/spiritual dimensions, but have limited depth, while others focus intensely only on a specific religious/spiritual dimension, but have limited range.

A Comprehensive Religious/Spiritual Assessment Tool

Following is a multi-dimensional religious/spiritual assessment tool that can be utilized with clients. It is designed to cover a range of issues, and includes a variety of questions of an exploratory nature that could be utilized. Appropriate use of this tool, however, is dependent on it's modification to the individual situation. The assessor needs to have a well-conceived rationale for what issues will be addressed, and when in the helping process those issues may be most appropriately explored. Questions can be modified and adapted to fit the specific client and situation (utilizing appropriate use of language, terms, and metaphors). Appropriate use for most clients would require careful limited selection of relevant issues (it is not intended to be given in its entirety).

I. RELIGIOUS AND SPIRITUAL HISTORY

1. Religious Upbringing

a. How would you describe your religious upbringing? Growing up, what were the religious and spiritual beliefs of your parents? Your siblings? Your extended family? How invested were they in them? What would you consider to be the most important beliefs they held? What were their religious and spiritual practices? What kinds of words would you use to describe your religious upbringing (strict, liberal, conservative, permissive, punishing, positive, negative, nurturing, deprivational, stunting, stimulating, non-existent)?

b. What kind of religious and spiritual training did you receive? What have you retained from this training? If you are not still practicing your earlier faith, why not?

c. Who would you consider to be your spiritual ancestors?

2. Life-Shaping Experiences

a. What kinds of experiences, events, persons, events, and crises shaped your religious and spiritual identity...positively...negatively?

3. Conversion/Peak/Mystical Experiences

a. Have you had anything you would describe as a "conversion experience?"

b. Have you ever experienced something you would call a "mystical" experience?

4. Spiritual Crises and Emergencies

a. Have you had any crises of faith...belief in your life? How did you handle them? How are you different now?

5. Current Social Environment

a. What are the beliefs and practices of the significant others in your life (spouse, partner, children, friends)? How do religious/spiritual issues affect your relationships?

b. What approach or religious/ and spiritual orientation are you using in your child- rearing? Are others (spouse) in agreement on the approach? What are the most important spiritual beliefs that you would like to instill in your children?

c. What relationships do you currently have that positively...negatively affect your spiritual self? How do other key people in your life view your faith? How does that affect you?

d. Do you have any clergy/church leaders/counselors that you respect...trust...confide in?

II. CURRENT BELIEFS AND PRACTICES

1. Religious Identity

a. Do you identify with any particular religion or faith? Would you consider yourself a religious person?

2. Commitment Level

    a. How central is your religion in your life? Your faith?

    b. How committed are you to your particular religion/faith?

3. Religious Identifications/Affiliations/Involvements

    a. Do you attend a particular church/synagogue/mosque/etc.? Do your friends attend the same place of worship that you do? Do you keep in touch with people from your religious group? How invested are you in your religious community? What is the attitude of your religious group toward outsiders?

    b. What kinds of social support do you receive from your religious community? What kinds of resources and opportunities are made available to you (financial, recreational, goods and services, other)?

4. Codification of Beliefs

    a. What are your most important beliefs? Do you adhere to any particular code... commandments... doctrinal requirements? Do you find that you are able to follow them? Do you have any sacred writings... books... scriptures from which you receive instruction? Do you read these writings? Are there any particular characters from these writings that you identify with?

    b. How, and to what extent, does your religious belief system have rules and/or norms about marriage... child-rearing practices... divorce... abortion... premarital sex... cohabitation... contraception... sex roles...? How do these beliefs affect your family life?

    c. What is sin? What would be the worst sin one could commit?

    d. What are your beliefs about human nature... human responsibility?

    e. What are your beliefs about an afterlife? How is it determined what happens to a person after their death? What do you believe will happen to you?

5. Rituals, Images, Symbols, Behavioral Enactments, Observances, Practices

    a. What have been some of the most significant religious rituals that you have participated in (baptism, communion, Bar-Mitzvah, rites of passage, membership, etc.)?

    b. Do you pray? How? How often? What do you pray about? What are your expectations about what will happen when you pray? Do you find it helpful to pray?

    c. How do you prefer to worship?

d. Do you participate in any kinds of "healing" rituals? What are your beliefs about healing?

e. What other kinds of religious rituals do you participate in?

6. *God Image, Theodocies*

a. Do you have a belief in a higher power? What name do you use for the Supreme Being? Do you have faith (trust) in this being? How do you experience God? What is your understanding about God?

b. What is God/Allah/Other like? What kinds of thoughts... feelings... memories... words come to your mind when you think of God?

c. How does God communicate to humans... to you?

d. Does God intervene in the events of this world? How? How does God regard human suffering? How concerned is God about your problems?

7. *Concepts of Evil and the Demonic*

a. Do you believe in evil beings? What names, if any, do you use for them? How do these beings/forces affect the world....your life? Have you ever had any experiences with the demonic that have affected your life?

III. SPIRITUAL MATURITY AND DEVELOPMENT

1. *Development Through Stages of Life*

a. As you have gotten older, how has your faith changed? Can you think of times that you have received help from your faith, as you have struggled with life events?

b. What kinds of spiritual conflicts are you now dealing with?

2. *Effect of Religious/Spiritual Identity on Life Style*

a. How do your beliefs affect your behavior? How do you decide what is right or wrong? How do you go about decision-making? How does your faith affect the way you handle guilt...fear?

c. Do your spiritual beliefs affect your ideas and practices regarding "forgiveness?"

d. How does your faith help you to cope with your current life circumstances?

e. How do your beliefs affect your physical health or self-maintenance?

3. Meaning of Life Issues

a. What gives your life meaning (makes life worthwhile)? Are you hopeful about the future... Why? When you get discouraged, what renews your sense of hope... vitality... purpose? Have you had any particular experiences that have shaken... affirmed your optimism? How satisfied are you with your life? Why do you think you are alive (what is the purpose)?

b. What are your goals for spiritual growth? What is your "growing edge?"

c. What does death mean to you? Are you afraid to die? What do you think happens after one dies? What do you believe will happen to you when you die? Have you thought about your own death? Have you experienced the death of someone you were close to?

d. How does your faith motivate you?

e. What is your ideal of mature faith?

4. Moral Frame of Reference

a. What are your key values? How did you develop them?

References

Abbot, A., Berry, M., & Meredith, W. (1990). Religious belief and practices. *Family Relations, 39,* 443-48.

American Psychiatric Association. (1994). *Diagnostic and Statistical Manual of Mental Disorders.* Washington, D.C.: American Psychiatric Association.

Bellah, R., Madsen, R., Sullivan, W., Swidler, A., & Tipton, S. (1985). *Habits of the Heart.* N.Y.: Harper Row.

Bergin, A. (1991). Values and religious issues in psychotherapy and mental health. *American Psychologist, 46*(4), 394-403.

Bergin, A., & Jensen, J. (1990). Religiosity of psychotherapists: A national survey. *Psychotherapy, 27,* 3-7.

Bullis, R. (1996). *Spirituality in Social Work Practice.* Washington, D.C.: Taylor and Francis.

Canda, E. (1988). Spirituality, religious diversity, and social work practice. *Social Casework, 69*(4), 238-47.

Canda, E. (1989). Religious content in social work education: A comparative approach. *Journal of Social Work Education,* Winter, 36-45.

Denton, R. (1990). The religiously fundamentalist family: Training for assessment and treatment. *Journal of Social Work Education,* Winter, 6-14.

Derezotes, D. (1995). Spirituality and religiosity: Neglected factors in social work practice. *Arete, 20,* 1-15.

Dombeck, M., & Karl, J. (1987). Spiritual issues in mental health care. *Journal of Religion and Health, 26,* 183-97.

Elhiany, A., McLaughlin, S., Brown, P., & Bertucci, G. (1997). *The role of religion and spirituality in social work education and practice*. Unpublished Paper.

Frankl, V. (1968). *The Doctor and the Soul*. N.Y.: Knopf.

Gallup, G. (1985). *Religion in America* [Report # 236]. Princeton, N.J.: Gallup Organization.

Gallup, G., & Castelle, J. (1989). *The People's Religion: American Faith in the 90's*. N.Y.: McMillan.

Gartner, J., Harmatz, M., Larson, D., & Gartner, A. (1990). The effect of patient and clinician ideology in clinical judgment: A study of ideological transference. *Psychotherapy, 23*, 98-106.

Goldenberg, H. (1983). *Contemporary Clinical Psychology (Second Edition)*. Monterey, CA.: Brooks Cole.

Jordan, C., & Franklin, C. (1995). *Clinical Assessment for Social Workers*. Chicago: Lyceum.

Karls, J., & Wandrei, K. (1994). *Person-In-Environment System*. Washington, D.C.: NASW Press.

Koenig, H., George, L., & Siegler, I. (1988). The use of religion and other emotion-regulating strategies among older adults. *The Gerontologist, 28*, 301-10.

Koenig, H., Kvale, J., & Ferrel, C. (1988). Religion and well-being in later life. *The Gerontologist, 28*, 18-28.

Lyddon, W., & Adamson, L. (1982). World view and counseling preference: An analogue study. *Journal of Counseling and Development, 71*, 41-47.

Mattaini, M. (1993). *More Than a Thousand Words: Graphics for Clinical Practice*. Washington, D.C.: NASW Press.

Netting, E. (1982). Social work and religious values in church-related social agencies. *Social Work and Christianity, 9*(1-2), 4-20.

Rauch, J. (1993). *Assessment: A Source Book for Social Work Practice*. Milwaukee, WI: Families International.

Veroff, J., Kulka, R., & Douvan, E. (1981). *Mental Health in America*. N.Y.: Basic Books.

Watson, P., Howard, R., Hood, R., & Morris, R. (1985). Age and religious orientation. *Review of Religious Research, 29*, 271-80.

Willits, F., & Crider, D. (1988). Religion and well-being: Men and women in the middle years. *Review of Religious Research, 29*, 281-94.

Worthington, E. (1986). Religious counseling: A review of published empirical research. *Journal of Counseling and Development, 64*, 421-31.

CHAPTER 16

THE FIELD OF CHILD WELFARE: SUFFER THE LITTLE CHILDREN

Gary Anderson

Social work practice takes place in a variety of settings and fields of practice. One of the most complex and challenging fields for social work is the field of child welfare. With the specter of abused and neglected children and the complications of working with multiple systems, this field of practice poses value questions and emotional dilemmas in addition to clinical and policy challenges for the social worker. Child welfare settings are some of the few places in which social workers are the predominant profession. It is also a field of practice that employs high numbers of social workers. Whether employed in child welfare or not, all social workers need to have some knowledge about child maltreatment and the system designed to respond to child abuse and neglect as all social workers have a professional and legal responsibility to recognize and report suspected child maltreatment.

There is a strong and positive relationship between child welfare and religion. Compassion for children and a commitment to family life are common ground for the Christian community and professionals concerned about the well-being of children. But there is also a degree of tension. Some in child welfare might question the church's vigilance in protecting children from abuse or neglect as demonstrated by the sexual abuse of children by clergy or other religious authority figures. Some might view various religious viewpoints as encouraging parents to be abusive and practice severe physical punishment in disciplining children. Hence child welfare authorities may view religion and churches as failing to see and appreciate child maltreatment and even at times allowing or encouraging such treatment. Conversely, religious people might be suspicious of the state's role and potential intrusiveness in parenting and interfering with the autonomy and integrity of the family. The Christian social worker in child welfare might find herself or himself in a position in which there is a shared concern for children and families, but also misunderstanding and, at times conflict, between the child welfare system and religion.

This chapter will begin with a brief description of the history, continuum and goals of the child welfare system. The congruence and tensions in child welfare and religion will then be explored. Finally, their common values and mission will be highlighted.

History

The American system of child protection and child welfare began in the earliest days of the United States as society responded to children who were orphaned or abandoned by their parents. Children were often placed in congregate care facilities—or orphanages—for at least part of their life to grow up under adult protection and supervision. There were a number of other responses to caring for mistreated or abandoned children. For example, in the mid-1800's Charles Loring Brace developed Orphan Trains to transport and place young children and sibling groups from Eastern cities with potential parents and homes in the Midwest and West (Cook, 1995).

In 1873, a child protection system was launched by the case of Mary Ellen in New York City. This young girl was being beaten by her stepmother and a "friendly visitor" tried to intervene to protect the child. There was no agency charged with protecting children from intrafamily abuse so the case was investigated by the Society for the Prevention of Cruelty to Animals. Soon after presenting this case in court, the private agency Society for the Prevention of Cruelty to Children was created. By the mid-1900's the child protection function was accepted by public child welfare agencies (Costin, 1991).

By the early 1900's the use of orphanages began to be replaced by using volunteer homes and families recruited to take in mistreated children. These homes—called foster homes—became the placement of choice from the 1950's to the present day. Although foster homes provided a family-like setting for vulnerable children, concern was expressed about the length of time children remained in temporary foster care, and the impact of separations and loss upon children. Research and practice experience pointed to the harmful effects of what was referred to as "drifting" in foster care, with no timely outcome or stable family life for the child. This drift was compounded by multiple placements for the same child, and inattentiveness to the needs of the child once in the foster home. After three decades of documenting the problems with placement of children in foster care and the length of the time that children spent in out-of-home care, the federal permanency planning law was passed in 1980. This law (Public Law 96-272) established permanency planning as the prevailing philosophy, value and strategy for child welfare. In the early 1990's there was a growing commitment to family preservation and family support legislation and funding to prevent the unnecessary placement of children in out-of-home care. Throughout the development of these child welfare systems in the United States the church has had a prominent role as sponsor and auspices for private child welfare services (Garland, 1994). For example, the child welfare agencies in New York City, apart from the city and state agencies, have been organized in three federations: Protestant, Catholic, and Jewish agencies.

Continuum of Care

The child welfare system in the United States has evolved to include a number of services in a continuum of care. This continuum suggests that there is a progression of seriousness, treatment need, and service commitment and cost from one service level to the next. This continuum includes:

- *Family Support Services*— the counseling and concrete services that provide supportive assistance to a family in response to a crisis, or absence of resources that if present would reduce stress or increase the ability of the family to meet the needs of its children.
- *Child Maltreatment Prevention Programs*— counseling and other services designed purposely to address and reduce the risk of child abuse or neglect.
- *Family Preservation Services*— oftentimes intense and short-term services targeted to families that are experiencing a crisis that has the potential to result in serious harm to the child, and that would result in out-of-home placement.
- *Crisis Nurseries/Respite Care*— special projects to provide relief for stressed parents who need to have some immediate and short-term assistance to provide some time away from their children/infant.
- *Emergency Shelters*— homes or residences with the capacity to house children for a number of days or weeks who need to quickly be removed from a dangerous setting. These settings could have a diagnostic capacity to determine the special needs of children awaiting placement in another setting. The shelter could also be a transitional setting providing an interim placement for a child while a proper setting is developed or identified. Children might be reunited with their families after a brief separation, assessment of the family, and the introduction of needed services.
- *Foster Care*— these are homes and family settings that provide temporary care for children who are unable to be with their parent(s). Foster homes can be provided by volunteer families

who are generally licensed and supervised by the agency and provided a modest board payment to meet the needs and expenses associated with the child in care. These homes can also be kinship or relative homes—the child is placed with a relative who provides a safe home for the child. Therapeutic foster homes are designed for children and youth with specific emotional and mental health challenges that require the special supervision and treatment resources that specially trained parents and professional staff can provide. Children generally enter foster care through a court order issued by the family or youth court in response to a petition alleging child abuse or neglect that was submitted to the court by a child protective service worker. Some children are voluntarily placed through an agreement between the child's parents and the child welfare agency.

- *Group Homes*— sometimes young people are placed in these congregate care facilities that provide a home-like atmosphere for a small number of youth supervised by live-in house parents or rotating staff members.
- *Residential Treatment Facilities*— provides housing, education, and counseling for young people in a congregate care setting that may be organized around dormitories or cottages. Residential treatment facilities are often responsible for helping young people with a number of challenges in addition to child maltreatment. These challenges could include working with young people with emotional, mental health, educational or developmental disabilities.
- *Adoption Services*— when it is determined that children cannot be reunited with their family, the legal system may terminate parental rights or parents may voluntarily relinquish their rights and the child welfare agency seeks to find an adoptive family for the child.

Intertwined in each service are relationships with other fields of practice, disciplines, and helping systems. For example, many out-of-home placements and services require court involvement, such as petitioning the court for custody, submitting case plans and the periodic review of these plans, and potentially, hearings, or trials to examine evidence and make recommendations. Health, mental health, and juvenile probation and law enforcement are some of those systems that interact extensively with child welfare service delivery.

The child welfare system encompasses a number of varied services and settings that are designed to separately meet the child and family's needs or provide a continuum of care if the child's needs change or intensify over time. Regardless of the setting, the American child welfare setting has a number of primary goals in service provision.

Goals

The American child welfare system has three primary goals: (1) making certain that children are *safe*; (2) working to secure *permanency* for children; and (3) when children are involved with the child welfare agency, it is the agency's goal to strengthen the child's *well being* while the agency is responsible for the child (Williams, 1996).

The first goal of child welfare is the *physical safety* of the child. The Child Protective Service division of the public child welfare agency is charged with responding to reports from the public and professionals alleging or suspecting that a child is in some form of danger. The perpetrator may be the child's parent or guardian, or another relative, adult or child/adolescent. Threats to safety include the physical abuse of children, a number of types of child neglect (including physical, medical, educational, or supervisory neglect), and the sexual abuse of children or threats to seriously harm or kill children. By law, professionals are required to report suspected child abuse and child protective service workers are empowered to investigate abuse and take steps to remove children from situations in which they are at serious risk or have been abused or neglected. For example, for show-and-tell, a kindergarten boy lifted the back of his shirt and showed his class the bruises and lash marks on his back as a result of a punishment from his father that morning. The school teacher immediately contacted the principal; who then called the child abuse hotline number to report the incident. A child protective service worker was assigned the case, proceeded to the school, witnessed the bruises, contacted the family court to obtain a temporary order of placement, and took the boy to a foster home that day. With the child physically safe, the work with the parents was begun by the worker.

The second goal of *permanency* is defined as providing children with family connections or the potential for a safe, stable and lifetime family. The commitment to permanency was informed by the research in child development that documented the effect of separation and loss on children, the impact of a child's sense of time and its correlation with length of stay in out-of-home care, and concern about children drifting in foster care. This drift was the tendency of children to remain in out-of-home care for long periods of time, typically years, without a viable plan to reunite the children with their families or provide another permanent option for the child. With foster care drift came the increased possibility of a child experiencing a number of foster care homes and placements. The outcome of long and ill-defined stays in foster care and multiple placements could include detrimental effects on the child's mental health and social adjustment resulting in the need for more intense placements. Without a commitment to permanency planning the child's psychological safety was at risk. For example, when the kindergarten boy was placed in foster care, the child welfare worker understood that this was a temporary arrangement to keep the child physically safe. Having accomplished some degree of safety, the goal of permanency became the worker's priority. So, the worker immediately began an assessment of the parents and family to form a judgement about the appropriateness, necessary steps and timing of reunification of the family. Family reunification is one means of achieving the goal of permanency. If the parents were unable or unwilling to provide a safe home for the child, another option for permanency, such as adoption, would be explored. For some older adolescents, a goal of establishing one's independence after age 18 or a guardianship arrangement might be considered in addition to reunification or adoption (Maluccio, et al, 1986).

The third goal of child welfare is to address the *well being* of children served by agencies or in out-of-home care. For example, when children are placed in foster care, the agency should provide for the medical care of the child and provide counseling or other support services to address the mental health needs of the child. Also needed is the assurance that children are receiving an appropriate education, recreation, and socialization.

These are worthy goals but their implementation has often been incomplete, at best. With regard to safety, the child welfare system has been buffeted by criticisms from two sides. Critics have charged that it has either responded too slowly, resulting in children being left in family situations that are dangerous because these situations were not reported to the authorities, or, if reported, the child protection sytem did not respond quickly, thoroughly, or decisively. Others have identified another troubling outcome. The child protection system has often moved too quickly, without adequate evidence, and unnecessarily intruded into family life and at least temporarily traumatically separated parents and children. The overrepresentation of minority children in foster care has added the concern that discriminatory practices have unfairly heightened this intrusiveness into families of color in the United States (Anderson, 1997).

With regard to permanency goals, the failure to implement permanency planning strategies and to internalize the necessity of permanency has allowed children to drift without their biological families and without the connection to another family that could become their psychological home. Some children in out-of-home care have not been well taken care of and their educational, health or mental health needs have not been adequately addressed.

The goals of the child welfare system are admirable. Their implementation is essential as they address the basic safety and mental health of the child. They provide a common focus for program planning, clinical practice and professional commitment.

Congruence with Christianity

A commitment to the safety of children, to their connection with loving adults and family members, and to the well being of children seems to be completely congruent with a Christian world and life view. For good reasons Christian churches provided early leadership in providing child welfare services. For a Christian social worker, working with vulnerable children and families would appear to be a natural expression of one's Christian beliefs and values.

The faith of the Jewish nation, its relationship with Jehovah, and its value on human life contrasted with the idolatry in Canaan where some worshipped Molech and required the human sacrifice of children. In Jesus' ministry (Matthew 19:13-15), he welcomed young children who were being kept away by the disciples. He spoke of the need to become like little children with an innocence of faith and response to the gospel (Matthew 18:2-6).

The connection between children and parents in families was respected and valued. When Jesus saw the grieving widow at Nain following the casket of her son, he understood her need for family and the importance of the parent and child relationship (Luke 7:11-17). This was also evidenced in other miraculous actions, including raising the daughter of Jairus (Luke 8:40-56). Among his final words on the cross, Jesus was concerned about his mother and proclaimed that John and Mary were to be as parent and child—preserving family ties and relationships (John 19:25-27). Throughout scripture there is the admonition to be sensitive to and assist the fatherless and the orphan (for example, James 1:27). One of the most serious threats by Jesus in his teaching was the warning against causing the stumbling of a child (Matthew 18:4-6).

It is consistent with scripture and the example of Jesus to be concerned with the safety and well-being of children and to strengthen their connections to family. The continuing leadership role of Christian organizations in the care of children is understandable and laudable. But this relationship between child welfare and Christianity is not without conflict and tension.

Tensions

That Christian people would have genuine compassion for the well-being of children seems natural based on the compassionate example of Jesus, the Christian ethic of love, and specific scriptural admonitions to care for children without parents or basic necessities. However, historically there have been a number of areas in which there is tension between the professional child welfare community and religion. Several topics of tension include: (1) the definition of child abuse and neglect; (2) the causes of child maltreatment; and (3) the view of the world.

1. *Definition.* In the United States there is no national child abuse and neglect law or definition. The definition of abuse and neglect varies from state to state. These definitions are oftentimes general and vague thus allowing multiple interpretations of conditions described as "harm" and "injury". This lack of clarity or allowance for a range of definitions reflects a conflict of values, or at least differing viewpoints, with regard to parenting, child raising, and discipline. The sanctity of the home and parents' rights to raise their children in the manner they choose may be in conflict with the value of protecting children from harm, and society's obligation to protect children and monitor parenting on behalf of children.

Consequently, within a community it is possible to find some persons who define abuse as significant injury that is life threatening or results in wounds and broken bones, whereas other community members might define any physical punishment as abusive. It is on this point that some criticize religion as allowing, if not promoting child abuse. The frequently cited "spare the rod and spoil the child" is viewed with horror by some child welfare professionals and viewed as the literal truth and interpreted as a directive to physically punish their children by a number of Christians (Meier, 1985; Radbil, 1974). In the public sector, corporal punishment is sometimes viewed as child abuse. Although few, if any, Christians would argue that the Bible promotes excessive or injurious physical punishment, the child welfare professional might be concerned about the support of physical punishment and failure to sufficiently warn against excessive punishment (Dobson, 1970; Lovinger, 1990; Wiehe, 1990). Defining only extreme, life endangering physical harm as abuse (particularly combined with a belief that child abuse could not occur in a Christian family) could lead to the failure to recognize and respond to potentially harmful situations (Pagelow & Johnson, 1988).

Specific areas of concern involving religion and child maltreatment have also been identified. In the mid-1980's the American Humane Association began to collect information on child abuse and neglect in cults and religious sects (AHA, 1984). Issues of medical neglect by parents who failed to secure critical medical treatment due to the family's religious beliefs have also been identified (Anderson, 1983; Bullis, 1991).

2. *Causation.* Broader than the issue of physical punishment, religion has at times been portrayed as providing the context or belief system that contributes to child abuse and neglect (Garbarino & Ebata, 1983; Garbarino & Gilliam, 1980; Kadushin, 1980; Salter, et al, 1985). The Bible is full of examples of killing infants and children, from the proclamation of the Egyptian Pharaoh in the days of Moses to the declaration of Herod the Great during Jesus' infancy. Yet it is not just jealous rulers who order the killing of children. The great flood drowned children, Abraham was asked to sacrifice Isaac, the death angel killed the firstborn children, the invading Israelites killed whole populations of children, and Jepthah's sacrifice was his adolescent daughter. Children suffer because of the actions of their parents.

A number of theories of child abuse point to the role of an authoritarian or patriarchal family structure in creating an atmosphere in which children (and sometimes women) are viewed as subservient to fathers and husbands (Horton & Williamson, 1988; Peek, Lowe & Williams, 1991). Equating patriarchy with authoritarian parenting styles, concern is expressed about physical abuse of children, emotional abuse or neglect, and a climate in which child maltreatment is justified or allowed. The child is expected to be obedient to the parent (Alwin, 1986). He or she is not allowed to display a "willful spirit" (Fugate, 1980; Hutson, 1983). The shaping of the child's will (sinful nature) and spirit, and discipline required for achieving maturity need to be firmly enforced by the parent (Hyles, 1974; Rice, 1982; Williams & Money, 1980). The implied relationship between patriarchal excess and child maltreatment is particularly noted in cases of child sexual abuse as the father or stepfather's actions are described as related to one's sense of power or powerlessness in the family and community (Pellauer, Chester & Boyajian, 1987). Parental actions are justified as preserving a family hierarchy, breaking the child's willful spirit, or responding to the child who is born in sin and needs to learn submission to authority (Walters, 1975; Miller, 1985).

3. *Viewpoint.* The first two dynamics—supporting physical punishment and providing a rationale or fertile ground for child maltreatment—portray religion as part of the child abuse problem. This "world-life view" describes religion as irrelevant to the problem of child abuse and neglect, and the church's attention to the spiritual world, the inner world, and the afterworld as diluting or replacing attentiveness to the

physical, material and present-day needs of children. Or there may be denial that a religious or Christian family would maltreat a child. Consequently, the church's knowledge of and support for public child protective and child welfare systems might not be present or strong.

Response

The child welfare system is intended to provide comprehensive assistance to children who are abused and neglected. This mission is informed by the permanency planning law—the commitment that children need to be raised in families with the potential of lifelong relationships. The Christian commitment to love one's neighbor and care for the helpless is congruent with this mission. There is a reasonable response to the critics of religion that affirms the critical role of Christians in social work and the Christian church in the child welfare service community.

There is a range of perspectives on Biblical passages that provide instruction in the raising of children. However, the abuse of children (or women) is not condoned (Alsdurf & Alsdurf, 1989; Campbell, 1985; Tomczak, 1982). The church has a crucial role in educating parents and supporting families. While acknowledging the authority of parents and the necessity to discipline children, there is also the admonition to love children and not provoke children to wrath due to one's parenting behavior.

While attentive to the physical and psychological needs of children and families, attention to the spiritual needs of parents and children does not have to be neglected or separated from its real life consequences. For example:

> A child abuse investigation discovered that a father had sexually molested his son and daughter. Picked up at their Christian school, the children were placed in emergency foster care and the child protective service worker immediately scheduled an appointment to meet with the parents.
>
> During this first interview, the father told the child protective service worker that the abuse had ended in recent months as he had a conversion experience and was now a genuine Christian. The worker expressed appreciation for this decision by the father but stated that the father's statement of belief needed to be demonstrated consistently by his actions. The father responded "Yes! faith without works is dead!"
>
> With his wife's support and the worker's support, the father confessed his guilt in court, entered counseling, apologized to his chil-

dren, and visited his children, who remained in foster care while he followed the court's order and case plan. Within six months, the family was successfully reunited as the father completed all required actions.

The church can support the spiritual, physical, and psychological needs of the family and recognize their connections.

Finally, the church and Christian individuals and organizations have historically and currently make a crucial contribution to services for children and families. Through its educational ministries, support services, and assistance to families, the church provides a significant network and number of family support services whose critical role in family preservation and the prevention of stress that may contribute to risk of child maltreatment, has not been fully recognized. The provision of formal child welfare services, such as foster care, group home care and residential treatment, and adoption services is frequently provided by private, church-related organizations under contract to the state's public child welfare agencies. These service providers are essential to meeting the need for placements and homes for children and young people who are removed from their homes or need to be placed in specialized settings to meet their safety and mental health needs. In addition to services provided by Christian or church-related organizations, there are significant numbers of foster parents and adoptive parents, licensed and approved by public agencies, whose motives, coping ability, and compassion are inspired by their religious faith and convictions and supported by their membership and involvement within faith communities.

One of the model programs that promotes a partnership between one's church and religious faith and the needs of children is the One Child One Church adoption initiative that encourages each church to encourage at least one of its member families to adopt at least one child waiting for a permanent home. This initiative, that began in an African-American congregation in Chicago, has been supported nationally by the federal government.

Why should a family care for its children? Why should a community care about the treatment of the children in its member families? The Christian response is simple and clear: affirming that children are God's creation and precious in His sight. Parent's are responsible for the nurturing of their children, and have reason to grieve or take pride in their children's accomplishments. In addition, the community's obligation to provide for children, particularly those without parents, is strongly affirmed in the Bible.

Conclusion

The child welfare system in the United States is a continuum of services designed to support families and protect children. When protection requires the removal of children from their parent's custody, the child welfare system's guiding philosophy of permanency planning informs plans and strategies to reunite children with their families. If this is not possible, the child welfare worker should develop another option that provides the possibility of a home and lifetime family for the child. Child welfare includes a professional concern for the child's well-being, including the child's physical health, mental health, educational and social needs.

The role of religion and the church has at times been presented with some concern regarding its impact on child abuse and neglect and responsiveness to at-risk children. The Church can serve as a primary source of family support and family preservation services for vulnerable families. Its members have a motive for becoming foster and adoptive parents, and a means of coping with the challenges of new parenting through prayer and the social support of the church. Church child welfare agencies have a long history of caring for children and families in crisis. This field of practice provides a setting in which a Christian social worker can express her or his care for children and commitment to families.

References

Alsdurf, J. & Alsdurf, P. (1989). *Battered Into Submission*. Downers Grove, Il: InterVarsity Press.

Alwin, D. (1986). Religion and Parental Child-Rearing Orientations. *American Journal of Sociology, 92,* 412-440.

American Humane Association. (1984). Child Abuse and Neglect in Cults and Religious Sects. *Protecting Children, 1,* 17.

Anderson, G. (1997). Achieving Permanency for All Children in the Child Welfare System. In G. Anderson, A. Ryan & B. Leashore (Eds.), *The Challenge of Permanency Planning in a Multicultural Society*. New York: Haworth Press.

Anderson, G. (1983). Medicine vs. Religion: The Case of Jehovah's Witnesses. *Health and Social Work, 8,* 31-39.

Bullis, R. (1991). The Spiritual Healing Defense in Criminal Prosecutions for Crimes Against Children. *Child Welfare, 70,* 541-558.

Campbell, R. (1985). *How to Really Love Your Child*. Wheaton, Il: Victor.

Cook, J. F. (1995). A History of Placing Out: The Orphan Trains. *Child Welfare, 74,* 181-199.

Costin, L. (1991). Unraveling the Mary Ellen Legend: Origins of the "Cruelty" Movement. *Social Service Review, 65,* 203-223.

Dobson, J. (1970). *Dare to Discipline*. New York: Bantam Books.

Fugate, R. (1980). *What the Bible Says About Child Training*. Tempe, AZ: Aletheia.

Garland, D. (1994). *Church Agencies: Caring for Children and Families in Crisis*. Washington D.C.: Child Welfare League of America.

Horton, A. & Williamson, J. (1988). *Abuse and Religion: When Praying Isn't Enough*. Lexington, MA: Lexington.

Hutson, C. (1983). *The Why and How of Child Discipline*. Murfreesboro, TN: Sword of the Lord.

Hyles, J. (1974). *How to Rear Children*. Hammond, IN: Hyles-Anderson.

Lovinger, R. (1990). *Religion and Counseling: The Psychological Impact of Religious Belief*. New York: Continuum.

Maluccio, A., Fein, E. & Olmstead, K. (1986). *Permanency Planning for Children— Concepts and Methods*. London and New York: Tavistock and Methuen.

Pagelow, M. & Johnson, P. (1988). Abuse in the American Family: The Role of Religion. In A. Horton & J. Williamson (Eds.), *Abuse and Religion: When Praying Is Not Enough*. Lexington, MA: Lexington.

Peek, C., Lowe, G. & Williams, L.S. (1991). Gender and God's Word: Another Look at Religious Fundamentalism and Sexism. *Social Forces, 69,* 1205-1221.

Pellauer, M., Chester, B. & Boyajian, J. (1987). *Sexual Assault and Sexual Abuse: A Handbook for Clergy and Religious Professionals*. San Francisco: Harper and Row.

Rice, J. (1982). *God in Your Family*. Murfreesboro, TN: Sword of the Lord.

Smith, E. (1995). Bring Back the Orphanages? What Policymakers of Today Can Learn From the Past. *Child Welfare, 74,* 115-142.

Tomczak, L. (1982). *God, the Rod, and Your Child's Bod*. Old Tappan, NJ: Revell.

Wiehe, V. (1990). Religious Influence on Parental Attitudes Toward the Use of Corporal Punishment. *Journal of Family Violence, 5,* 173-186.

Williams, C. (1996). *Keynote Speech: Mississippi Permanency Partnership, A Vision*. Jackson, Mississippi, June, 1996.

CHAPTER 17

ADOPTION AND ME: A NARRATIVE APPROACH

Mary Vanden Bosch Zwaanstra

Change, move, dead clock, that this fresh day
May break with dazzling light to these sick eyes.
Burn, glare, old sun, so long unseen,
That time may find its sound again, and cleanse
What ever it is that a wound remembers
After the healing ends.
    "Small Prayer" - Weldon Kees (1975)

"Outta my way, lady." Our fifteen year old son made his way to the back door. Dressed in jeans and a cowboy hat, Karl clutched a sleeping bag under one arm and a duffel bag and radio in the other hand. His jacket pockets were stuffed with his treasures. The runaway season was upon us again.

Beginning when he was around ten, fall evoked disaffection and restlessness in him with what was familiar and familial. Issues and events varied but the result was always the same. By the time of his November 11 birthday the stage was set. There would be a fight and he would leave.

This narrative explores a family's experience with adoption. I am the narrator and the mother. I relate the story from my perspective. It could, and perhaps someday it will, be told from the perspective of my husband or from that of any of our children: Karl, born in 1964; Kerrie, born in 1967; and Matthew, born in 1969. Karl is our son by adoption; Kerrie and Matthew are birth-children. Only Karl was "planned"; the others came along quite unexpectedly. In the third year of our marriage we joined the ranks of the infertile, having been informed that "it was statistically unlikely" that we would ever have children born to us. Adoption was the "cure" for our fertility problem. As is the case with policy arrangements generally, the practice of adoption produces both intended and unintended consequences. This narrative is about policy and its affects. Living it propelled me into the social work profession.

At one month of age Karl entered our family with a one page document detailing his birth weight and development since birth. He had gained two pounds, slept through the night and should be strapped on the changing table since he was a very active baby. That was the extent of it. Adoption practice in 1964 was grounded in two beliefs: nurture counted infinitely more than nature and anonymity was best for all members of the adoption triad. If their adult offspring were to be allowed access to identifying information, Michigan birth-parents were legally required to file the requisite written permission with the state. Few signed since they were not encouraged to do so. The professional community believed the birth-mother could and should release her child and go on with her life. Neither the adopted person nor the family established by adoption required more than a legal release from her. Everyone involved would live happily ever after.

We bought unquestioningly into this belief system. Without objecting to the quality or quantity of information supplied us, we took Karl into our hearts and acted like the parents we longed to be. Objecting to or even questioning adoption practice arrangements was not thinkable because it would challenge the authority of scientifically informed professional practice. More weighty was the power differential between the professional and the applicant-parent. The worker held the power to give or withhold the child. What prospective, hopeful parent-to-be with no other options would presume to challenge so potent a force?

We heard bits and pieces of information about Karl's birth-parents verbally related by the social worker in the Christian agency with which we chose to work. His mother was a college student, a biology major; his father was preparing to be a draftsman. They were from different religious backgrounds. The father disappeared when told of the pregnancy. The mother went to a "maternity home" to await the birth of her baby, hoping to keep her secret and spare her family embarrassment. It was standard fare in 1964. No written documentation of Karl's close or extended family history was offered, nor requested. We knew that Karl was born by Cesarean Section after an extended labor. Little was said about the quality of the pregnancy or labor and nothing about the specific events necessitating the Section. We were warned that he might have some "questions about his origins" as a teen. As our life together unfolded, we discovered that we needed all the information we could get. When Karl developed asthma there was "no recorded family history of asthma." When he became addicted to drugs and alcohol, we were reluctantly informed that his father and both grandfathers "perhaps" had alcohol problems.

Two explanations are germane. The agency and its workers were loath to dispense pertinent information; their primary loyalties were to secrecy commitments made to the birth-mother. In addition, information gathered was scanty and superficial; it was not considered important in the era which viewed the newborn as a blank slate upon which nurture would write the defining tale. Karl's early life in our family was manageable. It was pleasurable. He smiled easily and slept little during the day. He seemed unusually strong and loved to stand on his feet. He took to applesauce and pulled faces at meat. He was allergic to milk but we found a soybean formula that worked well. We responded to this busy, beautiful child by developing new schedules and priorities to match his need for action and attention. Beyond the necessities, Karl's life was filled with touching, talk and play. We walked him during his daily fussy time. We read books and explored the world. We sang and played peek-a-boo. He loved animals and we entertained a series of furry and crawly creatures over the years. He was loved. As time went on his intensity and impulsiveness gave us some pause. But we had both been raised in stable homes with positive parenting models. I was a pediatric nurse and my husband a seminary professor. We reassured ourselves that while we made mistakes, we were very adequate parents. Faith, hope and love would see us through. It would turn out all right.

In the months after we became a nuclear family, our church published its yearly directory. Karl's name was not included. We asked why. The answer was that he was not really "ours" until the adoption was legally finalized after a year. Until then he was not officially part of the fellowship and he could not be baptized as most newborns are in our church. In spite of its ostensible support of adoption and rich covenant theology, it was apparent that there were some rules about inclusion and exclusion of which we had been unaware. In the recesses of our minds we became aware that certain things were different for the adopted as compared with the non-adopted.

In preschool and kindergarten Karl was aggressive with other children. He hit, kicked, spat and fought. We were appalled and worried. We had him tested by a professional who found Karl to be of normal intelligence but socially immature. Time, it was suggested, was the antidote. We then spent a sabbatical year in the Netherlands and he attended kindergarten again. Karl's social skills needed more time to develop, we thought. He learned the Dutch language quickly. We lived in close quarters in a crowded society which valued privacy and decorum. Karl threw rocks at a car and we dealt with irate neighbors. He pried up a man-hole cover and dropped it on his three year old sister's toe causing much pain and loss of a toenail.

Upon our return, Karl entered first grade in the neighborhood Christian school with a new group of children. In second grade there were more children than could be accommodated in our neighborhood school and some children were selected to be bussed. Karl was one of them. Many parents strongly objected to this arrangement since they would have children in two schools. Karl was, however, an uncomplicated choice for the school since he was the only child attending from our family. At the new school he had to adapt to a new environment and reference group. At first it was difficult for him. He stayed for two years. He had the same teacher both years. She liked him and set firm but friendly boundaries. Then he was selected to return to the school close to home for fourth grade. That fall he looked forlorn. While driving home from a piano lesson he told me he felt like standing in the middle of the street and letting a car run him over. He could not elaborate on the misery he was feeling. At bedtime we talked again. He said solemnly, "I peed on the bathroom floor at school today and the teacher made me clean it up." I asked why. He cried and said, "Mom, if I don't do dumb things nobody pays any attention to me. No one wants to play with me or be my friend." The next morning, with a heavy heart, I called the teacher. She dismissed his feelings and my concerns: "Children work these things out best by themselves." Later, the principal judged that I was guilty of over-protecting my son. In his opinion it was a common fault among adoptive parents. There would be no help in the school system.

Karl's investment in the family had decreased markedly by the time he was eleven. He was using marijuana, though we were unaware of it at the time. The fall runaways began. At first he simply disappeared when it was time to cut the birthday cake and serve it to friends and neighbors, returning later in the evening. By the time he was fifteen he was gone for two weeks at a time. Then he began to run whenever there was a major conflict. We called the police, who never found him. I gave him the phone number and address of the local shelter for runaways and picked him up when he was ready to return. We talked, cajoled and set limits. But Karl preferred to be outside the limits, wherever they were set. Gradually fall became a fearful and chaotic time for all of us. Karl's behavior was disruptive. He was destructive. He slashed the orange chairs in the family room and sold his dad's gold class ring for the cash. We virtually stopped entertaining. Karl's unpredictability made our other children reluctant to have friends in to play or spend the night. In our isolation we felt like failures and freaks. Only other families had the luxury of normalcy. No other Christian family could possibly be like ours, we thought.

I began to read everything I could get my hands on about adoption. I became a sleuth. I became a pest at the adoption agency which maintained a stonewalling posture. I discovered much that surprised me. I learned that adoptive children were over-represented in the mental health system and first came across the term "restless wanderer" in reference to adopted persons (Sorosky, Baran & Pannor, 1975). I read about studies being done in

Scandinavia that followed adopted-away offspring of persons with mental illness. A genetic link to personality and behavior, particularly alcohol abuse and mental illness, was postulated. From John Bowlby (1969) I learned about loss, grief and attachment in the very young. From Rene Spitz (1965) I learned about infant-maternal bonding and the helpful effects of maternal regression in the service of forming a secure bond. From Thomas Verny (1981)I learned about the perils and importance of the intrauterine environment and prenatal period in human development. Verny states that an "emotional set-point," established at this time, is difficult to alter later. A sympathetic physician searched Karl's maternity home and hospital records and confirmed my suspicion that fetal distress had been a factor in the Cesarean decision. From Erik Erikson (1968), himself an adopted person, I learned how identity is shaped and how crucial it is to healthy development. I concluded that adoption policy and practice were based on politics and tradition and not on scientifically grounded principles. Slowly I began to trade isolation for openness. I discovered that ours was not the only adoptive family, Christian or otherwise, in distress. We organized a support group for adoptive families, many of which remain friends to this day. We tried to educate ourselves about what was happening to us and our children since we found little knowledgeable help in the professional community. I applied to graduate school in social work.

That fall I entered my graduate program; Karl turned fifteen. He continued to be moody and morose after running away in November. We called the adoption agency, but they had no help or insight to offer. On New Year's Eve Karl overdosed. We brought in the new year at the local emergency room. Karl was embarrassed and remorseful. He wanted to come home. We removed his bedroom door from its hinges and kept a suicide watch while, during the next two days, Karl descended into the depths again. We had to commit him. At the Christian psychiatric hospital family therapy was mandated. Our daughter cried, "How can I face my friends? They'll think I have a crazy brother and that I'm crazy too." Assumptions about the state of our marriage and family structure guided treatment. Our pathologies were labeled. We heard that Karl was the "identified patient," the "symptom bearer" in our family. When I suggested that Karl's adoption played a role, that he might have a biochemical disorder, my thinking was dismissed as inconsequential to the treatment plan. After a month, he was discharged home, no longer suicidal but singularly disinterested in continued treatment, which soon stopped. At home he kept to himself and to friends we did not know. We coped but with difficulty. Several years later we learned that long-term hospitalization of Karl was considered but rejected by the professional staff of the psychiatric hospital. They supported this decision by citing the possible iatrogenic effects of hospitalization on Karl and our own coping strength. Their thoughts and opinions were not shared with us. Neither were our ideas, opinions and preferences solicited.

When I applied for my first M.S.W. field practicum, the coordinator recommended that I not divulge the ongoing family crisis. It would, he believed, be looked upon with disfavor by social service agencies. I would be considered "sick." It was still the era of the "schizophrenegenic mother." Unable to compartmentalize my life so neatly or with integrity I gave voice to the stressors and found a warm welcome first in a gerontology program and later in a program for the persistently mentally ill and their families. Here I discovered, and came to fully appreciate, that cornerstone of social work thinking, the "person-in-environment." My clients, their families and the mental health system were powerful teachers. I was touched by the courage and strength of many clients and families.

Karl began high school the next fall. He played soccer with vigor. We went to his games and cheered along with the other spectators. As soccer season ended and November approached, the familiar pattern began again. Karl's drug use increased, and he carried a knife. He avoided questions. He came and went from home at will. He was involved in incidents of petty vandalism and harassment of younger neighborhood children. He refused to participate in activities with the family. He took the car for a drive though he had no license. Karl discovered he was physically stronger than his dad and became verbally threatening. He fantasized about our deaths. We were afraid that he would harm us. We slept behind locked doors. We visited a counselor at the juvenile court where we learned that to get help we would need to obtain release from our legal, parental responsibility for his behavior, supervision, and care. Essentially this legal process would declare us unfit parents and Karl, a Ward of the Court. Somehow we couldn't take that step. We were not bad parents and we would not abandon our son. Beyond a legal contract we had entered into a covenant, committing ourselves to be parents to him. We would seek help where we could find it and depend on available supports to ride out the storm.

On a 1979 November afternoon, after school and before either of us were home from work, Karl ripped the telephone from the wall, put his knife through a door, and verbally threatened his siblings. When he ran away it was a relief. All of us were completely exhausted. We rejected committing Karl because of the stigma and ineffectiveness of treatment. From some fellow adoptive parents we heard of a boarding school, run by a group of American Christians, for behaviorally disordered youngsters in the mountains of the Dominican Republic. We spoke to its representatives; we agonized. We found some aspects of the program not to our liking, but after considering the available options, made arrangements to enroll him. There were theological differences. The quality of the educational program was inferior to that of the local high school. It was costly and we couldn't really afford it. But the cost in suffering for the family as a whole from having him at home we judged to be greater. Karl wanted out of our family and was intrigued by the adventure of the "D.R.". He left in January, 1980 for what would be a year and a half stay and completion of a high school course of study. In spite of the criticism of some social workers and Karl's school, who thought we had "overreacted" and decided "prematurely," we were at peace. We knew our son was safe, and we felt safe too. We shed our tears and got on with our lives.

The program in the Dominican Republic was strictly behavioral. Karl earned privileges when he met the behavioral standards and lost them when he didn't. He ran once. But he knew neither the language nor the geography and quickly learned that conformity was his only ticket out. The rest of the family visited Karl there during his first summer. It was exciting to see him doing so well. He expressed some ambivalence about being in the program but pleasure with the progress he was making in school. By this time he had earned the right to be in a leadership role in his house and was rightly proud of this accomplishment. In the fall he wrote, describing the sadness he felt: "When my birthday comes I think about my birth parents. I wonder who they were and who I am. I feel like a variable that has no end. I could be anything or I could be nothing." One year later he returned for good.

We looked forward to Karl's return. But within twenty-four hours of his arrival large motorcycles and strange friends appeared in the driveway. Once again he was testing boundaries. He did not ask for advice or permission. He expressed no hostility. He simply pursued his own agenda in his own way. We were terribly disappointed but felt helpless to counter his personal choices. That fall he became eighteen. He commented, "I'm free at last." I replied, "Your dad and I are free too." That he was on his own, legally an adult, was understood by all of us. He entered college that fall and stayed for two years, finishing only a fraction of his courses and poorly at that. Typically he began a semester with enthusiasm that waned halfway through and finally evaporated altogether. His friends were not serious students. He was finally not allowed to return.

Karl lived at home infrequently after that, preferring the company of those with very different values from our own. He rapidly became a poly-drug abuser. His primary drug of choice was alcohol. He moved frequently often leaving things behind that had once been precious to him. I had given the children christmas tree ornaments each year, commemorating a trip or a special memory. Dated, these marked the history of their early years. Karl's collection was lost or stolen or perhaps disposed of during this period.

During his twenties Karl existed marginally. He worked sporadically at several low paying jobs where his attendance was often spotty. He married and divorced three times. He fathered a male child who was placed in an adoptive home. He dismissed his antisocial, self-destructive behavior, stating he would be dead before he was thirty anyway, so what difference did it make. Karl's nihilistic spirit was painful for us. We had tried to instill a love of life and of faith in him. But now we considered the possibility that he might destroy himself and perhaps others as well. Death seemed a distinct possibility and we thought about where we might bury him. We prayed that God would heal him or take his life and committed him to God's care. I wished that he could die while wanting for him the best that life can give. At times I wished that I could die too.

In the fall of 1994 as his third marriage disintegrated, Karl was jailed after his first DUI (Driving Under the Influence) arrest. This resulted in a stiff fine and loss of his driver's license. Shortly thereafter he elected to see a psychiatrist who listened carefully and told him he had likely been anxious and depressed throughout his life; his substance use/abuse was his attempt to self-medicate his fluctuating moods. The drug Paxil was prescribed. We could see how different Karl was within a week. He was initially ambivalent about this change. He did not know himself apart from the depressed state and had to learn to accept unfamiliar feelings and a more positive relational style. Gradually the clouds lifted and a different future seemed possible. After twenty years of substance abuse he was sober and could begin the process of rebuilding his life. He became both a successful full-time employee and college student, earning excellent grades while working full time. He moved in with a woman and her eight-year-old daughter. They enjoyed fixing up their house and planting flowers in the yard. We enjoyed an occasional picnic with them in their back yard around the umbrella table he gave her for Mother's Day last year. We gave thanks for these miracles in Karl's life and prayed for stability and future well-being.

But concerns about adoption policy and practice remain for me. I am repelled by the persistent romantic version of the adoption story. A bumper sticker, "Adoption not Abortion," in my opinion, typifies a simplistic approach to the complex realities of adoption. Open adoption is a move in the right direction since it recognizes the importance of both birth and adoptive parents to the adoptee. However, I remain concerned about the earlier generation of adoption triad members who must live under the onus of the closed system. Many remain in need and in pain, confined by earlier policy which, supported by the likes of Ann Landers, limits their well-being by denying them crucial information. In Michigan it is now legal for members of the adoption triad to engage an intermediary to search for another triad member with whom they desire contact while maintaining confidentiality. When Karl's birth-mother was contacted by the agency intermediary, she was indignant. Under no circumstances, distant or close, did she want anything to do with him. He would have been satisfied with so little from the woman whose abdomen bears the C-Section scar.

I am also concerned about current adoption practice. Somewhere there is a young child in an adoptive family. He is Karl's son. How much do they know about his genetic heritage and vulnerabilities? Do they know he is at-risk for depression and alcohol abuse? Are they teaching moderation or abstinence? Recent research suggests that co-occurring mental disorders and addictive disorders typically show up in genetically predisposed persons around the age of eleven (Kessler, Nelson, McGonagle, Edlund & Frank, 1996) Grafting a child to a family tree of strangers is a worthy endeavor. But it cannot be done without sufficient, reliable information. Whose responsibility is it to know and convey such information?

It is, furthermore, not ethically correct social work practice to place a child and leave the family to fend for itself. In this era of shrinking infant adoption and burgeoning international and "special needs" adoption, the practice of "place and run" is unconscionable. "Special needs" is often a euphemism for damaged, neglected, multiply-abandoned children who have often seen, heard and otherwise experienced what no child ever should. Of course these children need and deserve homes. However, the agency and the adoptive family must commit to collaboration with each other for the sake of the child for as long as it takes. And it may take a lifetime! In my opinion, the needs of the adoptee take ethical precedence over the claims of the birth-mother, the adoptive family or the agency. Adopted persons are precisely those with the most to lose and the least power. The state must also share the responsibility. The availability of post-adoption services in agencies, mandated in social policy is absolutely essential. In my experience, these are often considered an expendable luxury by administrators and politicians. In Michigan it is becoming very difficult to get Adoption Subsidy for special needs kids. It has always been nearly impossible in infant adoptions. This is short-sighted and cruel to all those whose lives are irrevocably affected. Social work advocacy is required here. Who will advocate for this marginalized group if not social workers? Who will demand that policy serve adopted persons in such a way that they can reach their full human potential? Professional helping that ignores environmental issues, including the policy and practice link, cannot rightly be called social work practice.

Diversity sensitive social work practice demands that the particular concerns of adoption triad members be heard and attended to by professionals tirelessly pledged to sort out situational complexities and act in the best interests of the members in creative ways. Much can be done when workers are willing to take risks rather than opt for "what we have always done." This also means rejecting traditional practices not supported by current knowledge. Perhaps we did not understand the interplay between nature and nurture correctly in 1964. But we now know that it is not an either/or question. We know that genetics plays a far greater role than we thought possible (Cadoret, Yates, Troughton, Woodworth & Stewart, 1995). We also know that a rupture of the first maternal-infant relationship often leaves a scar, remnant of a wound without conscious memory or words. Practice has not fully taken into account the effects of this rupture which every adopted person has experienced. Although rebellious youngsters appear similar, I would argue, with Cline (1979), that the underlying issue for adoptees is more often their failure to attach rather than their having been inadequately parented.

Professionals should be willing, and would do well, to accept knowledge from those closest to the issue: members of the adoption triad itself. We know and arrive at truth in different ways. One of these ways is through experience. Yet social work has been reluctant to take seriously the experientially acquired knowledge of persons closest to adoption. I passionately wish I could say that all the professionals we worked with over time listened carefully and demonstrated a spirit of consistent, supportive helpfulness. Some have done so and we are grateful for them. But in fact, the most helpful people have been the fellow strugglers, the adoptive families, who have lived out their innocently made commitments to parent children who are a mystery to them. These are the people who, more than anyone else, heard our grief and graced us with their presence and care. They gave us what we needed most — a shoulder to cry on and the hope that we would survive.

And we have survived. This story is one of hope even as it is one of pain. Our marriage is still intact and we are reasonably healthy. Karl's life is more stable. His siblings are also grown. Each is married and has children. It is, they say, unlikely that they could or would adopt. They have memories and some of them are painful. Because they experienced hurt in their relationship with Karl, they believe they could not bring needed objectivity to an adopted child. Each of us has coped in various ways. Some have opted for therapy while others have not. Our younger children maintain some distance from their brother. We have accepted the reality that they may never be warm friends.

Perhaps you are wondering why I would want to tell this story publicly. Simply said, it has long been a goal. Throughout this experience I often said, "Someday I'm going to write a book!" Perhaps this effort is the beginning of that project. But there are more compelling reasons. I am convinced that this is a story that must be told. Alcoholics Anonymous has a saying: secrets make you sick. In our family this document has provided opportunity for unpacking the past, a past not easily raised. This has been healing for each of us. I was fearful about giving it to Karl. He was doing so well. Would it set him back? Would he respond angrily or defensively? On the contrary, he was appreciative. He had no memory of some of the incidents described. We talked about hurts and gave and received apologies. We discussed parenting since he is now in a position to occupy the parenting role with his partner. He showed it to a co-worker, an adoptive parent struggling with a teen, as a means of encouragement and support. It cemented a friendship between them. It is my hope that parents with difficult children will understand that they are not alone, that things change, that they and their children can have relatively healthy relationships after the storms have passed.

Living this story has, furthermore, profoundly shaped the way I view the practice of social work. I am skeptical about claims of professional expertise. Although the social worker has acquired certain skills and understandings about people and the social environment, the worker doesn't know everything. The client is the expert in matters pertaining to their lived experience. When I wanted attention paid to adoption issues, genetics and biochemistry, I was not, I believe, trying to usurp the prerogatives of the worker or call into question the worker's competence. Nor was I attempting to deny any family problems. As a primary stakeholder and a thoughtful human being I considered my perspective important to the goals we were working on together. I expected to be a participant on the team; the deficits driven, worker-as-expert model didn't promote that. More than any hired helper, I longed for my son to be well and for the pain to end. Being a professional helper requires humility in balance with knowledge. It is my hope that clients and professionals alike will be encouraged to value and respect each other in the important relationships they forge together and do all they can to make these relationships humane.

Just as social work does not have all the answers to adoption's challenges, neither does the faith community. Many churches and Christians find emotional problems disturbing and difficult to respond to while physical problems are more readily accepted. As a result they find it hard to faithfully walk beside families in which there is an acting out youngster. Doesn't scripture, after all, instruct parents to train up children in the right way and infer the promise that children will then do the right thing? And isn't an acting out child evidence that the parents have failed in some fundamental way? Christians speak generally about "family values," but what does this buzz phrase have to say to families with difficult children? I support efforts to make and keep families strong and safe for all members. But I also feel for families that don't measure up to the model Christian family. We often carry shame, experience loneliness and grieve in isolation, while continuing to rub elbows with fellow church members either unable or unwilling to care sensitively or inured to our pain. Our grief is not only for ourselves but for our children who suffer, whose suffering we are powerless to end. We grieve because we long for wholeness, for God's shalom, for them, for us, for our families. We grieve because our prayers go unanswered and because we feel alienated from other Christians and from God.

It would probably be fair to say that most Christians oppose abortion and support adoption. I agree with them in general. Yet I often find this stance naive and superficial. While Christians rally to causes which support the right of the fetus to continued life, as a group they are far less concerned about how the child fares after it is born. How often have Christians rallied to demand that justice be done with regard to Adoption Subsidy funds or the right of adoptees to all of the available information about themselves held by various agencies? It seems to me that a consistent pro-life stance demands that the Christian community be at least as vigorous in advocating for measures to assure that adoptees have opportunities to become all that God desires and intends them to be.

There is little awareness, in my experience in the faith community, of the particular issues confronting adopted persons and their families. For example, those who are not adopted have difficulty putting themselves in the adoptee's experience of having very limited knowledge of their own history, or knowing a painful history. Most of us know what kind of people we came from, we have pregnancy and birth stories that are ours alone, we know how the pieces of our family tree fit together. Most of us know that our parents, siblings, grandparents and other extended family are part of who we are. We know ourselves by particular, sometimes peculiar ancestors, historical events and geographical locations. But none of this is true for the adopted person. The longings of the adoptee to know him/herself fully are both appropriate and normal, and do not imply rejection of the family by which the adoptee was "chosen." That Christians have all been chosen or adopted by God in Christ (Romans 8, 9; Ephesians 1) is sometimes used to normalize adoption, and to some extent the comparison works. However God's adoption is not the same as human adoption conducted according to the rules established by society. God adopts us, the human creatures he knows with the creator's perfect knowledge, out of pure grace. We continually turn away from him. He remains faithful to us. And He supplies us with a multitude of stories, recorded in the Old and New Testaments, designed to teach us who we are in relation to him. In human adoption neither are our motives so pure nor are our available resources so well designed. Still each of us—families, professionals, the Christian community—commits to diligently do the best we can with the limited information and finite resources we have at the time, trusting that God, who knows the whole, will bless our faithfulness.

References

Bowlby, J. (1969). *Attachment and loss*. New York: Basic Books.

Cadoret, R. J., Yates, W. R., Troughton, E. Woodworth, G. & Stewart, M. A. (1995). Adoption study demonstrating two genetic pathways to drug abuse. *Archives of General Psychiatry, 55*, 42-52.

Cline, F. W. (1979). *Understanding and treating the severely disturbed child*. Evergreen Consultants in Human Behavior.

Erikson, E. H. (1968). *Identity, youth, and crisis*. New York: W.W. Norton.

Kessler, R. C., Nelson, C. B., Mc Gonagle, K. A., Edlund, M. J., Frank, R. G., & Leaf, P. J. (1996). The epidemiology of co-occurring addictive and mental disorders: Implications for prevention and service utilization. *American Journal of Orthopsychiatry, 66*, 17-31.

Kees, W. (1975). Small Prayer. In D. Justice (Ed.), *The Collected Poems of Weldon Kees*. Lincoln: University of Nebraska Press.

Sorosky, A.D., Baran., A., & Pannor, R. (1975). Identity conflicts in adoptees. *American Journal of Orthopsychiatry, 45*, 18-27.

Spitz, R. A. (1965). *The first year of life: A psychoanalytic study of normal and deviant development of object relations*. New York: International Universities Press.

Verny, T. (with Kelly, J.) (1981). *The secret life of the unborn child*. New York: Summit Books.

ABOUT THE CONTRIBUTORS

Katherine Amato-von Hemert received a BA in History/Women Studies/Drama from Lake Forest College, a MA in General Studies in the Humanities, and a MA and PhD from the School of Social Services Administration, University of Chicago. Currently she is on the faculty of the College of Social Work, University of Kentucky, and an adjunct Professor at Lexington Theological Seminary. Her professional interests are researching the intersection of Christian congregation life and social service policy and program, the Medieval and Reformation history of poverty and social responses to it, along with the variety of religious influences in the history of the social work profession. Presently she is directing a research project examining Caucasian and African-American Protestant churches in four states (KY, CA, CO, GA) regarding congregational attitudes toward poverty and social welfare policy.

Gary R. Anderson received a BRE from Cornerstone College (Grand Rapids, Michigan), a MSW from the University of Michigan, and PhD from the School of Social Services Administration at the University of Chicago. Presently he is a Professor at Hunter College School of Social Work, of the City University of New York, in New York City. He has social work practice experience as a child protective service worker. He has published extensively in the areas of child welfare, ethics, and health care. He is currently the Principal Investigator for the National Resource Center for Permanency Planning at Hunter College and has recently been appointed Editor of the journal *Child Welfare*.

John E. Babler earned a BGS from the University of Texas at Dallas, a MSSW from the University of Texas at Arlington, and a MA and PhD from Southwestern Baptist Theological Seminary, Fort Worth, Texas. He is Assistant Professor of Social Work and Ministry-Based Evangelism at Southwestern Baptist Theological Seminary in Fort Worth, Texas. He has had direct practice experience in hospice social work, administration, and consulting for several years. Previous to his hospice experience, Dr. Babler worked as an administrator in a residential children's home, as an inner-city missionary, and on several church staffs. He has researched and written extensively in the area of spiritual care in hospice.

Timothy A. Boyd holds a BA from Wheaton College, a MA from the School of Social Services Administration at the University of Chicago, and a MA and PsyD from Rosemead Graduate School at Biola University. Currently he is an Associate Professor of Social Work and Psychology at Roberts Wesleyan College, Rochester, New York. His professional interest areas are cross-cultural psychology and international social work, counseling and education sevices for clergy and missions, and mental health services.

Rick Chamiec-Case earned a BA in Philosophy from Wheaton College, a MAR in Religion from Yale Graduate School, and a MSW from the School of Social Work at the University of Connecticut. He is presently Senior Vice President at ARI of Connecticut, whose mission it is to provide homes, jobs, and opportunities for people with disabilities and their families. He has several previous practice experiences in administrating clinical, case management, quality assurance, family support, staff training, and management information services for people with disabilities like mental retardation. He has written and presented at conferences on various topics addressing the integration of faith with different management and disability issues. He currently is the Executive Director of the North American Association of Christians in Social Work.

Diana Garland received her BA, MSSW, and PhD degrees all from the University of Louisville. She currently is Professor of Social Work at Baylor University in Waco, Texas. Her interests include church social work, family ministry, and child welfare. She is currently directing a national research project funded by the Lilly Endowment which is studying the characteristics of families in congregations and faith as a dimension of family life experience. She also serves as Editor of the *Journal of Family Ministry*. She has authored, or co-authored, or edited fourteen books, including *Church Social Work*, *Precious in His Sight: A Guide to Child Advocacy* and *Church Agencies*. In 1996, Dr. Garland received the Jack Otis Whistleblower Award from the National Association of Social Workers to honor her public stance against unethical practices of the administration of The Southern Baptist Theological Seminary.

Beryl Hugen received a BA from Calvin College, a MSW from Western Michigan University, and a PhD from the University of Kansas. He is currently a Professor of Social Work and Practicum Coordinator in the Department of Social Work and Sociology at Calvin College. He has practice experience in a variety of mental health and child welfare settings. Professional areas of interest include mental health (family and chronic mental illness), program evaluation, the integration of Christian faith and social work practice, child welfare, and social work history. Presently he serves on the Board and as Special Publications Editor for the North American Association of Christians in Social Work.

Lon Johnston holds a BA from Baylor University, a MSSW from Kent School of Social Work, University of Louisville, and a PhD from The Southern Baptist Theological Seminary. Presently he is Professor and Chair of the Department of Social Work and Sociology at the University of Mary Hardin-Baylor, Belton, Texas. His direct social work practice experience is in child welfare, medical social work, and inner-city churches. Professional interests include HIV issues, multiculturalism and human diversity, the homeless, and oppressed and vulnerable populations. He has been recognized by both professional and academic organizations for excellence in teaching and campus leadership.

Sarah S. Kreutziger earned a BA from Columbia College (South Carolina), a MSSW from the University of Tennessee, and a DSW from Tulane University. Presently she is Assistant Professor and Director of the Center for Life-Long Learning at Tulane School of Social Work. Previous social work practice experience has been as Director of Communications for the Louisiana Conference of the United Methodist Church and as a psychiatric social worker. Her research and practice interests are women's spirituality and religious beliefs and its impact on Amercian values, ethics, and social institutions, along with clinical services to individuals and families in health care and substance abuse. She has been recognized as social worker of the year in Florida and received several volunteer service awards.

Lawrence E. Ressler received a BSW from Eastern Mennonite College, a MSW from Temple University, and a PhD from Case Western Reserve University. He is currently a Professor of Social Work, Associate MSW Program Director, and Associate Division Chair of the Social Work and Social Sciences Division at Roberts Wesleyan College, Rochester, New York. His social work practice experience has been in individual, family, and organizational counseling, and mediation. Professional areas of interest include conflict management, research, church/state relationship, and family counseling. He has held leadership roles in NASW and in social work education at the state level, and served as President of the North American Association of Christians in Social Work.

David A. Sherwood received his BA from David Lipscomb College (Nashville, Tennessee), a MSW from Bryn Mawr Graduate School of Social Work, and a PhD in Social Work from the University of Texas at Austin. He is currently Professor of Social Work, MSW Program, at Roberts Wesleyan College, Rochester, New York. His professional interests include the integration of Christian faith and social work practice, ethics, practice with individuals and families, and social work in health care and with the elderly. He has written several articles on ethics and topics related to the integration of Christian faith and social work practice. Dr. Sherwood has served on the Board and as President of the North American Association of Christians in Social Work. He currently is the Editor of the journal *Social Work and Christianity*.

Janice M. Staral holds a BSW from the University of Wisconsin-Milwaukee, a MSW from the University of Michigan, and a PhD from the University of Wisconsin-Milwaukee. She presently is an Assistant Professor at Marquette University in the Social Work Program, within the Department of Social and Cultural Sciences. She has a particular professional interest in how social work can collaborate with churches in order to be a force for social change and social justice.

Mary P. Van Hook earned a BA from Calvin College, a MSW from Columbia University School of Social Work, and a PhD from Rutgers University. She currently is an Associate Professor of Social Work at Grand Valley State University (Grand Rapids, Michigan). Her social work practice experience includes clinical and supervisory roles in mental health and family and children's services. Her professional interests include family coping, integration of mental and general health care, incorporating religious issues into social work practice, and international issues regarding women and children. Dr. Van Hook presently is Editor of the journals *Rural Community Mental Health* and *Practice Forum of Health and Social Work*. In addition, her article "Christian Social Work" will appear in the next edition of the *Encyclopedia of Social Work*.

Mary Vanden Bosch Zwaanstra holds a Diploma in Nursing(RN) from Blodgett Memorial Medical Center School of Nursing (Grand Rapids, Michigan), a BA from Aquinas College (Grand Rapids, Michigan), and a MSW from Western Michigan University. She presently is an Associate Professor in the Social Work Program at Calvin College. Her practice experience has involved hospital nursing and social work, along with work in gerontology and mental health. She has been involved in education in both nursing and social work, including being the Dean of

Students at Reformed Bible College (Grand Rapids, Michigan). She has served on several Boards and community organizations. Her most extensive practice experience has been as an adoptive parent and consumer of social services.

Christianity
and Social Work

*Readings on the Integration of
Christian Faith and
Social Work Practice*

Beryl Hugen, Editor

NORTH AMERICAN ASSOCIATION
OF CHRISTIANS IN SOCIAL WORK

NACSW provides opportunities for Christian fellowship and professional learning, encourages professional
standards among Christian workers and agencies,
recruits Christian students to enter the social work
profession, and promotes a Christian philosophy of
social work and the development of professional
literature reflecting a Christian perspective. The
Association's services include:
- An Annual Convention and Training Conference;
- *Catalyst*, a bimonthly newsletter;
- *Social Work and Christianity*, a semi-annual refereed
  journal;
A growing array of publications including books,
  monographs, videos, etc.;
- Chapters in twelve states and in Canada.

For more information:
NACSW, Box 121, Botsford, CT 06404-0121
Phone/Fax: (203) 270-8780. Email: NACSW@aol.com

ISBN 0-9623634-6-4